OXFORD BROOKES UNIVERSITY LIBRARY
Harcourt Hill
A fine will be levied if this item becomes
overdue. To renew please ring 01865 483133
(reserved items cannot be renewed).
Harcourt Hill enquiries 01865 488222
www.brookes.ac.uk/library

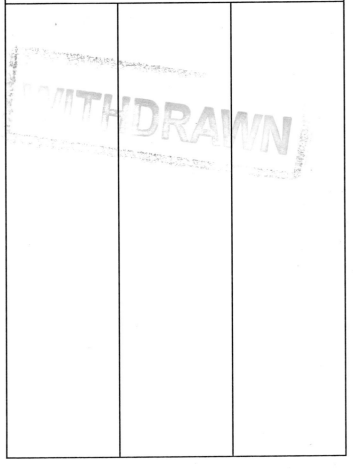

D0432847

Worship in Context

Liturgical Theology,
Children and the City

Stephen Burns

✛ EPWORTH

All rights reserved. No part of this publication may be
reproduced, stored in a retrieval system, or transmitted,
in any form or by any means, electronic, mechanical,
photocopying or otherwise, without the prior
permission of the publisher, Epworth Press.

Copyright © Stephen Burns 2006

The Author has asserted his right under the Copyright,
Designs and Patents Act, 1988, to be identified
as the Author of this Work

Extracts from The Book of Common Prayer, the rights in
which are vested in the Crown, are reproduced by permission
of the Crown's Patentee, Cambridge University Press.

Patterns for Worship (CHP 1989) copyright Central Board of
Finance of the Church of England, used by permission.
New Patterns for Worhsip (CHP 2002) copyright
The Archbishops' Council, used by permission
Common Worship (CHP 2000) copyright
The Archbishops' Council, used by permission
Methodist Worship Book copyright Trustees for Methodist Church
Purposes, used by permission of Methodist Publishing House

British Library Cataloguing in Publication data

A catalogue record for this book is available
from the British Library

ISBN 0 7162 0602 1/978 0 7162 0602 6

First published in 2006
by Epworth Press
4 John Wesley Road
Werrington
Peterborough PE4 6ZP

Typeset by Regent Typesetting, London
Printed and bound in Great Britain by
William Clowes Ltd, Beccles, Suffolk

CONTENTS

Part Four
Constructing Liturgical Theology:
Concluding Case Study

To Judith

ACKNOWLEDGEMENTS

Professor Ann Loades, CBE, of Durham University nurtured this piece of work in its original form as a doctoral study. In fact, she taught me theology at both undergraduate and postgraduate level over a decade and a half, and I am deeply grateful for all I have learned from her.

With Ann, Dr Alan Suggate of Durham University offered particular encouragement to me to publish this work, and I am grateful for his confidence in this study and for his nudging me to seek a wider audience for it.

Andy Lyons also read the entire manuscript and helped me in particular to think about connections with Methodist understandings and practice of worship.

Dr Natalie Watson of Epworth Press met the prospect of the book with enthusiasm, and throughout its production consistently exercised care and wisdom in her editorial guidance. I am grateful to Natalie and to Epworth Press for publishing *Worship in Context*. As an Anglican teacher in an ecumenical context – the Queen's Foundation for Ecumenical Theological Education, Birmingham – where I work and worship with Methodist friends and colleagues, it gives me great pleasure that this study, focused as it is on Anglican experience, should be associated with a Methodist press.

INTRODUCTION

This book is an attempt to begin a conversation about liturgical theology from a particular place and particular concerns. The work is grounded in a specific context – Gateshead – where I was parish priest; and it is shaped by concern about the possibilities of worship in deprived urban communities and among the young.

In constructing a conversation about these things, the book first introduces readers to *New Patterns for Worship*, an unusual and perhaps unique contemporary liturgical resource among the British churches. *New Patterns for Worship* was published by the Church of England in 2002, as part of the *Common Worship* range – in fact, as the 'teaching resource' for *Common Worship*. *New Patterns for Worship* merits close attention because it suggests fresh ways of resourcing liturgical celebration. It consists of basic structures for worship in the Anglican tradition, rubrics and instructions, a directory of resources, commentary about aspects of liturgical performance, and illustrative 'sample services'. In that it does not consist of full texts for particular services, but rather offers provisions for and teaching about how local communities might develop their own orders of service, it not only redefines inherited Anglican notions of 'common prayer', but also develops ways of enabling worship from which Christians in other denominational contexts can learn. *New Patterns for Worship* is of interest to Christians beyond the Church of England because it explores ways of enabling worship that other British churches may come to follow – or reject – on the basis of the promise of this Anglican development.

Something of the distinctiveness of *New Patterns for Worship* can be appreciated by comparison with the roughly contemporaneous *Methodist Worship Book*, published by the British Methodist Church in 1999. The Methodist book provides full orders – albeit rich seasonal ones – for Holy Communion throughout the year, but nothing like the 'directory' of resources to be compiled creatively locally, as in *New Patterns for Worship*. What perhaps makes this surprising is that the preface to the *Methodist Worship Book* stresses the value – as did its predecessor, the Methodist Service Book of 1975 – of both 'fixed forms' and 'freer expressions of worship'. The *Methodist Worship Book* in practice models one of these ways of worship, but, despite the encouragement of the preface, does little to model, *New Patterns for Worship*-style, how the two ways might be 'blended'. *New Patterns for Worship* therefore can be seen to represent a move on the part of the Church of England to embrace both form and freedom, such as is valued in other traditions, but which, at least on some accounts, may be being lost in those traditions,[1] despite aspirations to the contrary.

New Patterns for Worship emerged out of a series of liturgical experiments, and was in fact published in two previous editions – both known simply as *Patterns for Worship* – first in 1989 and then in 1995. *Worship in Context* sets the *Patterns for Worship* phenomenon in the context of contemporary ecumenical liturgical renewal, explores, in detail, its contents, engages its concerns and considers its promise for the future of liturgical provision in the British churches. Its affirmation and its critique relate to *New Patterns for Worship* as well as to the earlier editions (just *Patterns for Worship*).

The second major area explored in *Worship in Context* arises out of the first, for *Patterns for Worship* was particularly concerned to engage two types of congregation and their contexts which it considered to be marginal to the Church of England and its liturgical expression: that is, congregations in deprived urban settings, and congregations welcoming children. *Worship in Context*, then, develops *Patterns for Worship*'s concerns with urban and young people and attends to them in order to grasp an understanding of the contextual demands of Christian worship. Both of these concerns converged in Gateshead.

Worship in Context traces *Patterns for Worship*'s initial engagement with the challenges of worship among urban and young people, and it critiques both *Patterns for Worship* and *New Patterns for Worship* in view of more recent, sometimes radical, thinking in urban theology and what is sometimes called 'child theology'. It explores new thinking about the Church's mission among children and in the city. Even so, it does not simply critique various liturgical resources, but it also makes constructive proposals about what it might mean to continue to engage with its concerns in the present time. In order to do this, it looks particularly to North American liturgical theology, and its exploration of North American liturgical theology is the third distinctive feature of *Worship in Context*.

The work of three theologians in particular is explored in order to take a fresh look at some of the matters with which *New Patterns for Worship* is concerned. The writings of Gordon W. Lathrop, a Lutheran pastor and professor of liturgy at Lutheran Theological Seminary in Philadelphia, Don E. Saliers, a Methodist elder and professor of worship and theology at the Candler School of Theology, Emory University, Atlanta, and the now late James F. White, who was a Methodist elder and, across four decades, professor of liturgy at the University of Notre Dame, South Bend, Indiana, are studied to reframe and develop *Patterns for Worship*'s concerns with liturgical structures, participation and diversity. In the case of each of these liturgical theologians, a select range of themes in their work is explored in detail and their relevance to the debates around *Patterns for Worship* is highlighted. The chapters that especially concern Lathrop, Saliers and White might be read simply as orientations to the contributions of three influential and exciting liturgical theologians. However, set alongside material earlier in the book on *Patterns for Worship*, engagement with these scholars suggests the ecumenical, and to some measure, cross-cultural scope of *Worship in Context*.

Finally, the contextual character of the book is impressed

with a concluding case study that attempts a practical synthesis of the areas previous parts of the book have traversed. 'Liturgical Construction in Gateshead' explains some ways in which worship was celebrated in context and in conversation with the range of themes represented throughout the book. The end of the book suggests a beginning in practice to how conversation about liturgical theology might develop in service of the urban poor and the young.

Notes

1. See Lester Ruth, 'Extempore Prayer', Paul Bradshaw, ed., *New SCM Dictionary of Liturgy and Worship*, London: SCM Press, 2002, pp. 206–8.

Part One

Approaching Liturgical Theology:

Patterns and Participation

The two chapters that form Part One of this work are introductory in different ways. Together they provide narratives of the background necessary for the discussion that is to follow at later stages.

Chapter 1 sketches the larger context to which the following explorations belong, highlighting key moments and core concerns in the ecumenical liturgical movement. Covering such a large topic is necessarily selective and focuses especially on the insights of the movement as these found expression in the liturgical mandates emerging from the Second Vatican Council of the Roman Catholic Church, sometimes considered to be the most important thing to affect twentieth-century Protestantism! Of particular interest is the council's liturgy document, *Sacrosanctum concilium*, 'The Constitution on the Sacred Liturgy', which was the first of the council documents to be promulgated, on 4 December 1963. The chapter explores the wealth of literature emanating from this document through the key concept of 'participation', which has in turn been so influential in the life of churches of other Christian traditions. This paves the way for Chapter 2, when the focus turns to discussion about participation in the Church of England's recent liturgical revisions. As already stated in the Introduction, this Anglican document represents shifts in liturgical provision which are of interest to other churches.

Chapter 2 examines the Church of England worship resource *New Patterns for Worship*, published as part of the *Common Worship* series but having a longer history as *Patterns for Worship*. The chapter looks at the debates about children and the city that form its context and shape its content. As we shall see, *Patterns for Worship* was intended directly to address issues about participation in particular kinds of worshipping communities, specifically those in deprived urban areas, and those including children – concerns which converged in Gateshead, the setting in which *Worship in Context* developed. In its explorations of *Patterns for Worship*, Chapter 2 introduces the issues that constantly recur as foci of this present work – especially so in the following part, Part Two, 'Challenging Liturgical Theology'.

PARTICIPATION IN LITURGY

The ecumenical treasure of the Second Vatican Council

The notion of participation in the liturgy has become the keynote of liturgical renewal across the Christian traditions, and a vision of what it might entail came to clear and widely recognized expression in the liturgical documents of the Second Vatican Council. Those documents suggest that the participation of all is 'the aim to be considered above all else' in Christian worship. As 'The Constitution on the Sacred Liturgy', *Sacrosanctum concilium*, noted in its fourteenth paragraph,

> Mother Church earnestly desires that all the faithful should be led to that full, conscious, and active participation in liturgical celebrations which is demanded by the very nature of the liturgy, and to which the Christian people, 'a chosen race, a royal priesthood, a holy nation, a redeemed people' (1 Pet. 2.9, 4–5) have a right and obligation by reason of their baptism.
>
> In the restoration and promotion of the sacred liturgy the full and active participation by all the people is the aim to be considered before all else, for it is the primary and indispensable source from which the faithful are to derive the true Christian spirit. Therefore, in all their apostolic activity, pastors of souls should energetically set about achieving it through requisite pedagogy . . .[1]

Sacrosanctum concilium was the first of the documents of the council to be promulgated, on 4 December 1963. Being the

first of the directives to emerge from the council, *Sacrosanctum
concilium* can be regarded as having 'priority over all others for
its intrinsic dignity and importance to the life of the Church'.[2]
Within the document itself an important claim is made about
the liturgy being both 'source and summit' of the whole life of
the Church.[3]

If paragraph 14 of the *Constitution on the Liturgy* represents an important expression of the heart of liturgical renewal,
it is not surprising that its convictions find pulses and echoes
throughout the documents of the council. Paragraph 21 of the
same document speaks of the faithful being 'able to understand
[both texts and rites] with ease and take part in them fully, actively and as a community'.[4] Paragraph 30 speaks of acclamations,
responses, psalms, hymns, actions, gestures, silence and more
as means of 'active participation'.[5] The importance of a diverse
range of means aiding participation can also be seen by cross-
reference to *Apostolicam actuositatem*, 'On the Apostolate of
Lay People' of 18 November 1965. This speaks of lay people's
'life of intimate union with Christ in the Church' being 'main-
tained by the spiritual helps common to all the faithful, chiefly
by active participation in the liturgy'.[6] To facilitate this aim,
the rites themselves, the liturgy's leaders and the space in which
they are conducted are all called to aid the faithful. The rites are
to be 'short, clear, and free from useless repetitions . . . within
the people's powers of comprehension, and normally should
not require much explanation'.[7] 'Pastors of souls' are asked to
'ensure that the faithful take part fully aware of what they are
doing, actively engaged in the rite and enriched by it',[8] so that
'minds [may] be attuned to [. . .] voices'. Pastoral promotion
of liturgical instruction and 'participation, both internal and
external' in the 'mysteries of God' is encouraged.[9] Furthermore,
'Considerable freedoms' may be exercised by presiders to 'suit
[. . .] as well as possible [. . .] the needs, spiritual preparation
and receptivity of those who are to take part'.[10] And because
the Church is understood to find its 'principal manifestation
. . . in the full, active participation of all God's holy people'
in liturgy,[11] the Church's buildings are to be scrutinized as to

their suitability for facilitating the active participation of the faithful.[12]

These convictions of the bishops gathered for the Second Vatican Council have had import well beyond their own Roman Catholic Church, as we shall see in relation to some other theologians, traditions and contexts. Yet, from the start, many convictions of the bishops were not limited to the Roman episcopate, for in promulgating the Constitution on the Liturgy, the bishops to a large extent embraced the principles of the twentieth-century ecumenical Liturgical Movement. Indeed, in *Sacrosanctum concilium* the bishops amplified many of the perspectives of some of the actual authors of the Constitution who had been actively involved in the Liturgical Movement for some time.

Undoubtedly, 'nothing has symbolized more dramatically this "age of liturgical reform" than the Second Vatican Council'.[13] Consequently, the council may be seen to be the 'most radical thing to affect Protestantism in the twentieth century',[14] as Don Saliers suggests. And Protestant appropriation of the council has also had participation as a central concern: the 'call for "participation" can be seen as representing the leading edge of reform in the liturgies of all the Christian churches in the twentieth century, not just that of the churches in communion with Rome'.[15] Consequently, Gordon Lathrop writes of the key phrase of *Sacrosanctum concilium* 14 about 'full, conscious, and active participation' as an 'ecumenical treasure' of transdenominational significance.[16] If, then, some of the reforms mandated by the council looked to Roman Catholics like a 'Protestantization' of their inherited traditions of worship[17] – use of the vernacular being the most obvious first instance of this – the Protestant traditions have in turn been 'Romanized' by the ecumenical import of the council. These trends together have resulted in much greater consensus in terms of the shape and form of Christian worship across the traditions after the council than before. And the point of convergence between the traditions was typically centred on an understanding that the traditions were making a common rediscovery of the early

churches' liturgical practice as a measure and yardstick for contemporary change. This interest in the early centuries was mediated to the Church, both Catholic and Protestant, by the council
'fathers' as they absorbed the core concerns of the pioneers of
the Liturgical Movement,[18] and has remained at the centre of
concern for liturgical theology since.

However, before we consider the developing sense of the
subtleties involved in the notion of participation, a little more
attention to the Liturgical Movement will further help to set
the significance of the impact of the Second Vatican Council in
context.

The achievements of the Liturgical Movement

At the heart of the Liturgical Movement's achievements was a
gathering of concern to identify a shared inheritance of what
might be considered 'the essentials of Christian worship'.[19]
As has just been suggested, this was based largely on historical reconstruction of worship practice in the early centuries.
In particular, it is this endeavour to which the Second Vatican
Council gave unprecedented approval and energy.

Identifying a liturgical canon

In considering the concerns that have preoccupied those persons associated with the Liturgical Movement it is helpful to
keep in focus the notion of a liturgical 'canon', as this has been
significant to many subsequent commentators. Such a construct
is comparable in some ways to the canon of Scripture in so
far as it is constituted by elements which are considered to be
early, authentic and abiding, though of rite rather than biblical
text. And as with the scriptural corpus, there are varying views
about the precise content of such a canon. In the liturgical case,
many traditions tend to look for verification of their practice by
sifting records and assumptions of earlier times in ways which
justify the construal of their particular patterns of prayer.[20]

Nevertheless, quite considerable consensus about the essentials of Christian worship has been achieved, at least among the mainstream/old-line churches.

Included in the liturgical canon according to the Catholic and many (though not all) mainstream Protestant traditions are the Eucharist; those pastoral offices which correlate closely with the sacraments of the Catholic tradition – with a particular emphasis on initiation (a complex involving at least baptism, first Communion and confirmation); offices of daily prayer; and cycles of time expressed in seasons and feasts. Some of the elements of this liturgical 'canon' have greater or lesser influence in particular traditions, just as different elements are regarded as supreme in certain traditions and not others. For instance, the primacy of the Eucharist in the Roman and some other traditions might be regarded as being analogous to the primacy of the Gospel reading and preaching in many churches: the Gospel is an interpretative lens for all the other aspects of the lectionary chain.

Convergence of liturgical structures

If widespread recognition of a liturgical canon is a major achievement of the Liturgical Movement, another of its fruitful endeavours has been to facilitate the convergence of structures of liturgical rites. This is particularly the case in relation to Holy Communion regarded as a 'service of word and table' (the title now given to Eucharistic celebrations by the United Methodist Church of the USA, and some of the Uniting Churches of various lands), in which the disciplined, lectionary-based reading and proclamation of Scripture has a central place. The recovery of the related integrity of word and sacrament has had a major impact on Christian worship in every continent. Protestants are shifting to a more regular, and symbolically richer, sacramental celebration, while the following imperative of *Sacrosanctum concilium* has set the tone for changes in much of the Roman Catholic world: 'The treasures of the Bible are to be opened up more lavishly so that a richer fare may be provided for the faithful at the table of God's word.'[21] The value placed on proclamation of Scripture in the revised Roman rites might be regarded as another expression of their Protestantization. The increasing frequency of sacramental celebration that the Liturgical Movement encouraged can conversely be seen as a Romanizing of a number of Protestant traditions.

Shared appropriation of ancient texts

As structures of rites converged in these ways, the texts of rites have similarly become a focus of ecumenical consensus. Recovery and study of early liturgical texts and rubrics has led to their incorporation into many recent expressions of liturgical creativity. The most vivid example of this is perhaps the common use of *The Apostolic Tradition*, once assumed to be by Hippolytus, in the formulation of modern texts for Eucharistic prayer.[22] Its particularly vivid phrase, 'he stretched out his hands when he should suffer', expressed in the third Eucharistic prayer of the Roman Rite as 'for our sake he opened his arms on the cross' has helped to popularize the Hippolytan inheritance in the prayers of many other contemporary traditions.

Shared attention to sources

Finally, alongside the recovery of such primary texts of prayer as *The Apostolic Tradition*, the Liturgical Movement has encouraged and facilitated shared attention to secondary sources. A contemporary example is *Sacrosanctum concilium* itself and, more recently again, the so-called Lima Document – the 111th paper of the Faith and Order Commission of the World Council of Churches, *Baptism, Eucharist and Ministry* – is perhaps the contemporary text par excellence in this category.[23] Such secondary texts have also clearly helped to shape celebration of rites across denominational lines, providing alternative 'authorities' to the texts around which Reformation and Counter-Reformation controversies were centred, be they the documents of the

Council of Trent, Luther's *Catechism*, Zwingli's treatise *On the Lord's Supper*, Cranmer's revised liturgies, or whatever.

These various means of liturgical consensus form an essential background to the discussion that follows, for it has been liturgical theologians who have – perhaps primarily – been involved in shaping these contemporary ecumenical endeavours in the period after Vatican Two. They have certainly been active in the work of aiding understanding of potential reasons for consensus by tracing the 'essentials of Christian worship' through their historical trajectories, and reconceiving them for maximal contemporary relevance. By focusing on the rites of worship, in a way that is distinctive from the work of other kinds of theological scholars – systematicians, for instance – they have pioneered a particular kind of approach to the practice of worship. They are less dependent than some other theological colleagues on the secondary sources of the medieval and Reformation period where so many attempts at ecumenical convergence have faltered. They have also been the creators of a new wave of secondary theology, so often being those who have both written and shaped the texts, rubrics and rites of their traditions, and the first to offer commentaries on the revised rites for which they are responsible. In this respect, liturgical theologians are often powerfully situated at the interface of the 'rule of prayer' and the 'rule of faith', in that they may revise and write the Church's liturgies and then comment as experts upon them, and so in different but related ways shape the understanding of the Church.

Orientation in liturgical theology

Pioneers of liturgical theology: Benedictine and Orthodox influences

While it may be argued that liturgical theology, broadly conceived, is one of the most ancient and basic theological areas of all, it is with its contemporary form that this work engages.

Following from the previous discussion, 'liturgical theology' as it is conceived here, can be understood in relation to its roots in the twentieth-century Liturgical Movement and is especially associated with the refinement of liturgical reflection generated by the reforms of the Second Vatican Council. However, it is notable that while the Liturgical Movement had its roots in Europe, liturgical theology is now most advanced and developed in the continent of North America. An important thread of connection between the Liturgical Movement and liturgical theology is that Benedictine communities and authors are at the heart of the promotion of liturgical theology in its present, Americo-centric form,[24] just as Benedictines pioneered the movement that was contemporary liturgical theology's antecedent. And contemporary, Americo-centric liturgical theology is now a thoroughly ecumenical enterprise, just as the Liturgical Movement itself was instrumental in establishing the conditions in which it became appropriate to designate the twentieth as 'the ecumenical century'.[25]

This being said, in terms of reference to written authorities, the most single influential secondary text of contemporary liturgical theology is the work of an Orthodox theologian, Alexander Schmemann. And so, alongside the Benedictine influence, any discussion of contemporary liturgical theology wisely finds orientation from Schmemann's *Introduction to Liturgical Theology*, the seminal text in its academic field.

A priest of the Russian Orthodox Church, Schmemann studied theology in Paris under Roman Catholic teachers. Some of them were Benedictines and came, around the time of Schmemann's writing of his *Introduction*, to find an important role at the Second Vatican Council.[26] Following the publication of the *Introduction*, Schmemann himself spent much of his teaching career in the United States, at St Vladimir's Seminary, New York City, whose press initially published his book. The *Introduction* reflects Schmemann's deep experience of Christian worship on two continents and in at least three different contexts; and although concerned specifically with his own Orthodox tradition, it is widely regarded across Christian confessions as having shaped the discipline of the ecumenical enterprise of liturgical theology as it has evolved to this day. First published in 1965, *Introduction to Liturgical Theology* is so influential as to be regarded aptly as a 'primer' for liturgical theology subsequent to it.

For example, in the first pages of his 'Introduction' to the *Introduction*, Schmemann makes a number of points that have formed a generation of liturgical theologians across the Christian traditions: he states that 'liturgical theology' as he is to expound it is 'comparatively recent', and thus to be distinguished from much of what had passed as liturgical study hitherto. The distinction he identifies between liturgical study in earlier modes and the liturgical theology which is to be his own particular concern hinges on the latter's concentration on 'the meaning of worship', as opposed to 'the study of "rubrics"' (which had, in his view, too often been considered a clerical or churchly, but not theological, business). He therefore intended his work to amend 'the neglect of liturgics' by theologians, as well to develop the more positive but still underreached 'historical and archaeological interest in worship' of much liturgical study that he considered to fall short of a genuinely theological appreciation of liturgy.

Schmemann's seminal vision of liturgical theology as a matter of 'the elucidation of the meaning of worship' is elaborated in various ways in the *Introduction*, perhaps most importantly in terms of 'giving a theological basis to the explanation of worship and the whole liturgical tradition of the Church' by finding and defining 'the concepts and categories which are capable of expressing as fully as possible the essential nature of the liturgical experience of the Church', and by then connecting these 'with that system of concepts which theology uses to expound the faith and doctrine of the Church'. In the *Introduction*, Schmemann is also concerned to present 'the separate data of liturgical experience as a connected whole, as, in the last analysis, the 'rule of prayer' dwelling within the Church and determining her 'rule of faith'.[27]

These trajectories expanded the range of liturgics at the time

Schmemann wrote, pointing liturgical study in a consciously theological direction and focusing the agenda he wished to introduce. Yet although his work has remained a reference point against which subsequent liturgical theologians have defined their own understanding, they have by no means assented to all the details of the content of the *Introduction*. That the vision and the detail in the work have gained different levels of assent from others can be seen in the way that subsequent scholars of liturgical theology have become conscious of the particularities of the 'data of liturgical experience' in their own ecclesial traditions, contrasting their experience with Schmemann's Orthodoxy. This has led to some of the debates about the content of the canon of Christian worship, as hinted above. One of the discipline's richest areas of development has emerged out of such debates, although conversely it has frustrated the possibility of arriving at an agreed definition of liturgical theology. It is now typical of the discipline that rather than focusing on a narrow definition it is commonly conceived in topographical images,[28] as a 'geography' with 'borders' within which two 'distinguishing characteristics' are contained, but about which prescriptive understandings are considered to be problematic. As Dwight Vogel suggests, a common contemporary view is that liturgical theology 'must deal with the liturgy and it must be theological in nature. To say more, or to attempt to define terms too precisely, would be to impoverish our geography.'[29] This broad approach to the discipline therefore embraces a number of perspectives shaped in unique ways by the traditions of worship from which they arise. Schmemann saw his own work very much as a service to the Liturgical Movement, which he regarded as having 'created the necessary conditions for liturgical theology by its focus on worship'. The service that Schmemann saw liturgical theology being able to offer was in terms of helping the movement to avoid subsiding into expressions of either contemporary fashions or nostalgic primitivism, as at least some of the movement's proponents would, he believed, have encouraged it to do. Schmemann's own enterprise has not been free of such criticism itself, and it is implied in the recent works of Catherine Pickstock among others, although in her reference to the crafters whose hands shaped the liturgical documents of Vatican Two, she does not name him. This notwithstanding, liturgical theology as it has been shaped by Schmemann's influential vision has not only reflected but also actively formed aspects of ecumenical consensus about worship.

Primary and secondary modes of liturgical theology

Defining the relationship between the two rules – the 'rule of prayer' and the 'rule of faith' – is one matter to which Schmemann renewed attention. The origins of such a distinction are commonly ascribed to Prosper of Aquitaine. Writing about the intercessions of the Good Friday liturgy of his fifth-century ecclesial context, Prosper comments at one point: *legem credendi lex statuat supplicandi*. This much-used phrase is variously translated, and has had a great many meanings loaded on to it by liturgical theologians, each with a distinctive range of implications for the relationship between the two 'rules'.[30] We have already noted the wide definition of liturgical theology for which one of the most recent commentators, Dwight Vogel, settles: that it 'must deal with the liturgy and it must be theological in nature'. And as quotations from Schmemann have indicated, for some theologians prayer, regarded as primary theology, is regarded as heavily – if not wholly – determinative of secondary, reflective theology, so that doctrine is understood by them to be derived from the liturgy. For others, the Church's theological traditions possess a greater power of critique in relation to liturgical experience, and are considered to have a more explicit role in the adjustment and evolution of liturgical practice. Typically, an awareness and sympathy with scripturally-grounded Reformation arguments about aspects of medieval liturgical celebration or familiarity with forms of contemporary liberation theologies shape this latter position.

Furthermore, in the latter case at least, theological traditions that prioritize the perspectives of particular oppressed groups may relegate much of the Church's received tradition.

They receive the tradition as deficient – as at best ancillary to liberative 're-constructions' with little historical authority in themselves.[31] What supporters of this approach are prepared to concede and which Schmemann and others – notably, Aidan Kavanagh – will not is the role of worship as primary theology, theology 'in the first instance',[32] which places all attempts to reflect upon it into secondary position.

Even among those who refuse to concede this point, the relationship between the 'rules' of prayer and belief may be 'expanded' to include a third 'rule', *lex agendi*, the rule of 'living' or of what has been called 'belief enacted'.[33] Among contemporary liturgical theologians, Kevin Irwin is especially associated with this adjustment to Prosper's dictum, and it has come to be quite commonly adopted by others. The expansion reflects the close interest many liturgical scholars have given to the pursuit of social justice and communal expressions and representations of holiness. It may also, in many cases, be informed by the scriptural connections between liturgy and life as hinted at in the phrase 'living sacrifice', used by Paul in his letter to the Romans (Romans 12.1–2). The phrase *lex agendi* is usually used in the sense of embracing 'liturgical spirituality', the 'living out in life of some of the implications of the liturgy . . .', and 'the challenge to live what is celebrated'.[34] In this respect, it has meant that attention has been cast on some of the mediating factors between forms of Christian life and the meaning of liturgical texts. So it has highlighted a diverse range of aspects of liturgy, such as symbol, gesture, movement, environment and art, which have, with time, come to be recognized as each in their own way aspects of participation in liturgy, and constitutive of liturgy's primary theology. In this sense, these elements of liturgy do more than simply mediate between liturgy and life, but are in themselves parts of the experience of worship.

Liturgy as embodied activity

Conviction about the vast and varied range of elements relevant to participation has had major implications for liturgical study in the contemporary period. They are probably not yet fully understood, but have initiated a whole-scale shift away from a more traditional focus on rite alone – and especially away from prescribed texts.[35] In the academy, this can be seen not only in the desire to attend more comprehensively to the subtleties of symbol but also in the valuing of careful description in the work of liturgical theology. For instance, a felt need among liturgical scholars for more descriptive attention to worship events became a focus of the 1974 gathering of the North American Academy of the Liturgy and led to a shift that has been incorporated into the discipline since then. Recognizing the inadequacy of 'comparative textual inquiry', the academics gathered in 1974 resolved to 'undertake a detailed enquiry of case studies of liturgical celebrations drawn from actual parish life'.[36] In fact, the study of fifteen Roman Catholic congregations across the United States, published as *The Awakening Church*, was one notable result of this shift. For that study, a team of scholars observed people as part of worshipping congregations, conducted extensive interviews with worshippers about their experience of worship events, and gathered to reflect upon their findings, producing papers and responses about their work. Don Saliers, one of the contributors, expanded the range of ecclesial traditions examined by simultaneously undertaking a related study of 13 United Methodist congregations.[37] As a result of such initiatives, in the era since these first major studies, seminaries in the United States have often begun to make descriptive accounts of worship a greater focus of courses in liturgy. For example, James White outlines a number of instructions for his students about 'what to observe' when they seek to understand worship as they describe it:

> [Observers] must look beyond the words that are said and sung. They should be instructed to note: who the people are (age, race, sex), what roles each group plays (including the ordained clergy and choir), what is the architectural setting of the worship, what visual arts are present, how people arrive and leave, what actions happen (such as offering,

receiving communion, baptism, etc.), what leadership roles are apparent (usher, reader, presider), who sings and how, the uses of music, the use or not of printed materials, use of the body (handclapping, hands raised), and how strangers are treated.[38]

The observation that 'much more is done in worship than is said'[39] finds expression also in James White's preferred description of worship: 'speaking and touching in God's name'.[40]The tactile, the kinetic, the aural and visual environment are all now commonly regarded as part of the primary theology of worship.

Here, we may perceive the evermore complex and subtle ways in which 'participation' is understood. As we shall see, Don Saliers – among others – is concerned with 'resistance and vulnerability to the non-verbal and symbolic dimensions of liturgical celebrations in specific social-cultural contexts'[41] in ways which deepen appreciation of what participation may mean. In his own contributions to *The Awakening Church* project he discovered that 'in our preoccupation with reformed texts and rubrics, we may have neglected the most difficult challenge: to uncover the intersection of human hopes and fears, longings and hungers, with the symbolic power and range of liturgical rites authentically celebrated'.[42] Interviewees were almost wholly concerned with what Saliers names the 'expressive' dimensions of participation, while 'the inner relations between the formative and expressive power of primary symbol' were neglected. He calls attention to the nature of symbolic participation in order to deepen ongoing appropriation of the council's core mandate at paragraph 14 of *Sacrosanctum concilium*.

Inculturation

Futhermore, since the Second Vatican Council a wealth of literature has also evolved around the minimal hints about widening participation in worship offered by paragraphs 37–40 of the Constitution. They read in part:

Even in the liturgy the Church does not wish to impose a rigid uniformity in matters which do not involve the faith or the good of the whole community. Rather does she respect and foster the qualities and talents of the various races and nations. Anything in these people's way of life which is not indissolubly bound up with superstition and error she studies with sympathy, and, if possible, preserves intact. She sometimes even admits such things into the liturgy itself, provided they harmonize with its true and authentic spirit.

Provided that the substantial unity of the Roman rite is preserved, provision shall be made, when revising the liturgical books, for legitimate variations and adaptations to different groups, regions and peoples, especially in mission countries. This should be borne in mind when drawing up the rites and determining rubrics. (37–8)

'Sacraments, sacramentals, processions, liturgical language, sacred music and the arts' are each mentioned in paragraph 39 as the possible focus of adaptation, yet paragraph 40 concedes that 'in some places and circumstances [. . .] an even more radical adaptation of the liturgy is needed', though it prescribes boundaries around who may legitimately make changes.[43]

These short paragraphs are concerned with what has come to be called 'inculturation' and are headed 'Norms for Adapting the Liturgy to the Temperament and Traditions of Peoples'. The term inculturation was not used in an official way to describe the processes imagined in paragraphs 37–40 until 1979. Then, in an address concerning biblical interpretation, Pope John Paul II used the term to 'express[. . .] one of the elements of the great mystery of the incarnation'.[44] Studies of inculturation in the liturgical realm have been especially developed by Anscar J. Chupungco, who writes in turn: 'liturgical pluralism is an incarnational imperative, rather than a concession of Vatican II.'[45] A key example of what liturgical inculturation, in the spirit of the Constitution 37–40, might mean is the Roman Rite authorized for Zaire in 1987, which incorporates African images, prayers (involving ancestors, for instance), music and dance.[46]

Among contemporary liturgical theologians, the attention paid by David Power to embodied celebration of liturgy is an important contribution to the unfolding implications of liturgical inculturation. Power has been particularly trenchant in his critique of the assumption that liturgical celebration can be regarded as homogeneous, whatever impressions may be given by use of shared texts. Noting the plasticity of popular devotion among Roman Catholic people in different cultures around the world, he has argued that liturgical inculturation has often failed 'because people are rarely invited to express [their faith] in their own way. Rather, they are given models of doctrinal belief to follow, instead of being expected to generate their own expressions.'[47] And from this observation his critique has expanded to a number of 'imposed' or assumed liturgical traditions and gestures which change in meaning from one culture to another and so may at best diminish their authenticity or at worst alienate participants from the liberating experience they have been found to convey in other cultures. Consequently, Power is hostile to the notion of liturgy as 'the work of the elite' and calls for the incorporation of 'indigenous' traditions of popular devotion into corporate celebration.[48] It is easy to imagine how the comparative study of liturgy across different cultures might have given its own particular impetus to a whole-rite focus for liturgical theology in the contemporary period. These concerns are clearly relevant to the agenda of *Patterns for Worship* and its desire to relate to particular local cultures.

The concerns of *The Awakening Church* and similar projects with deepening appreciation of participation through attention to meaningful symbol and the concerns of liturgical inculturation marry in Saliers's oft-repeated statement that worship is 'always culturally embodied and embedded'. This statement serves well as a summary of the range of elements constituting the malleable notion of 'participation' that now contributes to primary theology as this is understood by contemporary liturgical theologians.

Liturgical theology and sacramental theology

Given a sense that primary theology may now be recognized to be any aspect of a liturgical event, and their configuration in ritual events, it can be appreciated that the distinction between liturgy as primary theology and reflective theology (such as sacramental theology) as secondary theology is not simply about the use of different kinds of texts – prayer texts, or reflective theological texts. This in turn has led to an understanding of liturgical theology which is drawing sacramental theologians' attention away from secondary texts and inviting their engagement with many aspects of the primary modes of prayer and its links with living. Liturgical theology may therefore be seen to have an important contribution to make to the systematic agenda of contemporary theologians, encouraging sacramental theology to envision an inclusive focus on the whole rite, and more.

Gathering fragments from Chapter 1

Our next chapter focuses on one particular product of contemporary liturgical reform, *New Patterns for Worship*, a recent and – as we shall see – unusual Church of England document. This present chapter is included primarily because the commitments of the Liturgical Movement form a theological background to *New Patterns for Worship* that is not explicit in the pages of *New Patterns for Worship*, nor widely appreciated. Yet the concerns that this chapter has outlined need to be in view in order to have a sense of the wider context to which *New Patterns for Worship* belongs (as with all liturgical texts produced in the mainstream churches in the last decades of the twentieth century).[49] That the concerns of the Liturgical Movement are so little discussed or understood in the general culture of the Church of England, and that the Liturgical Movement's concerns are not clearly related to the liturgical texts produced for use in the denomination, is problematic. That the rubrics accompanying liturgical texts – and the things with which rubrics have traditionally been concerned – also do not unfold with anything approaching clarity the perspectives of the Liturgical Movement is an even greater problem and one that this present work seeks to redress as it develops in what follows.

Notes

1. *Sacrosanctum concilium*, 14, Austin Flannery, ed., *Vatican Council II: Conciliar and Post-Conciliar Documents*, New York: Costello, 1975, pp. 7–8.
2. Address (4 December 1963) by Pope Paul VI; quoted by German Martinez, 'Reform, Liturgical, History of', Peter C. Fink, ed., *New Dictionary of Sacramental Worship*, Collegeville: Liturgical Press, 1991, pp. 1066–72, p. 1068.
3. The conviction about the priority of liturgy is embedded in *Sacrosanctum concilium* itself, which states that 'the liturgy is the summit towards which the activity of the Church is directed; it is also the fount from which all her power flows' (paragraph 10), Flannery, ed., *Vatican Council II*, p. 6.
4. *Sacrosanctum concilium*, 21, Flannery, ed., *Vatican Council II*, p. 9.
5. *Sacrosanctum concilium*, 30, Flannery, ed., *Vatican Council II*, p. 11.
6. *Apostolicam Actuositatem*, 4, Flannery, ed., *Vatican Council II*, p. 770.
7. *Sacrosanctum concilium*, 34, Flannery, ed., *Vatican Council II*, p. 12.
8. *Sacrosanctum concilium*, 11, Flannery, ed., *Vatican Council II*, p. 7.
9. *Sacrosanctum concilium*, 19, Flannery, ed., *Vatican Council II*, p. 9.
10. *General Instruction on the Roman Missal*, 313, Flannery, *Vatican Council II*, p. 199.
11. *Sacrosanctum concilium*, 41, Flannery, ed., *Vatican Council II*, pp. 14–15.
12. *Sacrosanctum concilium*, 124, Flannery, ed., *Vatican Council II*, p. 35. Cf. *General Instruction on the Roman Missal*, 253: 'The church (or other place) should [. . .] be suitable for the ceremonies and such as to encourage the people to take their full part.' Flannery, ed., *Vatican Council II*, p. 189.
13. Don E. Saliers, 'The Nature of Worship: Community Lived in Praise of God', Robin Leaver and James Litton, eds, *Duty and Delight: Routley Remembered*, Norwich: Canterbury Press, 1985, pp. 35–45, p. 38.
14. Don E. Saliers, 'Christian Spirituality in an Ecumenical Age', Louis

Dupré and Don E. Saliers, eds, *Christian Spirituality III: Post Reformation and Modern*, London: SCM Press, 1989, pp. 520–44, p. 538. Among other examples, see also Adrian Hastings's assessment that 'the [Second] Vatican Council was the most important ecclesiastical event of [the twentieth century], not just for Roman Catholics, but for all Christians': Adrian Hastings, *A History of English Christianity 1920–1990* (London: SCM Press, 3rd edn 1991), p. 525.

15. Gordon W. Lathrop, 'Strong Center, Open Door: A Vision of Continuing Liturgical Renewal', *Worship* 75 (2001), pp. 35–45, p. 36.
16. Lathrop, 'Strong Center', p. 36.
17. Hastings, *History*, p. 525, among many possible examples.
18. Among a wealth of literature, see introductions to serve orientation in John Fenwick and Bryan Spinks, *Worship in Transition: The Twentieth Century Liturgical Movement*, Edinburgh: T&T Clark, 1995; Virgil C. Funk, 'Liturgical Movement, the (1830–1969)', Peter C. Fink, ed., *New Dictionary of Sacramental Worship*, Collegeville: Liturgical Press, 1991, 695–715, especially pp. 710–11; Gordon Wakefield, *An Outline of Christian Worship* (Edinburgh: T&T Clark, 1998), chapter 9: 'The Liturgical Movement'.
19. See Gordon W. Lathrop, *What Is Essential in Christian Worship?*, Minneapolis, Minnesota: Fortress, 1996, volume I of the 'Open Questions in Worship' series, which represents one of the most recent and best expressions of this consensus, appropriating it for the North American Lutheran tradition.
20. These issues will be explored in some detail below, especially in relation to the work of James F. White.
21. *Sacrosanctum concilium*, 51, which initiated work on the lectionary which has formed the basis for reading across the churches, through its influence on the Common Lectionary and Revised Common Lectionary. Flannery, ed., *Vatican Council II*, p. 17.
22. See Ronald C. D. Jasper and Geoffrey Cumming, eds, *Prayers of the Eucharist: Early and Reformed*, Collegeville: Liturgical Press, 3rd edn 1987), pp. 31–8. For recent critique of Vatican Two's liturgical reform, and particularly the reliance of its crafters on the Hippolytan construct, see Catherine Pickstock, *After Writing: The Liturgical Consummation of History*, Oxford: Blackwell, 1998, pp. 171–5; also, David Torevell, *Losing the Sacred: Ritual, Modernity and Liturgical Reform*, Edinburgh: T&T Clark, 2000, pp. 146–9.
23. *Baptism, Eucharist and Ministry*, Geneva: WCC, 1982, and a wealth of material flowing from it.
24. Not least through Benedictine sponsorship of the primary journal of contemporary liturgical theology, *Worship*, among many examples.

25. Horton Davies, *Worship and Theology in England: The Ecumenical Century, 1900 to the Present*, Grand Rapids: Eerdmans, 1996. See also James F. White, 'Writing the History of English Worship', *Christian Worship in North America: 1955–1995: A Retrospective*, Collegeville: Liturgical Press, 1997, pp. 51–8.

26. For a brief history of the liturgical movement, see Funk, 'Liturgical Movement, the (1830–1969)', Fink, ed., *New Dictionary of Sacramental Worship*, pp. 695–715.

27. Alexander Schmemann, *An Introduction to Liturgical Theology*, New York: St Vladimir's Press, 1965, pp. 16–17.

28. The geographical image may originate from the quotation from Joseph Gelineau's *The Liturgy Today and Tomorrow*, London: DLT, 1984, much loved by Don E. Saliers and quoted, for example, in *Worship as Theology: Foretaste of Glory Divine*, Nashville, Tennessee: Abingdon, 1994, p. 139. Saliers uses the geographical images in his own introduction to *Worship as Theology*, p. 13. And it is picked up by Gordon W. Lathrop, '"O Taste and See": The Geography of Liturgical Theology', Byron Anderson and Bruce T. Morrill, eds, *Liturgy and the Moral Self: Humanity at Full Stretch before God: Essays in Honor of Don E. Saliers*, Collegeville: Liturgical Press, 1998, pp. 41–53.

29. Dwight W. Vogel, 'Liturgical Theology: A Conceptual Geography', Dwight W. Vogel, ed., *Primary Sources of Liturgical Theology: A Reader*, Collegeville: Liturgical Press, 2000, pp. 3–14, p. 13.

30. For overviews and suggestions of best translations and meanings, see Paul De Clerk, '"Lex Orandi, Lex Credendi": The Historical Sense and Historical Avatars of an Equivocal Adage', *Studia Liturgica* 24 (1994), pp. 178–200; David W. Fagerberg, *What Is Liturgical Theology? A Study in Methodology*, Collegeville: Liturgical Press, 1992; Kevin W. Irwin, 'Liturgical Theology', Fink, ed., *New Dictionary of Sacramental Worship*, pp. 721–33; Kevin W. Irwin, *Context and Text: Method in Liturgical Theology*, Collegeville: Liturgical Press, 1994; Maxwell Johnson, 'Liturgy and Theology', Paul Bradshaw and Bryan Spinks, eds, *Liturgy in Dialogue: Essays in Memory of Ronald Jasper*, London: SPCK, 1994, pp. 203–27; Vogel, 'Liturgical Theology'.

31. Marjorie Proctor-Smith, *In Her Own Rite: Constructing Feminist Liturgical Tradition*, Akron, Ohio: OSL, 2nd edn, 2000; see also, Rosemary Radford Ruether, *Women-Church: Theology and Practice of Feminist Liturgical Communities*, San Francisco: Harper and Row, 1985.

32. Aidan Kavanagh, *On Liturgical Theology*, Collegeville: Liturgical Press, 1984, is the classic argument of this point. For theology 'in the first instance', see pp. 74–5.

33. See Irwin, 'Liturgical Theology', Fink, ed., *New Dictionary of Sacramental Worship*, p. 726.
34. Irwin, 'Liturgical Theology', Fink, ed., *New Dictionary of Sacramental Worship*, p. 726.
35. Aidan Kavanagh, 'Textuality and Deritualization: The Case of Western Liturgical Usage', *Studia Liturgica* (1993), pp. 70–7.
36. Don E. Saliers, 'Symbol in Liturgy, Liturgy as Symbol: The Domestication of Liturgical Experience', Lawrence J. Madden, *The Awakening Church: Twenty-Five Years of Liturgical Renewal*, Washington DC: Liturgical Press, 1992, pp. 69–82, p. 69.
37. Saliers, 'Symbol in Liturgy'; also, *Worship as Theology*, especially chapter 11: 'For the Sake of the World: Liturgy and Ethics'.
38. James F. White, 'Forum: Some Lessons in Liturgical Pedagogy', *Worship* 68 (1994), pp. 438–50, pp. 442–3. A similar set of questions has recently been published in a liturgical textbook arising from the British setting in Susan J. White, *Groundwork of Christian Worship*, Peterborough: Epworth, 1997, pp. 235–7.
39. White, 'Forum', p. 443.
40. James White, *Introduction to Christian Worship*, Nashville: Abingdon, 1980, p. 22.
41. Saliers, 'Symbol in Liturgy', p. 71.
42. Saliers, 'Symbol in Liturgy', p. 71. I assume that there is an intended allusion here to the opening of *Gaudium et spes*, 1: 'The joy and hope, the grief and anguish of the [people] of our time, especially of those who are poor and afflicted in any way, are the joy and hope, the grief and anguish of the followers of Christ as well'; Flannery, ed., *Vatican Council II*, p. 903.
43. *Sacrosanctum concilium*, 37–40, Flannery, ed., *Vatican Council II*, pp. 13–14.
44. Pope John Paul II, 'Address to the Pontifical Biblical Commission', quoted in Mark R. Francis, *Shape a Circle Ever Wider: Liturgical Inculturation in the United States*, Chicago: Liturgy Training Publications, 2000, p. 58.
45. Anscar J. Chupungco, 'The Theological Principle of Adaption', Dwight W. Vogel, ed., *Primary Sources of Liturgical Theology*, Collegeville: Liturgical Press, 2000, pp. 247–52, p. 252, referring to *Gaudium et spes*, 58. See also, Anscar J. Chupungco, *Liturgical Inculturation: Sacramentals, Religiosity, and Catechesis* (Collegeville: Liturgical Press, 1992).
46. See Chris Nwaka Egbulem, 'An African Interpretation of Liturgical Inculturation: The Rite Zairois', Michael Downey and Richard Fragomeni, eds, *A Promise of Presence: Essays in Honor of David N. Power*, Washington DC: Pastoral Press, 1992, pp. 227–50; see also Aylward Shorter, *Toward a Theology of Inculturation*, London: Geoffrey Chapman, 1988, pp. 191–5.

47. David N. Power, *Worship: Culture and Theology*, Washington DC: Pastoral Press, 1990, pp. 67–8.
48. Power, *Worship: Culture and Theology*, p. 83.
49. Questions arising from consideration of 'mainstream' and 'marginal' liturgical traditions are addressed in Part Three of the present work, particularly with respect to the views of James White.

2

NEW PATTERNS FOR WORSHIP

New Patterns for Worship was published by the Church of England in 2002, as part of its *Common Worship* resources. Its preface suggests that, within the *Common Worship* range, it has a particular role, 'to educate and train those who plan and lead worship'.[1] Its intent was also explicitly concerned with mission, enabling congregations 'to enjoy God in worship in such a way that others are attracted to join in'. The 2002 edition has two precedents, in that the book was published in slightly different forms first in 1989 and then in 1995. In this chapter, we explore the initial vision for *Patterns for Worship* that emerged into the *Common Worship* resource.

The ecumenical significance of *New Patterns for Worship*

Some of the clues as to what makes *Patterns for Worship* so worthy of attention are already given in the preceding paragraph. Others will become clear as the chapter progresses. *Patterns for Worship* remains unusual – if not unique – among the range of liturgical resources published by churches in Britain, consisting as it does of rubrics, resources, commentary and sample services. It radically redefines inherited Anglican notions of 'common prayer'. Whereas once this was associated with set forms, as we shall see, in *Patterns for Worship* common prayer is linked to clear structures around which large amounts of variable material may be used. This is somewhat in contrast to other contemporaneous liturgical resources, as may be seen by reference to the *Methodist Worship Book*

(1999) and *Worship from the United Reformed Church* (2003).

The preface of the *Methodist Worship Book* repeats words from the preface of its predecessor, the *Methodist Service Book* of 1975: 'These forms are not intended to curb creative freedom, but rather provide norms for its guidance', adding that 'within our heritage, both fixed forms and freer expressions of worship have been, and should continue to be, valued'. Although the book then offers excellent summaries of 'guidance for ordering a morning, afternoon, or evening service'[2] and likewise for 'a service of holy communion',[3] with some pages of 're-source material',[4] by and large the book offers full, fixed orders of service. So, for example, orders for Holy Communion are arranged sequentially through the seasons of the liturgical calendar, providing forms for Advent, Christmas and Epiphany, Ash Wednesday, Lent and Passiontide, Easter, Pentecost and Times of Renewal, and three orders for 'Ordinary Seasons'. These impressive orders include a rich range of material, and mark each season with distinctive tones and emphases, but, organized in such a way, they offer little guidance about how these fixed patterns might be amended at local level. In fact, although through many of the services, 'basic elements' are marked with an asterisk symbol to indicate that they are an integral part of the order, while 'other sections may be omitted',[5] there is little guidance anywhere in the *Methodist Worship Book* about just how fixed forms, such as those provided by the book, and freer forms, which the preface and rubrics encourage, might each be incorporated into one service. The experience of at least some, if not many, Methodists, that the rich orders for Communion in the worship book are used in sacramental celebration, but that services of the word are often organized without reference to the resources of the worship book, suggests that there may be a widely felt uncertainty – or lack of desire or interest – about 'blending' liturgical forms and freer expressions of worship within contemporary British Methodism. What *Patterns for Worship* may then suggest to Methodists is ways to enable the blending of form and freedom, which their own book espouses but unfortunately does not foster as it might.

Likewise, *Worship from the United Reformed Church* includes a preface that repeats its predecessor, *A Book of Services* (1980), which stated: 'The orders found here are not prescribed. It is not expected that they will be used in our churches to the exclusion of others. Yet we believe most of these services reflect the ethos of our Church and of its inherited traditions.' The preface goes on to note that in the book 'rubrics have been kept to a minimum, thus encouraging worship leaders to develop styles appropriate to their situation'. The introduction to the book's Communion Orders suggests that 'the service may either be used as it stands or it may be shortened by the omission of some of the suggested items'. As with the *Methodist Worship Book*, though, the sense is of a choice between using the orders as set, or omitting parts of them, without clues in the book as to how these forms might incorporate freely extemporized or local material. Perhaps the assumption behind both the *Methodist Worship Book* and *Worship from the United Reformed Church* is that leaders of worship who are likely to be using those resources already know and have the gifts and skills to blend the form and freedom. This assumption would, however, cut against the observation that extemporization is increasingly being lost in some traditions that have valued it. Nor is the assumption easily reconcilable with the common experience of worship in some free-church traditions employing orders in books, and then somewhat slavishly, or else being entirely extemporized or organized according to patterns that their denominational liturgical resources do not espouse. One reason why *Patterns for Worship* might be valuable in such situations is that it that does not simply assume that leaders will know how to employ such freedom well, but teaches principles for its exercise as well as providing resources for local and occasional material, and examples of extemporized material. In so far as this is the case, *Patterns for Worship* may indicate the kind of liturgical resource that other traditions will in future come to produce in order to nurture the aspirations that have been inherited as important within those traditions.

Patterns for Worship in the Church of England

Patterns for Worship was published by the Liturgical Commission of the Church of England in July 1989, almost half-way into the period of the authorization of the *Alternative Service Book 1980 (ASB)*. One of its key aims, at the request of the house of bishops, was to 'provide greater freedom' in liturgical celebration, so that services of worship might be either 'enriched or shortened'. Two particular issues were at the centre of the bishops' concern to see such provision made available: the widespread but unauthorized use of 'family services' in many parish churches and the special needs of worshipping congregations in 'urban priority areas' (UPAs).[6] The main purpose of this second introductory chapter is to explore these issues and to trace the ways in which they were discussed in the Church of England leading up to and beyond *Patterns to Worship*, through to the present moment in which we read and write.

In the interval between the *ASB* and *Patterns for Worship*, a number of reports related to 'family services' and to worshipping congregations in UPAs had received considerable attention in the church's general synod, most notably *Faith in the City* (February 1986) and, to a somewhat lesser extent, *Children in the Way* (February 1988). Both of these reports critiqued the *ASB*, and their 'urgently expressed' convictions relating to the church's worship were acknowledged by the bishops to have led to their commissioning of *Patterns for Worship*. These reports on cities and on children, and the further reports to which they led, will be explored in greater detail below, though we may note at this initial stage their shared central critique of the church's inheritance of liturgical worship. *Faith in the City* suggested that 'a 1300-page Alternative Service Book is a symptom of the gulf between the Church and ordinary people in UPAs', and so commended requests from UPA parishes for 'short, functional service booklets or cards, prepared by people who will always ask "if all the words are really necessary"'. *Children in the Way* also suggested 'the need for new liturgies to serve all-age worship and in particular a form of Eucharist suitable for when children are present' (bishops' notes 2 and 3).

Following the bishops 'prefatory note' to *Patterns for Worship*, the Liturgical Commission themselves presented their work with an acknowledgement that 'the coming of the *Alternative Service Book* in 1980 marked a new stage in the development of Anglican worship'. The commission suggested that the *ASB* looked 'both backwards and forwards': back to 'the principle established by Cranmer of having all the texts for worship available in one book' and into the more recent past in order to 'distil the best' of the series of experimental booklets produced from the middle of the 1960s, and forward to 'a new era of flexibility in the Church of England worship' (*sic*).[7] This aspect of forward-lookingness in the *ASB* may be overstated by the commission – perhaps in order to down-play their own innovation in *Patterns*? – as it was undoubtedly the specific foci of concern with urban deprived and 'all-age' congregations in the post-*ASB* period which led to the freedoms permitted in the later book. Nevertheless, they cite as a sign of emerging flexibility in the *ASB* the recurrence of permissive rubrics, that is, what are sometimes referred to as 'soft spots' – those 'open-ended phrases' in its rubrics – allowing for 'other suitable prayers', 'other appropriate words' and such like, as alternatives to the printed texts for prayer. *Patterns for Worship* developed this principle and although in its 1989 edition it was neither authorized nor commended for congregational use – except in specially authorized 'liturgical experiments' (bishops' note 4) – it is *Patterns for Worship* that will almost certainly come with time to be recognized as a more significant shift in the Church of England's approach to liturgical provision than the *ASB* itself. As the bishops acknowledged, *Patterns* expanded the 'bounds of choice and variety . . . more widely than [had] been customary' (bishops' note 5), though, significantly, the bishops also recognized that this expansion would be likely to cause 'anxiety' to some in the church perhaps more content with the *ASB* or *Book of Common Prayer* (1662) than those consulted and supported by *Faith in the City* and *Children in the Way*.

The structure of *Patterns for Worship*

The make-up of the first edition of *Patterns for Worship* was markedly different from both the *BCP* and *ASB*, and its make-up was key to its novelty. It consisted of three main parts.[8] Part One offered a range of templates for worship, outline services consisting of minimal prayer texts and rubrics. One of these, sample service 6, 'The Lord Is Here: The Eucharist', was intended as a direct embodiment of the kind of order required in response to the criticisms of *Faith in the City*. It is divided into five sections: 'We prepare', 'The ministry of the word', 'We pray', 'The Eucharistic prayer' and 'After Communion'. Later versions standardized these headings to place consistent stress on action, the second heading becoming 'We hear God's word', the fourth, 'We give thanks' and so on. Rubrics are kept to a bare minimum, and only congregational texts and their necessary triggers are printed. For instance under the heading 'We prepare' we find:

Singing, greeting and prayer, which may include

This is the day that the Lord has made.
Let us rejoice and be glad in it.

Lord, direct our thoughts,
teach us to pray,
lift up our hearts to worship you
in Spirit and in truth,
through Jesus Christ. Amen.

or

Almighty God,
to whom all hearts are open . . .

[the text of the collect for purity follows].

A confession using imagery from the story of the forgiving father or prodigal son and an absolution emphasizing the 'fellowship of [God's] table' follow, then the 'Peruvian Gloria' and the rubric that 'the president says the Collect – the prayer for the day' conclude the section. The whole rite is presented in this relatively Spartan style, with explanations of specialist terms (for instance, 'collect'). The presentation of the whole order amounts to no more than four A5 pages of minimal text, a radically different alternative to a 1300-page book.

Part Two, the bulk of *Patterns for Worship*, consisted of 're-source sections' offering alternatives for every liturgical element of services, including 'samples of new lectionary material' and (in the 1989 edition only) Eucharistic prayers. Although the Eucharistic prayers were never authorized (and edited out of the 1995 edition), it is clear from anecdotal evidence that they did enjoy wide use – well beyond the parishes granted permissions in liturgical experimentation. Also, the provisions in the book for use of A Service of the Word – a list of rubrics requiring use of alternative texts within a flexible structure – allowed for contemporary expressions of 'the third service' which had enjoyed unofficial status in many parts of the Church of England for a long time.[9] Using the resources of this section, it was also possible for the Service of the Word to restructure or replace the synaxis at the Eucharist, allowing much greater flexibility in the presentation of Eucharistic worship. Acknowledging that

> the needs of the UPA parish for worship reflecting local culture, language and concrete expression are not best met by a group of experts at the centre laying down all the words of the liturgy, but by creating the framework and the environment which will enable a new generation of worship leaders to create genuinely local liturgy which is still obviously part of the liturgy of the catholic Church.[10]

Part Two presented alternative texts for liturgical greetings, introductions to confession, confessions, absolutions, introductions to the peace, blessings and other elements of the rite. Many of these alternative texts make explicit reference to cities, as in the echoes of Hebrews 12.22–4 in an opening greeting: 'We have come to the city of the living God, to the heavenly Jerusalem . . .' or the reference to Jesus weeping over the sins of the city (Luke 19.32) in a *kyrie* confession.

Most unusually, Part Three of *Patterns for Worship* was a 'commentary', the inclusion of which was a remarkable feature of a Church of England prayer book, commentaries having never been part of the tradition's liturgical literature. This commentary section took the form of 'the stories of four entirely imaginary congregations' whose circumstances and reasons for employing various elements of the resource sections were described. Although perhaps tending at times towards caricatures of congregations in different traditions or divergent social circumstances, the point of these imaginary congregations was to underscore the particularity of in fact every congregation, while an ancillary aim of the commentary section was to highlight the Liturgical Commission's conviction that 'worship is not worship until you do it',[11] a point that the commentary style could expand and explore in ways that were not possible in prayer books consisting of prayer texts alone. Apart from the contextual considerations that surface in the descriptive accounts of the churches, the accent on performance underlined the charge of insufficiency against a worship book consisting simply of texts – either those for prayer or rubrical – such as the *BCP* or the *ASB*. In retrospect, however, although the commentary section mentioned some aspects of the performative, non-textual elements of worship, it is with regard to such elements of rite that even *Patterns for Worship* is weakest, with the result perhaps that too often new, flexibly arranged texts were in the practice of many of the congregations that employed them easily left competing with unrevised approaches to use of space, gesture, symbol and ceremonial.

Anxiety about this departure in style of presenting the

Church's liturgy inevitably focused on the notion of common prayer, as in *Patterns for Worship* the *BCP* was clearly being considered deficient for pressing needs in the late twentieth century. The sense of common prayer that the commission suggests was feasible in the climate of the Church in their times was defined around a number of marks which they considered to maintain continuity with historic Anglican tradition:

- a recognizable structure for worship
- an emphasis on reading the word and on using psalms
- liturgical words repeated by the congregation, some of which, like the creed, would be known by heart
- using a collect, the Lord's Prayer and some responsive forms in prayer
- a recognition of the centrality of the Eucharist
- a concern for form, dignity and economy of words . . .
- . . . a willingness to use forms and prayers which can be used across a broad spectrum of Christian belief.[12]

These ideas were later expanded by one of the commission members, the late Michael Vasey, in the foundational contribution – 'Promoting a Common Core' – to *The Renewal of Common Prayer*,[13] a series of essays amounting to a rationale by the commission of their purposes in the post-*ASB* period. The notion of promoting a common core has remained at the heart of the task of liturgical revision in the Church of England to the present day,[14] and outlines of services noting minimal text and rubric are now gathered in the major landmark of revision, *Common Worship*, which has been published in stages since 1997. For instance, *Common Worship* includes its own Service of the Word adopted from *Patterns for Worship*.

However, progress towards *Common Worship* also involved a considerable share of the 'anxiety' picked up the bishops in 1989. Following tensions in the Church's General Synod the commended version of *Patterns for Worship*, published in 1995, omitted the Eucharistic prayers included in the earlier edition, and when new Eucharistic prayers were again revised for approval in 1996 they were again rejected – although, like their forebears, they enjoyed wide use, in the later case due to their publication as a booklet, *Six Eucharistic Prayers as Proposed in 1996*.[15] Authorized new prayers for the Eucharist had to wait for the core book of *Common Worship* published in late 1999, though in some respects *Common Worship* represents a retreat from, rather than an advancement of, the vision of *Patterns* a decade before. Its collects, based on the *BCP* opening prayers, have been much lamented in many parishes, and are one example of direct contradiction of the request from the bishops in 1986 which supported the call in *Faith in the City* for the exercise of the criterion of whether 'all the words are really necessary'.[16] Perhaps more significantly, however, the suggestion of *Faith in the City*, promoted by *Patterns for Worship*, that 'short, functional service booklets or cards' should be popularized, has arguably happened not due to the force or right of arguments embraced by the bishops and Liturgical Commission in the late 1980s, but rather due to the unforeseeable widespread use of computing technology in the intervening period. At the same time, *Faith in the City*, which with its follow-up reports *Living Faith in the City* and *Staying in the City* caused considerable interest and debate for a number of years after its publication, is no longer so highly regarded for its relevance to the contemporary urban situation – not least owing to changes precipitated by the revolution in new technology.

In contrast to *Faith in the City*, *Children in the Way* never received the same sustained attention from the Church, although further reports in its mould have been produced – most notably *Youth a Part*[17] – at the same time as numbers of the young involved in Church of England worship have declined considerably. Interestingly, however, this decline has happened most sharply in a predominantly rural diocese, Carlisle – a 62 per cent decline through the decade of the 1990s. Decline in urban areas, if acute, is not quite as drastic.

Faith in the City and its legacy for liturgy

It has been suggested that *Faith in the City* was the most important Anglican document of the twentieth century.[18] The report by the Archbishop of Canterbury's Commission on Urban Priority Areas, published in 1985, took a comprehensive approach to 'the serious situation that has developed in the major cities', that situation being the continuing decline of quality of life in 'what have been designated "Urban Priorities Areas"'. Undoubtedly, the whole report was forceful and had an important impact on Church and society, though it may be noted that the Church has been more effective in responding to at least some of the parts of it directed to the Church than governments or any other body has been to those parts attending to the state of the nation. Perhaps few parts of the commission's concerns have received as much steady attention as their comments about worship in UPA churches, which formed part of the section of the document entitled 'Developing the People of God'. Although the section specifically relating to worship is relatively small – amounting to just under 3 pages of the 398-page publication – it is remarkable that the commission's reflections and proposals have shaped the evolving liturgical resources of the whole Church of England, not only its urban congregations. In the following paragraphs, the authors of *Faith in the City*'s reflections on worship are recalled, interspersed with some commentary upon them.

In the report, two particular characteristics were demanded of the church in the UPA environment, that it be 'locally rooted and outward looking' (6.99). Many of the comments that followed this demand gave some substance to what might be entailed in the achievement of a locally rooted and outward-looking church. The theological notion of incarnation was immediately introduced to provide a broad and basic rationale for the demand for local roots. As an 'indispensable characteristic of a worshipping community' the '"incarnational" side of the Christian religion' is said to call the church in UPAs to 'live in and be part of the local world' (6.100). This is said to involve, at the very least, 'talk[ing] people's language, so that they have a chance of hearing and understanding'. Next, however, a key qualification was introduced to shape this incarnational require-ment, as the commission wrote of a necessary tension between incarnation and transcendence. They stated that worship is (in whatever context) worship of a transcendent and 'Other' God. So the necessity of worship to 'emerge out of and reflect local cultures' relates to God who is to be 'found, worshipped and served through the realities of UPA life' (6.101). Although not explicitly stated, the tension between transcendence and incarna-tion serves to resist the limits of narrow self-reference, which may be as unhelpful for coping within the horizons of 'UPA life' as it would be over time in any other situation. Nevertheless, it is held that 'certain aspects of UPA life will necessarily greatly affect the formation of the worshipping life of the UPA church' (6.102). Local life is to be 'gathered up' and 'informed' by wor-ship, and one facet of what this is likely to demand is an accept-ance at least of the 'positive aspects' of working-class culture, two of which are identified as the strong senses of 'family' and 'community'. Other aspects of UPA life which are said to be needful of attention are the tendencies to relate through 'feeling rather than the mind' and to communicate non-verbally rather then verbally, as well as to employ 'informal and flexible . . . urban language'. While it might be feared that too-easy assump-tions were being made about the marks of other people's lives, this important paragraph of the report (6.102) introduced a key principle which itself transcends the many possible flaws of the particular examples used to illustrate it. The principle, taken up vigorously as a result of the report, and in various ways, is that worship in UPAs must 'reflect a universality of form with local variations'. Here the theological themes of transcendence and incarnation find their liturgical counterparts – universal and local forms – to be balanced in the practice of an urban congregation's worshipping life. The next paragraph, 6.103, recognized that greater involvement of congregations in wor-ship is desirable in UPA churches, and this point is illustrated with some biting examples that uncover the racism that may be operative, though perhaps unacknowledged, in practices that deny participation.

Paragraph 6.104 relates to some possible further features of the 'working-class culture' which was the concern of paragraph 6.102, in that 'local UPA people' are said to be concerned that 'things . . . be more concrete and tangible rather than abstract and theoretical'. The importance for many UPA congregations of traditional and contemporary symbols – crucifixes and banners, for example – is noted, as is a particular 'love to tell the stories of their lives'. The following paragraph, 6.105, encouraged UPA congregations to resist formality – for the sense of 'go[ing] through the correct motions from start to finish' inhibits people from 'coming and going' from the church as they feel the need. And the next paragraph (6.106) draws attention to the potential of worship as a form of evangelism,[19] which is said to be likely to be most attractive when 'lively and participatory' – an expression, in positive mode, of the complaint of paragraph 6.103, perhaps? The balance between transcendence and incarnation reoccurs in some measure at this point also, as it is said that worship that is appropriately evangelistic will combine 'a sense of the presence of God while showing concern for the real things in people's lives'.

Various commissions attending to UPAs have been more successful at avoiding a patronizing tone about the people who live in such areas than the group responsible for *Faith in the City* at paragraph 6.107, which is a low point of the liturgical section of the document. Here, they were concerned about the sense of 'inferiority' which might be imposed upon UPA dwellers when 'their debts, their court cases, their sufferings at the hands of their husbands', and other such 'realities', are not faced. There can be little question that such realities occur in UPAs, though much greater care is needed when others write about such matters, in order to ensure that any supposed sense of inferiority is not further magnified. The point that the commission is making is expressed without the grating overtones in the principle delineated in paragraph 6.108, that 'worship will put the harsh realities in a new light. It may enable people to withdraw for a time from the pressures, but it will be "withdrawal with intent to return", not evasion'. When in paragraph 6.109 the commission stressed the importance of attention to 'the ordinary', we should note that this will of course include realities that may be bright and delightful as well as harsh.

Paragraph 6.110 noted 'many' suggestions from UPA contexts that small service booklets or cards be provided as an alternative to the *ASB*, which the commission had already recognized earlier in the report as being severely problematic in a non-book culture. This proposal has been of great significance for the whole Church, and it has carried implications far wider than the UPA church itself, for whom the commission acknowledged that 'the work of reforming the liturgy has really only just begun'. If resources for liturgical worship were to be presented as single service booklets or cards, rather than a combined book, a more expansive need again was for appropriate permissions to be given for 'informal and spontaneous acts of worship'. The Way of the Cross was cited as an example of the kind of informal and spontaneous form which would 'complement' formal liturgies (6.111); though the commission insisted that occasions for increased informality and spontaneity demand care and preparation, as do more formal occasions, as both are concerned with and express 'beauty' and 'excellence' (6.112). Finally, although informality may be readily associated with small groups, the commission asserted that 'glorious occasions' would continue to have a most important role in complementing smaller gatherings (6.113).

It has already been noted that these proposals have shaped an agenda for the whole Church, not only UPA congregations, to a quite remarkable extent. Of course, in their own way some of the proposals magnify aspects of liturgical renewal that also gathered strength from other sources, and some of these will become apparent as this work progresses. The stress on participation is perhaps the most obvious example, receiving as it does a much fuller theological understanding in the documents of the Second Vatican Council than its practical or ethical underpinnings in this particular Anglican report.[20] For whereas *Faith in the City* related its stress on participation to its combative approach to racial exclusion, the Constitution on the Sacred Liturgy required 'full, conscious, and active participation' because such participation 'is demanded by the very nature of the liturgy' and is the 'right and obligation' of the baptized as 'chosen . . . royal . . . holy . . . redeemed' (paragraph 14, cf. 1 Peter 2). Some other developments suggested by the report have affected the whole Church rather than the church in UPAs but have emerged separately from the report's recommendations – as in the massive and pervasive expansion of electronic technology to enable very widespread use of service booklets and cards well beyond the UPA environments in which the commission deemed them to be especially necessary.[21] While this was both felt to be desirable and found to be helpful, what is not always so readily recognized is that it perhaps severed many besides UPA dwellers from a sense of the resources of the 'ecology' of their worship and doctrine, which may be represented by a prayer book of rites for a whole life cycle and for a range of human conditions. Narrowing this wider 'habitat', cards may limit spirituality and related resources to a restricted range of foci – and perhaps for many to a single, Eucharistic focus. Perhaps, particularly in a culture conscious of its postmodernity, use of a prayer book including many resources expressing different moods for different occasions could suggest a possibility of integrity and fullness of life under God that extracted samples of a limited style may not. Such questions notwithstanding, the commission's work on worship in UPAs has prompted some significant changes in the worship of the Church of England which have carried implications for the wider Church and shaped its shared liturgical tradition.

Five years after *Faith in the City*, the follow-up report *Living Faith in the City* was published. It dedicated some attention of its own to matters of worship. In the chapter 'Celebrating Faith: Worship in UPAs' some of the key concerns of the original report are reiterated, and two especially significant consequences were identified: the work of a sub-group of the Liturgical Commission to prepare services responsive to the needs of the UPA parishes; and the fresh impetus by clergy and congregations to explore forms of worship arising from their own experience. This new impetus was said to have resulted in forms of worship which included the 'bright', 'beautiful', 'banal' and 'bizarre', and so the two consequences of the original report are in this follow-up related to one another – and it was suggested that one aspect of the work of the Liturgical Commission might be to 'rein in' some of the forms of worship emerging from the fresh impetus of the original report.

The Liturgical Commission had by the time of *Living Faith in the City* published *Patterns for Worship*. *Living Faith in the City* commended *Patterns* for its jettisoning of 'excess verbiage', its 'orientation towards congregational participation' and its provision of services on small, foldable cards. It drew particular attention to the conviction of the members of the Liturgical Commission themselves when they wrote in the introduction to *Patterns*: 'The needs of a UPA parish for worship reflecting local culture, language and concrete expression are not best met by a group of experts at the centre laying down all the words of liturgy, but by creating the framework and the environment which will enable a new generation of worship leaders to create genuinely local liturgy which is still obviously part of the liturgy of the catholic Church.' And it recognized that, if accepted by synod, this statement by the Liturgical Commission could prove both 'exciting' and 'revolutionary' (3.4), as indeed it has.

Echoing the bishops' concern about anxiety, *Living Faith in the City* recognized Eucharistic revision as a particularly 'painful nettle' to grasp in the light of *Faith in the City*'s call for more pictorial, concrete images and shorter texts for prayer. For a tradition which had expressed its unity in a particular notion of common prayer – the shared use of a particular, limited set of carefully nuanced prayers – the diversification of options and a more poetic or pictorial mode of speaking within them represented a range of potential threats, in addition to the loss of the 'ecology' of a particular rite, as noted above. As also noted, as it happens *Patterns for Worship*'s Eucharistic prayers did not receive synodical authorization and were not published in the commended version of the prayer book in 1995, despite *Living Faith in the City*'s affirmation of the Liturgical Commission's conviction that 'the forces of tradition, inertia, fear of insecurity and upheaval should not be allowed to prevent the continuing growth and development of the liturgy which is necessary to meet the needs of those in our cities' (3.5).

Taking up the observation brought in to focus in *Faith in the City*'s paragraph 6.104, that UPA dwellers appreciate being able to tell stories, *Living Faith in the City* 3.6 suggested that the Liturgical Commission attend to lectionary provision which included scriptural material excluded by the two-year cycle of the *ASB* which would cohere with enjoyment of stories. Following from this, it suggested that consideration be given to the question of how opportunity within the liturgy for UPA dwellers to tell their own stories might be facilitated, yet in such a way as not to disrupt the movement of the liturgy. In the intervening years, both of these suggestions may have come to fruition in so far as adoption of the Revised Common Lectionary has enabled a greater sweep of Scripture to be voiced, including its great stories.[22] Churches within the charismatic tradition, among others, have also taken up freedoms granted with the authorization of the Service of the Word, and have modelled to churches in other traditions ways in which congregational response to scriptural reading may be developed.

Finally, *Living Faith in the City* insisted that care, preparation and training would remain as important as ever in the context of more informal and spontaneous worship, and that 'in an age when the tv set and video player are to be found in most homes, the demand for visual as well as spoken presentation becomes increasingly insistent in worship', so that the Church must respond (3.7). One appropriate way to engage in appropriate preparation and to enable training of those with public forms of participation was said to be the development of opportunities for communal preparation for the presentation of worship, which would 'nurture prayer' and grow 'spiritual confidence' as well as evoke livelier liturgies (3.8).

After thinking about the work of the Liturgical Commission,

Living Faith in the City suggested that dioceses themselves be able to designate 'areas of Liturgical Experiment'. This would in effect be a means of testing the balance between universality and locality by allowing certain congregations, with appropriate permissions, to explore diverse forms of worship without culpability of illegality (3.9), and yet would allow their explorations to be accountable beyond their own particular local circumstance. It commended the notion of 'people liturgy' – informal, perhaps, but deep communal expressions emerging without centralized directives (as was believed to have been encountered in the responses to the Hillsborough football stadium disaster) as an element with which such experimental practices should work (3.10). (In the intervening years, popular responses to the death of Diana, Princess of Wales, including the funeral service itself, perhaps represent some other possibilities for consideration.) Exuberant as well as solemn moods might appropriately find expression in such 'people liturgies'. The final point on worship in *Living Faith in the City* focused on the role of 'celebration', especially when congregations meet in 'drab and depressing situations', and an explicit link between celebration and the biblical motif of feasting was encouraged (3.11).

Staying in the City: Faith in the City Ten Years On, published in 1995, devoted less attention to worship than previous reports. But it accompanied an authorized form of *Patterns* that had clearly developed many of the suggestions of *Staying in the City*'s predecessors. It did, however, reiterate the link between 'appropriate forms of worship' and evangelism (4.103) and in its update on the work of the Liturgical Commission drew attention to the theoretical and theological elaboration which the commission had offered on *Faith in the City*'s proposals about worship. This led the Liturgical Commission to publish, in *The Renewal of Common Prayer*, some extended reflections on how a common core might be promoted as a unifying and identifying strand of Anglican worship, as well as some thinking about liturgy in its social and congregational context. *Staying in the City* rightly suggested that *The Renewal of Common Prayer* indicated the seriousness with which the Liturgical Commission took *Faith in the City*, in that they 'felt it necessary to address these broader questions before embarking on the nitty gritty of liturgical revision' in terms of texts (4.132). And the principles developed in response to these broader questions were, *Staying in the City* suggested, employed in *Patterns for Worship* even to the extent that the Service of the Word 'consists almost entirely of introduction notes and a balanced "menu" rather than liturgical text' (4.133). (Indeed the Service of the Word might be regarded as an illustration of the title of the larger book – it is little more than a pattern for worship.) A more oblique note was struck in *Staying in the City*'s final comment reviewing the work of the Liturgical Commission, noting that liturgical language needs to be both 'simple and direct' and to allow '"space" for individuals to bring to it deeper levels of meaning' (4.134). This is a possibility which was of course emphatically not opened up by the General Synod in its refusal to authorize the commission's work on Eucharistic prayer, either for the 1995 edition of *Patterns for Worship*, or again in 1996.

Another important publication relating to UPAs, and also post-*Patterns* in its 1995 form, was the 1995 essay on 'Praise' in the Archbishop of Canterbury's Urban Theology Group's collection *God in the City*.[23] Although not a liturgy, nor a liturgical theology, it suggested important theological perspectives with direct reference to the situations described in *Faith in the City*. For instance, responding to the notion that in areas shot through with poverty, powerless and other disadvantages, the last thing that Christians ought to do is undermine the sense of the seriousness of the situation by being 'too joyful', David Ford and Alistair McFadyen assert that 'no account of a situation is truly realistic if it is disconnected from the transforming God' and warn Christians in UPAs against living 'in the grip of . . . false normality' which denies an account of God's presence.[24] Worship, they asserted, may create an environment that involves the affirmation of personal dignity and also celebrates the dignity of others, so worshippers may 'praise open' an alternative culture with a different future.[25] They may also exercise judgement on their present social circumstances, if praise can be seen as 'a witness to the ultimate contradiction of idolatry and sin' which UPAs may represent as places where 'there is a specially intense convergence of the negative consequences of our society's habitual idolatries'.[26] According to Ford and McFadyen, praise may help worshippers: 'imagine how things might be different'; 'find multiple ways of remembering who God is and who people are in God's sight'; 'resist "problem–centred" mentalities'; 'analyse situations so as to expose the idols that dominate them'; 'not to despair when good things prove fragile or short-lived'; and 'imagine time differently', repeating and teaching stories which can vie for allegiance over against other less helpful narratives by which people may live:

> It seems a weak gesture 'just' to worship. What are we doing every Sunday, every day, as we 'waste' time on this? We are resisting the most dangerous of temptations – to turn stones to bread, manipulate the world to suit ourselves, dazzle with successful gestures – in favour of a message that says to love God with all we have and are, and to worship God alone. And when we do that in the extreme situations of UPAs there is a sign of faith, hope and love that is desperately needed elsewhere too.[27]

Undoubtedly, these are important possibilities, though Ford and McFadyen do not engage directly with liturgies,[28] even *Patterns for Worship*, to suggest how such things might happen.

Children in the Way and its legacy for liturgy

Children in the Way: New Directions for the Church's Children did not receive the wide readership nor range of attention given to *Faith in the City*, though, in their preface to *Patterns*, the bishops clearly recognize its importance for the Church. Like *Faith in the City*, very little of the report is spent making liturgical recommendations, although a later, related report, *Youth a Part*, is much more explicit about engaging young people in worship, and so both *Children in the Way* and *Youth a Part* are considered here in terms of their evaluation of the young in the Church's worship.

Children in the Way itself belonged to a line of documents on its subject, and a quote from its most important predecessor, *The Child in the Church*, opens the report:

> The Church that does not accept children unconditionally in its fellowship is depriving those children of what is rightfully theirs, but the deprivation such as the Church itself will suffer is far more grave.[29]

The powerful language of deprivation in this quotation resonates in the light of the above consideration of *Faith in the City* and introduces a vigorous point of critique for churches that may then be seen to aid and abet already virulent forms of 'multiple deprivation' in UPAs. The language of deprivation also serves as a reminder that both *Child in the Church* and *Children in the Way* were written before the widespread acknowledgement of forms of child abuse, deprivation being one, though the latter report was aware of the realities of abuse and represented an early church-based engagement with some of the issues (1.11–13). *Children in the Way*'s timely consideration of child abuse may be seen as an illustration of a conviction it makes at a later point, where stress is laid on the need for the Church to engage in societal issues as the basis on which it 'is more likely to be judged by people outside its own community', although such engagement is paired to a detrimental comment about 'the niceties of the ordering of Church worship' (2.24) with the implication that worship is of no or little interest or importance. While abuse forms one aspect of awareness that the authors of *Children in the Way* brought to their work, a more pervading awareness for them was that children had 'become the centre of attention in our society today' (1.4), not least as consumers.[30] It was primarily this changed position of the child in society with which they wished the Church to engage.

Unlike later reports on the topic, *Children in the Way* demonstrated some optimism about the levels of young people's involvement in the life of the Church of England; it noted that 'some 400,000 children are regularly involved' (2.14) in a variety of ways. Sunday Schools, uniformed organizations, networked youth groups and choirs are among such forms of involvement. Significantly, and in a chapter whose title is relevant to the point – 'Children on the Edge' – the report stated that 'an introduction to Christianity through worship only can be an ambivalent experience' (2.12), and so although 'school models', especially Sunday School, are seen to have some limitations (3.10–12) they are nevertheless regarded as very important in the Church's mission among the young. The report extends special wariness to 'family services', which are recognized to be variously successful in helping attract and hold young people and their families in the church (4.27). A particular weakness of such services is identified as their dependence in many cases on the charisma of a leader, such that when particular charismatic leaders are not available the services flounder (5.12). Although not explicitly stated, there is considerable unease with this focus on a particular person, the unstated underlying assumption presumably being that authentic worship is necessarily God-centred. And the tendency for such family services to be non-Eucharistic is doubtless behind the report's recommendation that new liturgies for 'all-age worship' be developed, and in particular a form of Eucharist especially inclusive of children (recommendation 4.3). The call in the same recommendation for 'full consultation with leaders and parents of young children' is developed further still in *Youth a Part*, published in 1996, which, although having older children as its focus, demands that they themselves become much more central in the consultative processes of the church, not least in relation to worship.

The Archbishop of Canterbury's foreword to *Youth a Part* articulated part of the 'challenge' of fostering the young in the worship of the Church as balancing 'experimentation with flexibility and accountability whilst at the same time finding ways to help the members of [alternative worship] services remain a part of the Church of England' (viii). This statement reflected a much less buoyant mood about the potential of the Church of

England to hold young people, and stands in marked contrast to the optimism of *Children in the Way*'s authors who cited their 400,000 young fellow-worshippers. In a distinct change of mood, *Youth a Part* charted an alarming decline (1.13–15): young people were acknowledged to be departing rapidly from the Church, increasingly less willing to consider confirmation (5.34), and 'conspicuous by their absence' in 'most church congregations'.[31] Enormous gulfs (cf. 4.2) between 'youth cultures' and 'Church cultures' are expounded by the report's authors as the reasons for the decline, and worship is understood by them to be symptomatic of Church culture with which young people are likely to struggle. A recurring point is the strong challenge that 'the primary frontier which needs to be crossed in mission to young people is not so much a generation gap as a profound change in the overall culture' (2.11 and 4.14).

The report demanded that 'spiritually invigorating' (3.14) worship be made available to and for the young, amending the notable marginalization of their contributions to worship (4.1). 'Liturgy that is youth friendly – forms of prayer and praise that are authorised by canon' and the possibility of young people being 'able to participate in, rather than be an observer of, worship' (4.3) are said to be needed. Because 'liturgy and the style of worship can . . . exclude young people' (4.3), 'the Church has to be prepared to ask young people how they feel about worship and to engage in a real dialogue with openness and with a willingness to try new things and to change' (4.4). 'Youth congregations' (4.11) and 'alternative worship' (4.13–16) are cautiously commended, and attention is drawn to the 'messages' which may be given by the timing of such events: 'if they are tucked into a time when the "real congregation" will not be affected there is an implicit message that the group is marginal and not part of the main church' (4.18).

Whereas *Children in the Way* stated that

if children are to continue in the way of faith, if they are to continue on the path to which the Church welcomed them at baptism, then they must be aided and supported by the adult fellow-Christians who are also on that journey and must be acknowledged as those who sometimes lead the way,[32]

the tone of official reports changed in the intervening years to *Youth a Part*'s more urgent and sharp demands:

> Young people must be taken seriously if they are to stay within the Church, or if the Church wants to attract young people into its work and mission . . . because they *are* the Church of today . . . (4.29)

For *Youth a Part*'s authors, this meant at least that the young 'plan, lead and take part in worship, and help develop new ways to worship' (recommendation 6), for which 'a bank of resource material' needed to be developed (recommendation 6.1). Furthermore, 'liturgical experimentation' needed to be licensed (recommendation 6.2), and liturgical revision groups also needed to undertake to consult with young people themselves (recommendation 6.4).

Gathering fragments from Chapter 2: Constructing a conversation

Youth a Part shows little awareness or appreciation of *Patterns for Worship*, and many of its recommendations would seem to suggest that the provisions of *Patterns* are inadequate to engage youth cultures, despite the considerable development in liturgical flexibility in the Church of England that *Patterns for Worship*'s recommendations represent. *Youth a Part* could, then, be seen to have raised a number of very sharp challenges about the worship of the Church which are at least as difficult as those articulated in *Faith in the City*. Perhaps the central question the documents read together may generate is how the different concerns and demands of the urban documents and those relating to the young are in turn to be related to the common core that the Liturgical Commission was concerned to promote. Part of the purpose of this present work is to discuss these matters, as mutual testing grounds. Surely, a 'core' that excludes the needs of the young or UPA dwellers will be inadequate according to these influential documents, while, according to the Liturgical Commission, worship formed outside the core will be impoverished. Each of these claims will in the course of this work be tested in relation to the subtle and illuminating writings of three liturgical theologians, Gordon Lathrop, Don Saliers and James White, who are in turn a major focus of the following study not least for what they can contribute to the consideration of issues concerning 'common prayer' and cultural diversity in liturgical celebration, such as *Faith in the City* and *Children in the Way* and their related documents promoted. The theological discipline, liturgical theology, which White, Saliers and Lathrop represent and lead has flourished in the period since 1980 as the Church of England has revised its liturgy, though it remains little examined in England or elsewhere in Britain. So the contributions of these authors will provide a context in which to attend to the notions regarded as essential by the Liturgical Commission in *Patterns for Worship* and the *Renewal of Common Prayer*, and will provide a solid basis for their critique and expansion, as the liturgical theologians are tested in their own turn by the special challenges of the contexts under consideration. For, perhaps surprisingly, the discipline of liturgical theology has not to any great extent focused the specific issues that were brought to the fore by *Patterns for Worship*: deprived urban congregations and children as congregants. A mutually critical and enriching dialogue might then enlarge both the insights of liturgical theology and the contextual concerns of some in the English Church.

While both the principles and achievements of *Patterns for Worship* and the theological writings of noted liturgical theologians are important features of this present study, so is the context in which it is written, as the preface of this work noted. Gateshead is one of the places that was visited by the authors of *Faith in the City*; it is repeatedly mentioned in their text, and much of what follows is devoted to the attempt to understand the needs and challenges of deprived urban congregations, as well as of congregations wishing to include children in gatherings for worship, from a 'practical', particular location. To underline just one reason for this study's relevance, we may note that *Patterns for Worship* is now, at least in part, being incorporated into the range of material being published as *Common Worship*, which will become the alternative service book of the Church of England, alongside the *Book of Common Prayer* (1662), for the foreseeable future. The place of *Patterns for Worship* material in *Common Worship* will therefore to some measure determine the longevity of the perspectives it represented and of the resources it offered to the Church in its perceived need. It is in this context interesting to note that in at least *Common Worship: Daily Prayer* there are no rites specifically said to be for children, or for use with children among the group of worshippers using the book. *Daily Prayer* is an adult prayer book in so far as it acknowledges no concessions to children as members of a daily praying Church. This is despite its publication at a time when the Church appears to be wanting to affirm the 'sacramental belonging' of children in terms of their Eucharistic participation, and despite precedents of liturgical prayer designed to include material for children in the recent prayer books of other provinces of the Anglican Communion, Family Prayer in the *New Zealand Prayer Book – he Karakai Mihinare o Aotearoa* being a significant example. Yet that there are no resources for children speaks a great deal about children's 'belonging' and concern for their flourishing in Christian faith and habits of worship. So our conversation matters.

Notes

1. *New Patterns for Worship*, London: Church House Publishing, 2002, p. x.
2. *The Methodist Worship Book*, Peterborough: Methodist Publishing House, 1999, p. 51.
3. *Methodist Worship Book*, pp. 221–2.
4. *Methodist Worship Book*, e.g. pp. 52–9.
5. *Methodist Worship Book*, p. 115.
6. See the Prefatory Note by the House of Bishops printed in *Patterns*

for Worship: A Report by the Liturgical Commission of the General Synod of the Church of England, GS 898, London: Church House Publishing, 1989, pp. v–viii.

7. *Patterns for Worship*, p. 1.

8. The structure of *New Patterns for Worship*, London: Church House Publishing, 2002, is slightly different. For a brief discussion of its contents, see Stephen Burns, *The SCM Studyguide to Liturgy*, London: SCM Press, 2006, chapter 5.

9. Bryan Spinks, 'Not So Common Prayer: The Third Service', Michael Perham, ed., *The Renewal of Common Prayer: Unity and Diversity in Church of England Worship*, London: SPCK, 1993, pp. 56–67.

10. *Patterns for Worship*, p. 2.

11. *Patterns for Worship*, p. 264.

12. *Patterns for Worship*, p. 5.

13. Michael Vasey, 'Promoting a Common Core', Michael Perham, ed., *The Renewal of Common Prayer*, London: SPCK, 1993, 81–101, p. 101.

14. The notion also relates to discussion in synod as to how a minimal number of key texts might come to be 'known by heart' among Anglicans as a basic bedrock of contemporary Anglican spirituality. In ensuing debates the image of the 'knapsack' was used to suggest the scale of this common core, and the devotional prayer book *An Anglican Companion*, edited by Alan Wilkinson and Christopher Cocksworth, London: Church House Publishing/SPCK, 2nd edn 2001, develops the idea and suggests some possible contents of a spiritual 'knapsack'.

15. Colin Buchanan and Trevor Lloyd, eds, *Six Eucharistic Prayers as Proposed in 1996: The Official Texts for Final Approval with Introduction and Commentary*, Grove: Cambridge, 1996.

16. Disappointment with the *Common Worship* collects has led not only to a series of *Common Worship: Additional Collects*, London: Church House Publishing, 2003, in a very different, simpler, style, but also to widespread use of the lectionary-based International Consultation on English in the Liturgy (ICEL) collects produced by the Joint Liturgical Group and published as *Opening Prayers: The ICEL Collects for Cycles A, B and C*, Norwich: Canterbury, 1998. (Incidentally, *Opening Prayers* is dedicated to Michael Vasey, who wished to promote their use in the Church of England.)

17. *Youth a Part: Young People and the Church: A Report by the Board of Education*, London: Church House Publishing, 1996.

18. David F. Ford and Laurie Green, 'Distilling the Wisdom', Peter Sedgwick, ed., *God in the City: Essays and Reflections from the Archbishop of Canterbury's Urban Theology Group*, London: Mowbray, 1995, pp. 16–24, p. 16.

19. '*Faith in the City* and similar reports have made us uncomfortably aware that the forms and patterns which cradle-Anglicans have, perhaps too easily, accepted as the norm are exceedingly blunt instruments of evangelism when placed in the hands of those who have the task of proclaiming the gospel to an increasingly indifferent and sometimes even hostile world', Donald Gray, 'Postscript', Michael Perham, ed., *Towards Liturgy 2000: Preparing for the Revision of the Alternative Service Book*, London: SPCK, 1989, pp. 101–2, p. 102.

20. See *Sacrosanctum concilium*, 14. See extended discussion following.

21. This is exemplified in *Electronic Patterns for Worship*, London: Church House Publishing, 1995, and in *Visual Liturgy 4.0 for Common Worship*, London, Church House Publishing, 2003, for use with computers. For discussion of some of the general issues, see Susan J. White, *Christian Worship and Technological Change*, Nashville: Abingdon, 1994.

22. Fritz West, *Scripture and Memory: The Ecumenical Hermeneutic of the Three-year Lectionaries*, Collegeville: Liturgical Press, 1997, is an extended study of the lectionary. For continuing critique of the lectionary, from a feminist perspective, see Marjorie Procter-Smith, 'Feminist Interpretation and Liturgical Proclamation', Elisabeth Schüssler Fiorenza, ed., *Searching the Scriptures, Volume 1: A Feminist Introduction*, London: SCM Press, 1993, pp. 313–25, and Marjorie Procter-Smith, *In Her Own Rite: Constructing Feminist Liturgical Tradition*, Akron: OSL, 2nd edn 2000. Also, Elizabeth J. Smith, *Bearing Fruit in Due Season: Feminist Hermeneutics and the Bible in Worship*, Collegeville: Liturgical Press, 1999.

23. David Ford and Alistair McFadyen, 'Praise', Peter Sedgwick, ed., *God in the City*, London: Mowbrays, 1995, pp. 95–105.

24. Ford and McFadyen, 'Praise', p. 96. The insight is developed by Alistair McFadyen in 'Sins of Praise: The Assault on God's Freedom', Colin E. Gunton, ed., *God and Freedom: Essays in Historical and Systematic Theology* (Edinburgh: T&T Clark, 1995, pp. 32–56, and *Bound to Sin: Abuse, Holocaust and the Christian Doctrine of Sin*, Cambridge: Cambridge University Press, 2000, chapter 1: 'The Loss of God: Pragmatic Atheism and the Language of Sin', pp. 3–13.

25. Ford and McFadyen, 'Praise', p. 98.

26. Ford and McFadyen, 'Praise', p. 102.

27. Ford and McFadyen, 'Praise', p. 104.

28. Similarly, another of David Ford's works on 'praise', *Jubilate: Theology in Praise*, London: DLT, 1984, co-authored with Daniel W. Hardy, is not generally regarded as liturgical theology; see Kevin Irwin, *Liturgical Theology: A Primer*, Collegeville: Liturgical Press, 1990, p. 9.

29. British Council of Churches Consultative Group on Ministry among Children, *The Child in the Church*, London: British Council of Churches, 1984, cited in General Synod Board of Education, *Children in the Way: New Directions for the Church's Children*, London: Church House Publishing/National Society, 1988, p. 1.

30. See, more recently, Rowan Williams, *Lost Icons: Essays on Cultural Bereavement*, Edinburgh: T&T Clark, 1999, chapter 1: 'Childhood and Choice'.

31. *Youth a Part*, Introduction, p. 1.

32. *Youth a Part*, Introduction, p. 3.

Part Two

Challenging Liturgical Theology:

Children and the City

Part Two of this work seeks to deepen appreciation of the central concerns of *Patterns for Worship*, and to impress their continued relevance for contemporary liturgical theology. It indicates, in chapters 3 and 4 respectively, how the situation of British urban churches and of congregations incorporating children has shifted even in the period since *Patterns for Worship's* publication, effectively suggesting that the good work of *Patterns for Worship* needs to be repeated in a new time. In doing so, it exposes and explores issues that I am convinced liturgical theology has not yet fully grasped. 'Urban deprived' congregations, and those including children remain a challenge for liturgical theology and for communities celebrating liturgical worship.

This part of this study, then, sets out an evolving agenda which I believe an adequate liturgical resource and liturgical theology needs to engage. And so as well as referring back to *Patterns for Worship*, which was the focus of Chapter 2, it also looks forward, anticipating the discussion which is to follow in the next part of this work, Part Three. In Part Three I introduce three theologians – Gordon Lathrop, Don Saliers and James White (who are in turn the centre of my attention in chapters 5, 6 and 7 respectively) – as fruitful dialogue-partners with whom to engage many of the problems and possibilities with which *Patterns for Worship* was concerned. As I hope to show, each in their own way offers clarity and direction to the issues at the heart of *Patterns for Worship*. However, notwithstanding my appreciation of the three liturgical theologians, it remains, to my mind, that the liturgical theology they have developed has also not yet given as it might explicit, necessary and generous attention to the lives of the young and the poor. While the thrust of the book is about the contribution of liturgical theology to thinking about the concerns expressed in *Patterns*, Part Two also stands as a question mark against liturgical theology that does not engage the realities of lives considered here. Part Two, then, is meant to grate. It seeks to invite a liturgical theology that consciously articulates a more fully inclusive vision and range of resources.

3

THE CHURCH IN THE CITY

Twenty years after the publication of *Faith in the City* and the production period of the first version of *Patterns*, this chapter continues their concern with the Church in the city by exploring key features of contemporary urban theology and seeking to draw out some of their implications for the worship and mission of the Church in a new time. The chapter proceeds in a series of steps: first, it locates urban theology among a wider range of contextual theologies that have been such an important feature of the theological landscape in the latter part of the twentieth century. Second, it suggests an organizational schema for understanding different emphases in the emergence of urban theology, consisting basically of three 'waves'. Third, the chapter maps these waves of urban theology onto a broader, interdisciplinary range of perspectives on the modern city, identifying some major resonances. Then, having in these ways made some engagement with urban theology, the chapter turns to more specific questions about the possibility of particular 'urban subjectivities' which may call for or require distinctive approaches to liturgy in the city. Some perspectives on the religious expressions of urban subjectivity are introduced, and finally some connections to liturgical concerns are made in that context.

Context and theology

In Antonio Skarmeta's novel *Il Postino* (The Postman), the character Mario Jiménez makes a tape recording of sounds collected around the island, Isla Negra, which is his home, in order to send it to his friend and associate, the poet Pablo Neruda. Mario's tape pays extraordinary attention to the details of his environment, as he records the breeze moving chimes, waves breaking, the movement of a motor boat on water, the beating of his unborn baby's heart through the wall of his girlfriend's stomach:

> [H]is life and work were reduced to pursuing the waxing tide, the waning tide, and the rough waters churned up by the winds.
>
> He tied the Sony to a rope and lowered it into crevices in the rocks where crabs sharpened their claws and the seaweed clung for dear life.
>
> He rode out beyond the breakers in his father's boat, and wrapping his Sony in a piece of nylon, almost managed to capture in stereo the crashing of the six-foot waves that brought the driftwood tumbling onto the beach.
>
> On calmer days, he was fortunate enough to catch the hungry snapping of the gulls' beaks just as they fell vertically upon sardines and then took off along the surface of the water, having secured their prey.
>
> Then there was the time some pelicans – those anarchic, questioning birds – flapped their wings along the water's edge . . .
>
> The magical Japanese machine was recording the sounds of bees at daybreak just as they reached their solar orgasms, their noses clinging passionately to the calyxes of coastal daisies; of stray dogs barking at the stars that fell into the Pacific Ocean as if it were New Year's Eve; of the bells on Neruda's terrace rung manually or capriciously orchestrated by the wind; of the foghorn from the lighthouse as it expanded and contracted, evoking the sadness of a ghost ship lost in the fog on the high seas; and of a tiny heartbeat in Beatriz Gonzalez's belly . . .[12]

We could argue that Mario's project serves as a vivid analogy of what contextual theology seeks to achieve: careful attention to the particularities of a specific environment. The value of a contextual theology lies precisely in its detailed particularity. Indeed, it has led to attention to context becoming one of the most important features of modern theology, as increasingly it is recognized that the particularity of a social situation informs theological reflection and action. Whole schools of theology have now developed which are 'constructed with maximal concern for [their] relevance to the cultural context in which [they occur]'.[2] Vincent Donovan's text *Christianity Rediscovered: An Epistle from the Masai*,[3] on Donovan's experience of missionary work among an African people, is widely regarded as a classic of contextual theology, though the subject can also be approached through other forms of literature. Skarmeta's novel has already been mentioned, and perhaps none is better than Margaret Craven's extraordinary story *I Heard the Owl Call My Name* about the young priest Mark Brian's life and death among the indigenous people of the village of 'Kingcome' in British Columbia, Canada.[4]

As contextual theology takes its themes from the situations in which it develops, it does not usually begin from 'a conventional academic syllabus' by considering items on the systematic agenda: God, Christ, salvation, Church, sacraments and so on.[5] Rather, it begins and proceeds by attending to context through listening to those who inhabit a particular environment – hence the importance of testimony, understood very broadly. A powerful example of such testimony can be seen in the insistence of a 'peasant' in conversation with the late Archbishop Oscar Romero, as he powerfully forces the view that, although they share the same faith, they 'carry it in different containers'.[6] The exchange provided Romero with one of several encounters with the poor of his land which radically changed his perspectives and led to the politicization of his archiepiscopate.

In addition to testimony, gathering perspectives from the social sciences is also important to a great deal of contextual theology, and the descriptive and analytic value of social-science material is highly valued as it is in turn brought into dialogue with more traditional sources in theological construction: Scripture and commentators upon it, representative figures in the Christian traditions, texts and practice in liturgy etc. Robert Schreiter offers a sense of this wide range of potential dialogue-partners involved in developing a contextually sensitive theology: 'being a theologian is a gift, requiring sensitivity to context, an extraordinary capacity to listen, and immersion in the Scriptures and the experience of other churches . . .'.[7]

Given the importance of such dialogue and its developments, contextual theology is better understood as a related 'family' of theolog*ies* rather than as a single entity. This family would include liberation and feminist theologies as some of its most well-known members. Most of the theologies specifically identified as contextual are among those which have gained ascendancy since the early 1970s; and together they have argued for recognition that in fact all theology, preceding it or contemporaneous with it, is indeed also contextual. What they mean is that every theologian is affected by his or her 'blood' and 'bread' – blood: family, race, gender, sexuality, psychology; bread: location, livelihood, dependencies, socio-economic status and so on.[8] John Vincent makes the point:

> All theology is, and has always been, contextual. All theology is done in the first place by listening to the questions which arise for people, and those questions are determined by their contexts. Even and especially theologies which come to us as dogmatic were created originally within and by their contexts.[9]

Liberation theologians have shaped all subsequent contextual theologies, in so far as they have all come to share its emphatic insistence that the starting place of theology is its context. Since Gustavo Gutiérrez's classic *Theology of Liberation*, first published in 1971, liberation theologians have consistently stated that theology is 'a second act, a turning back, a reflecting, that comes after action'. Theology is 'not first . . . it arrives later on', following analysis of a particular situation – and, they would add, a resolve to confront and alleviate poor living conditions.[10] That situation, as liberation theologians are likely to see it, is 'the present life of the shanty towns and land struggles, the lack of basic amenities, the carelessness about the welfare of human persons, the death squads and the shattered lives of refugees', which result, in Gutiérrez's words, in the 'premature and unjust death of many people'.[11] Gutiérrez writes that

> poor and exploited people, the ones who are systematically and legally despoiled of their being human . . . do not call into question our religious world so much as they call into question our economic, social, political and cultural world. Their challenge impels us towards a revolutionary transformation of the very bases of what is now a dehumanising society.

He continues,

> The question, then, is no longer how we are to speak of God in a world come of age; it is rather how to proclaim him Father in a world that is not human and what the implications might be of telling nonhumans that they are children of God.[12]

Feminist theology, which might minimally be defined as 'a movement that seeks change for the better for women',[13] may begin with a similarly committed stance: the recognition that, apart from both massive disparities in opportunity and injustices in what is for many the 'privileged West', human life in large parts of Asia and North Africa suffers from a persistent failure to give girl children and women medical care, food, or access to social services similar to that which men receive. Together, this amounts to the charge that 'sexism is not something that hurts women's feelings, sexism is something that kills millions and millions of girls and women each year'.[14] In the case of both liberation and feminist theology, explicitly *theological* reflection is 'bracketed out' of the first stage of the process of reflection upon particular situations, as the first stage is occupied with acknowledgement of a situation, albeit in its sometimes profound horror. A related method is now also familiar in articulate forms of pastoral theology – as developed, for instance, in John Patton's book, *From Ministry to Theology: Pastoral Action and Reflection* (the title of which conveys the order of shifts in attention: 'from . . . to, action . . . reflection').[15]

Introducing urban theology

'Urban theology' is an emerging discipline in the wider landscape of contextual theology. It is marked by an acute consciousness of the distinctive situations in which it is developed. Clearly, not all urban situations are alike, and care should be taken to resist assumptions that may emerge from use of generalizations such as 'urban theology'.[16] Yet as with other forms of contextual theology, because the Latin verb *contexere* means to 'braid', 'weave', 'connect',[17] one task of any urban theology should be to understand 'interweavings' between one context and another, as well as, where possible, between contexts, Christian tradition and interdisciplinary perspectives. Another dimension of this last point can be seen in the dynamics of two widespread trends in the modern world: urbanization and urbanism, which reveal in different ways the interconnections between different contexts. The first trend, urbanization, is focused upon *places* – cities – marked by their large size, the density of their human and human-made environment, and by cultural heterogeneity. Urbanization is a massive world-wide trend, as an estimated half of the world's population now lives in cities, as compared with under 10 per cent one hundred years ago, and as population growth in urban areas has escalated dramatically in the past quarter century. Urbanization on such an enormous scale is especially focused around the Pacific Rim, though it is apparent in every continent. Urbanism is another world-wide trend, in which the varied *cultures* of cities – the values, products and lifestyles of their inhabitants – are reflected into their environs, which are coming increasingly to be linked to the cities by means such as the mass media, which are usually situated in cities. Urbanism, then, is a process by which cities come to dominate wider society as non-urban hinterlands become less and less influential.[18]

The vitality associated with influence and cultural creativity is one obvious factor of urban reality. Indeed, creative vitality is often an intrinsic element in the definitions of cities. Twentieth-century understandings of cities have characteristically stressed the proximity of intense, diverse cultures, enabling personal and social transformation. Yet because lively and chosen cultures can tend in urban environments to be the principal reference points for personal identity, the possibility of personal disassociation and social disintegration also emerges, as those in close physical proximity may live very different lives, with little sense of shared 'community'.[19] As a result of this, 'worlds within cities' emerge,[20] geographically juxtaposed, but intensely different in terms of their particular cultures and their prospects. The possibility of creative enclaves generates staid enclaves, and those whose populations cope with – and benefit from – the opportunities of new cultural interaction become separate from those who do not, and the urban environment becomes spatially segmented. The spatial boundaries between these different environments often become especially 'charged environments' as those places at which the relative poverty of the inhabitants of the poorer 'world' may be seen most starkly.

The designation 'urban priority area', used by both *Faith in the City* and *Patterns for Worship*, identifies spatial casualties of urbanization: that is to say, those parts of cities and urban environments in which social *disintegration* has been most acute. The designation does not refer to those areas which have flourished as diverse cultures have mixed and enriched one another, so providing new opportunities for their inhabitants, but rather to their spatially and culturally distinct neighbours. The subtitle of Michael Pacione's study, *Britain's Cities* – 'Geographies of Division in Urban Britain' – is powerfully descriptive, and Pacione's work itself is one of the most salient recent examples of concern which outlines and expands upon an 'anatomy of multiple deprivation' in such areas: it refers to a circle of low pay, dereliction, delinquency, unemployment, poor services, one-parent families, poor housing, ill-health, powerlessness, stigmatization, vandalism, poor schooling and homelessness, all of which are held together by the central problems of poverty and crime.[21] John Vincent, of the Urban Theology Unit (one of the most longstanding theological engagements with urban life in Britain) in his book *Hope from the City* helpfully puts 'faces' onto this 'anatomy', insisting from a Christian perspective that the issues are discussed and addressed with a focus on: low-paid *people*, derelict *human* environment, delinquent *children*, segregated *people*, and so on.[22] Such a humanizing perspective may be a distinctively religious or theological approach to the issues involved, and it is very much a feature of a wealth of theological literature associated with and emanating from *Faith in the City*.

This recognition brings us forcibly to one point that characterizes urban theologies: that, like liberation or feminist theologies, theology aware of its urban context is likely to involve recognition of an intolerable state of affairs. For example, *Faith in the City* underlines the plight of inner-city Britain as a 'grave and fundamental injustice'.[23] Conscious of an immediate environment marked by such injustice, Anthony Harvey suggests in his 'theological response' to *Faith in the City* that a contextual theology in an urban setting might then

> begin with genuinely urban and working class perceptions and build up a repertory of resources from all parts of the Christian tradition which would become the theological equipment of these local 'theologians' in the same way . . . as traditionally trained ministers are equipped with a smattering of Bible, doctrine, history, ethics, and liturgy.[24]

Some of the most contextually sensitive 'urban theology' in Britain has in fact arisen in the light of the Church of England report *Faith in the City*, which was pivotal in the provision of guidelines, adopted from those used by the Evangelical Urban Training Project, for parish audits as a basis for understanding the distinctive characteristics of local areas. In very recent years, however, rapidly evolving new dynamics in urban settings have loosened the descriptive and analytical relevance of *Faith in the City*, at least in part measure. This has in turn led to fresh forms and foci of urban theology, although the challenge to maintain a focus on particularity, and especially the particularity of the circumstances of *the poor*, has remained vibrant within many evolving modes of urban theology, as we shall see below. It is attention to this kind of particularity that we wish to insist upon in this work, with special reference to the liturgical resources and liturgical understandings engaged in by urban congregations. First, though, we may consider ways in which urban theology has been refined since *Faith in the City* and the other Church of England documents which formed its direct legacy.

Three 'waves' of urban theology

At least until recently, almost all urban theology in the British situation has taken its point of reference from *Faith in the City*. Yet that document itself represented a *development* in the discipline of urban theology as it was being appropriated and developed in the UK. The Anglican report and its Methodist counterpart, *The Cities: A Methodist Report*, developed a perspective on cities that was distinct from what in hindsight was recognized as the naivety of previous forms of theological reflection on urban life, particularly those versions of 1960s urban theology, in particular a notable example being Harvey Cox's *The Secular City*. Cox's text adopted a basically optimistic slant on urban forms of life, so that, for example, he found himself able to interpret 'urban anonymity' as a form of 'deliverance from the Law' in the spirit of Paul. So, for instance,

> Urbanization can be seen as a liberation from some of the cloying bondages of pre-urban society. It is the chance to be free. Urban man's [*sic*] deliverance from enforced conventions makes it necessary for him to choose for himself. His being anonymous to most people permits him to have a face and a name for others.[25]

Admittedly, Cox is concerned to establish 'responsible living' amidst anonymity,[26] yet his stress falls on the 'glorious liberation' that a metropolis may permit, freeing inhabitants from the 'saddling traditions and burdensome expectations of town life'.[27]

In sharp contrast to Cox's early optimistic excitement about the hopeful possibilities of city living, the later form of urban theology of which the Anglican and Methodist reports are indicative, interpreted cities as scenes of various kinds of crisis. They took as their focus particular dynamics concentrated in the spatial areas designated as 'urban priority areas' and, in ways very unlike the bourgeois tones of Cox's early seminal text, the church reports lamented a range of forms of deprivation afflicting UPAs. So *Faith in the City* called both 'church and nation' to attend to 'a vicious circle of causes and effects' that sustain 'the decline of the quality of life' in UPAs.

Part of the legacy of *Faith in the City* was two publications by a group convened by Peter Sedgwick, which became known as the Archbishop of Canterbury's Urban Theology Group. The group's two books were published in 1995 and 1998 respectively, the first, *God in the City*, being a 'collection of essays and reflections' by its members, the second, *Urban Theology*, being a 'reader'. (The first of these publications was mentioned in Chapter 2, above.) The work of the group arose out of the critique of one of their members, David Ford, who in various papers examining *Faith in the City* had pointed out a lack of theological vigour in the report itself while he at the same time suggested some relevant theological themes to animate and enrich the report's key convictions.[28]

The *Urban Theology* reader may be regarded as marking an end of the line of at least semi-official Anglican studies consciously referring back to *Faith in the City* (the Urban Theology Group disbanded on the book's publication). In the themes explored by the reader, it is obvious that it clearly relates to the era of the initial report itself, the 1980s, without great – if any – conscious awareness of the changes overtaking cities at the time of publication in the late 1990s. Perhaps the most notable omission is any serious reference to the rapidly advancing trend towards globalization, of which the migratory patterns of asylum seekers and refugees are just one instance. The reader's overlooking of vast contemporary trends perhaps indicates a certain decline in attention to urban issues in certain theological circles in the 1990s, and it perhaps also suggests the enormously powerful influence of *Faith in the City* (for good reasons, because of the agenda's own seriousness and importance) that it nevertheless overwhelmed other questions and perceptions for a surprising length of time and to a very large extent.

However, change in British government in the late 1990s re-invigorated more general attention to life in cities and brought British cities to a point of renewed focus in politics. For instance, two initiatives, the Social Exclusion Unit and the Urban Task Force, have each received a high national profile in their consideration of the problems and possibilities of cities, and each have had considerable influence on government practice. In addition to this, a series of government white papers has highlighted an effort to shift political weight away from centralization towards more local governance. In this new political climate, the inadequacy of *Faith in the City* has slowly begun to become apparent to a number of theologians alerted to the growing range of issues unimagined in the era of *Faith in the City*'s ascendancy. For example, Andrew Davey suggested some first hints of dissent from *Faith in the City* in a review for the Church of England's Board of Social Responsibility's journal *Crucible* when he proposed that the Open University series of course-books, Understanding Cities, presented an approach to urban life appropriate to the contemporary situation with which successors of *Faith in the City* in the theological field would need to engage. He began to publish his own such engagement in his *Urban Christianity and Global Order* of 2001, and has continued to do so in numerous other publications since. Unlike the urban theology reader published by the group of Anglican theologians, trends such as globalization shape the whole perspective of the Understanding Cities series and, in turn, the others who have learned from it. The three volumes of the series, *City Worlds*, *Unruly Cities* and *Unsettling Cities* (and their related video material), are also closely related to another publication co-written by some of the same authors who were also largely responsible for the Open University texts. The related document, *Cities for the Many Not for the Few*, arose out of conferences sponsored by the Open University and the universities of Bristol, Durham and Newcastle, and engaged directly with UK government policy under the Labour administration, especially the work of the Urban Task Force. In particular, it critiqued the keynote report of the Urban Task Force, *Towards an Urban Renaissance*, also commonly known as the 'Rogers Report' (as it was chaired by Lord Richard Rogers of Riverside). And although not engaging in any formal theological reflection, nor involving any professional theologians, these publications have provided a basis for a third wave of urban theology – following Cox et al. in the 1960s, and then *Faith in the City* and its trail of spin-offs from the mid-1980s to the mid-1990s. The OU and related texts are just now beginning to be appropriated by professional theologians in their reflection. Philip Sheldrake, for instance, in his *Spaces for the Sacred* of 2001, suggests that the Rogers Report in itself may be marked by a 'scriptural vision', whether or not its author was conscious of this possibility. And so Sheldrake writes that, 'In his definition of a sustainable city of the future, it is interesting that Richard Rogers adopts seven principles that are scriptural as much as or more than purely functional.'[29] Sheldrake succinctly summarizes these apparently biblical principles as follows:

> A city will need to be just (fundamentally accessible to all and participative), beautiful (with an aesthetic that uplifts the spirit), creative (able to stimulate the full potential of all its citizens and able to respond easily to change), ecological (where landscape and human action are integrated rather than in competition), 'of easy contact' (where communication in all senses is facilitated and where public spaces are communitarian), polycentric (integrating neighbourhoods and maximising proximity), and finally diverse.[30]

The recent work of Laurie Green is also representative of this most contemporary wave of urban theology. Formerly a member of the Archbishop of Canterbury's Urban Theology Group, he has since the folding of the group gone on to consider factors not conceived by the group in its time, and particularly the impact of globalization. His publications in this area, notably *The Impact of the Global – an Urban Theology* of 2000, have provided a focus for a new initiative, the Urban Bishops' Panel, an intercontinental concern that stretches across the Anglican Communion, established at the Lambeth Conference of 1998.

A very significant commonality between these representative texts of what we have labelled the third wave of urban theology and the perspectives of those in the OU team and its related manifestations is that they are forcefully asking questions about *vision* for cities – about 'what and who cities are for, and what kinds of societies they might most democratically embody'[31] and 'why cities – what are cities for?'[32] Sheldrake insists that such questions are both theological and spiritual,[33] and notes their omission from many influential texts in urban studies. For instance, he cites, rightly, the obvious interdisciplinary textbook co-edited by Richard T. LeGates and Frederic Stout, *The City Reader*, and this weakness is not made good in the second edition of 2000. Likewise, Doreen Massey and other co-writers for both the OU series and *Cities for the Many . . .* point out the lack of framing vision in current government-related documents. The third wave of urban theology can be seen, therefore, to have a potentially major contribution to make to wider public discussion at the present time.

Meanwhile, it is important to note the shift in terminology employed in the UK by New Labour, which has also contributed to the awareness of outmoded aspects of *Faith in the City* and earlier forms of urban theology. For the language that *Faith in the City* identified as central to the 'grave and fundamental injustice' attending Britain's urban priority areas – namely, 'poverty' – was sidelined by New Labour in favour of the notion of 'social exclusion'.[34] A mark of the powerful analysis of *Faith in the City* might be that it did in fact link poverty to the dynamics of exclusion, although it fervently held economic poverty at the centre of its analysis of the grave situation it identifies. For example:

Poverty is not only about shortage of money. It is about rights and relationships, about how people are treated and how they regard themselves; about powerlessness, exclusion and lack of dignity. Yet the lack of an adequate income is at its heart.[35]

If a downside of the newer terminology of exclusion is that it detracts from the poverty that remains at the core of the urban crisis, a positive counterpoint of this is that notions of exclusion are *dynamic* – involving active and passive agents – and so, with appropriate thought, questions of power can perhaps be more openly brought to the surface of discussion by use of the newer terms. Nevertheless, the shift in language has exposed some of the key weaknesses of theological and churchly understandings of cities, still often employing more generally superseded terms. As a third wave of urban theology develops, a fundamental task for it will be to appropriate the renewed possibilities of the political climate. Fundamental also, however, will be that this third wave of urban theology can at the same time remain continually aware of abiding realities – like poverty – which might otherwise be disguised by shifting rhetoric.

Mapping urban theology onto other urban studies: the shape of the city

A sense of the spatial concentration of difference in cities can be quickly discerned in the most basic identification of ethnic, cultural and 'lifestyle choice' ghettoes, as indicated by the popular designation of areas as 'the Chinese quarter', 'the theatre district', 'the gay village' and so on. With these very different areas in mind, Steve Pile writes in *City Worlds* from the Understanding Cities series, that

> living in cities has consequences for people's way of life. They are brought into close proximity with people who might be very much richer or poorer than they; or from an entirely different country; or have completely opposite views of lifestyle, politics, religion and so on.[36]

Cities are often celebrated for their capacity to accommodate diverse cultures in geographical proximity, enabling great vital-

ity and creativity in the resulting mix of social juxtapositions.
This potential for the blossoming of diverse but proximate communities is a feature often marked out by urban commentators as the central achievement of urban life, and in turn it is
seen as allowing persons and communities to be transformed
by encounter with the strange, or difference, made accessible by
geographical nearness. So it is said that the fact of the heterogeneity of urban life 'tends to break down stable identities because
there are great opportunities for people to form relationships
with others: to meet, to mix – and to change'.[37] One important
social consequence of this is that by allowing for participation
in these various communities without participants needing to
reside in them, cities permit wider possibilities to attach to the
notion of 'community' than is customary in more rural circumstances in towns and more so villages. And, importantly, this at
least partially redefines 'community' in terms of *interest*, rather
than geography.

Pile continues the quotation cited above with awareness that
urban heterogeneity may itself be experienced as much as being
threatening as well as being exciting and hopeful, for

> the consequences of this [heterogeneity] are uncertain – it
> is impossible to say how an individual will react to all this
> diversity. But it does suggest that the city exaggerates and
> contrasts, disorganizes and reorganizes, and changes speed
> (faster and slower), manifesting itself as an intensity that
> cannot be found elsewhere.[38]

In refraining from wholesale commendation of urban life, Pile's
reserve strikes a note that is not always sounded by other urban
commentators, and the uncertainty of which he speaks is absent
from some positive assessments of the intensity of urban life,
either religious, like Cox's, or from other perspectives. Pile's
tone stands in obvious contrast, for instance, to the positivity
inherent in the keyword of the architect and urban planner Le
Corbusier's vision, the 'radiant' city. Those less cautious than
Pile may be less ready to acknowledge that urban geography is
also marked by spatial arrangements which are *not* primarily

shaped by interest and choice, and that ghettoes of a different kind – less glamorous than the 'theatre district', for instance – are created by high concentrations of the economically poor. In Michael Pacione's incisive phrase, already noted and particularly apposite at this point, is that cities are marked by 'geographies of division'. It helps to magnify the point that although the language of poverty is not central in government-led discussion at the present time, vogue references to the 'socially excluded' catch something of the dynamic of geographically poor areas being actively contained by more powerful 'communities' which may converge on a variety of shared interests. The dynamics of exclusion can be pernicious, if more subtle than the physically (sometimes electrically) 'fenced communities' that are increasingly being created in many world cities by the middle classes in order to preserve residential enclaves of their own.

One of the OU team's complaints about the Urban Task Force's *Towards an Urban Renaissance* was the absence from its vision of the sustainable city of what they called 'a whole side' of contemporary cities. They refer to that 'side', which, although not named as such, is what were previously referred to as 'urban priority areas', those poor geographical areas that were the concern of the churches' reports. The dependence of Lord Rogers's proposals on the flourishing of forms of the New Economy, as opposed to majority 'elementary occupations', may be one aspect of this absence or oversight. But what is missing from so many upbeat assessments may take many forms, affecting the lives of large numbers of people who may themselves miss out on much of cities' creative potential. As the OU team suggests,

the vibrancy of urban life, bringing as it does diversity in close proximity, is certainly about creative intermingling, cultural mixture, and exploratory potential. But for many it is also about the desperate search for privacy, sanctuary, and anonymity, about coping with loneliness, fear and anxiety, about being seen, heard and recognised, about jostling for space, work and welfare, about resentment, anger and intolerance.

The absence of these latter aspects from the Rogers Report is exposed directly as they continue with further echoes of Pile's conclusions about the heterogeneity of cities, cited above:

> In part there is an absence in this Report of ethnicity, and of the general mixity of cities. And in part there is an absence of what we might call the underground of the unseen city: not just the illegality but the car-boot sale, the huge networks of hobby groups, the myriad of everyday concerns . . .[39]

Because the churches have moved well beyond the arguable naivety of what was labelled above as the first wave of urban theology, they too may have a very strong and important contribution to make in helping others, even governments, avoid falling for notions of utopian harmony or images of cities which effectively marginalize the perspectives of the socially excluded. Duncan Forrester's theological explorations in *On Human Worth* of the dangers even, in sophisticated ways, of 'talking behind people's backs'[40] – by which he means excluding some from discussion, or assuming others' experience to be the same as one's own – is just one of many lively and forceful theological arguments that open a space for a critique of any kind of 'centralized' or imposed 'solutions' to other people's perceived problems.

Even so, the OU team notes that there is 'much to be welcomed' in the Rogers Report at a time when 'after years of Conservative neglect' 'the positive tone on urban possibility is overdue'.[41] Pacione's book *Britain's Cities*, published in 1997, the year in which New Labour came to government, can be seen to chart a range of aspects of the neglect that the Rogers Report seeks to remedy, and which were also the focus of the Church reports. Pacione's articulation of aspects of life in certain geographical areas includes this concentrated summary of the realities of the side of cities that the OU-related authors suggest are out of focus in the Urban Task Force's work:

> The spatial concentration of poverty-related problems, such as crime, delinquency, poor housing, unemployment and

increased mortality and morbidity, serves to accentuate
the effects of poverty and deprivation for particular localities. Neighbourhood unemployment levels of three times
the national average are common in economically deprived
communities, with male unemployment rates frequently in
excess of 40 per cent. Lack of job opportunities leads to a
dependence on public support systems. The shift from heavy
industrial employment to service-orientated activities in
major urban regions, and the consequent demand for a different kind of labour force, has also served to undermine
long-standing social structures built around full-time male
employment and has contributed to social stress within families. Dependence upon social welfare and lack of disposable
income lowers self-esteem and can lead to clinical depres-
sion. Poverty also restricts diet and accentuates poor health.
Infant mortality rates are often higher in deprived areas and
children brought up in such environments are more likely to
be exposed to criminal sub-cultures and to suffer educational
disadvantage. The physical environment in deprived areas
is typically bleak, with extensive areas of dereliction, and
shopping and leisure facilities that reflect the poverty of the
area. Residents are often the victims of stigmatization which
operates as an additional obstacle to obtaining employment
or credit facilities. Many deprived areas are also socially and
physically isolated and those who are able to move away do
so, leaving behind a residual population with limited control
over their quality of life. Although support groups, community organizations and pressure groups can engender social
cohesion and make tangible gains, the scale and structural
underpinnings of the problem of multiple deprivation generally precludes a community-based resolution of the difficulties facing such localities.[42]

This kind of analysis is continuous with the claims of *Faith in
the City* itself, and can be regarded as updating the state of the
difficulties exposed so readily by the churches in 1985. Through
the climate of 'neglect' the churches also provided a vital minis-

try, as noted above, that nuanced the sharp focus on the issues identified so forcefully by Pacione and others. As noted above, representatives of the churches, perhaps more than others concerned with the issues, typically encouraged a 'humanizing' perspective on urban priority areas, so that as awareness grew of an 'anatomy' of multiple deprivation in UPAs, the focus fell on the people afflicted by it. So this 'anatomy' was given a 'face', as it were.

Striking faces in the anatomy of deprivation

Although the issues have received less attention from theologians in the UK, in the US, Pamela Couture in the same period drew particular attention to the fact that this 'face' is likely to be female and/or young, addressing the trend towards the 'feminization of poverty' and, crucially, the effects of poverty upon children's lives.[43] For example, alongside the very real disadvantages of economic poverty, Couture identifies some contours of a poverty of 'tenuous connections' that afflicts the lives of children, often in addition to socio-economic deprivation, and found within its matrix. This very personal aspect of impoverishment – tenuous connection – is in her account especially concentrated in cities, in which children may be more likely to be separated from their extended families, a factor which, she asserts, may well destabilize a crucial element in children's social ecology, particularly in an environment in which relations with other adults in social institutions in the neighbourhood are vulnerable, and this apart from the children's families' socio-economic (in)security. The economic forces that prevail in a neighbourhood, alongside other influences upon its milieu – government programmes and social services, and – not least – belief systems used by family or neighbours in order to make meaning to life – are other factors which may feed into each other and foster tenuous connections in children's lives, so that this exacerbates the experience of poverty.[44]

In response, Couture develops an argument for the Church's role in such circumstances as an agent seeking to influence all

of the systems of which children are part, and with responsibility for the 'promoting the resilience' of children and children's caretakers as they seek children's flourishing. Certainly,
where such children and the other people in their lives remain
in danger of still being overlooked in current government policy
– despite white papers that apparently promote their inclusion
– there is a special urgency that their experience of urban priority areas is noted.

Another striking face in the anatomy of deprivation is that of
the asylum seeker, for a notable recent feature of the urban British landscape is the constant influx of asylum seekers to many
deprived urban communities. The presence of this group of persons, in all their diversity – and sometimes very visible 'difference' – requires us to recognize that places remain the focus of
particular experiences of acute need. 'Sanctuary' is often a very
uncertain state of affairs, despite the fact that the rhetoric of
regeneration may be more and more current about the places in
which it is in some measure available. Asylum seekers bring their
own configuration of problems that very easily become knotted
in to the already debilitating arrangement of social problems as
well as, of course, in many places in the UK, bringing a black or
brown 'face' to the anatomy of urban deprivation. Among the
particular challenges faced by asylum seekers are very considerable language difficulties, adjustment to unfamiliar climactic
conditions, widespread resistance to the recognition or revalida-
tion of professional skills, racism, inadequate and disorganized
provision and social isolation, often magnified by emotional
instability associated with post-traumatic stress, apart from the
need for physical healing.[45]

Testimony by some children caught up in the situation of
seeking asylum indicates the kind of experience such children
may have endured and other experiences they may crave. Inger
Hermann relates her experience of working in a Hamburg
school as religious educator:

> [One child asks:] 'Is praying and that any use?'
> We reflect. Can people influence God? Doesn't God do
> what he wants anyway?

'I believe that the devil does what he wants and God can't do anything anyway. You see that on the TV,' says Dragomir, a passionate Croat.

'And if people do such devilish stuff, kill others and that – I mean criminals and such people – does God still love the criminals?' Mario wants to know.

Otto, 'Of course, they're God's children'.

Mario, 'Even when they do shit?'

Otto, chewing, 'My mother loves me even when I do shit'.

Mario, 'Idiot, God isn't your mother'.

Dragomir, 'Then my father. My father hits me sometimes, but he still loves me. He said he would visit me even in prison'.

. . . Otto, 'Wait a minute, I think that God loves me, whether or not I do shit, because God can't do anything but love. Isn't that right? Only we humans can do lots of other things, kill and so on'. Otto breaks off and sinks into philosophical reflection.

Dragomir (top of the class – why is he in this school?) sums up: 'The devil can do shit, God can only love, and only humans can do everything: shit and love'.[46]

We may note that persons such as Dragomir, Mario and Otto are not always central to some of the new modes of urban theology, however much their plight is itself an aspect of globalization. One danger of some newer urban theology is that, in its concern to harness fresh interest in the *potential* of cities, such theology may become 'gentrified' – like cities themselves – and so 'overlook' or even 'hide' some people and their experience.

The danger to be avoided, if at all possible, is expressed by the OU team in relation to both UPAs and to the newer phenomenon of middle-class fenced communities that are, arguably, an extreme of the tactics of exclusion that operate so pervasively in contemporary cities. The team laments the trends that lead to cities being constituted as 'mosaics of geographically inward-looking communities',[47] spatially proximate but disengaged from any attempt to facilitate the 'creative intermingling, cultural mixture, and exploratory potential' which are cited above as being within the capabilities of cities at their best. And, beyond the polarities of utopia and UPAs, Philip Sheldrake's modelling of a new phase of urban theology makes a crucial point related to the hope to avoid this danger:

> Theological reflection on cities in recent years has tended in England to focus largely on what have been called, especially in Anglican terms, 'urban priority areas'. This may actually produce an unbalanced result. If there are sinful structures of exclusion and social deprivation these are not limited to particular districts within cities but effect, or perhaps I should say 'infect' the city as a whole, both as built space and human community. If there is a message of liberation and trans-formation that the Christian gospel proclaims, it must be an integral one for the concept of the city as a whole.[48]

In this regard, perhaps one of the strongest challenges of the 'whole' city focus, inclusive of those who may most vigorously resist the 'infection' of their own enclaves by the excluded – comes from Robert Furbey in his critique of the New Labour rhetoric of urban 'regeneration':

> Recent British urban policy, for all its seeming 'inclusiveness', utilises the idea of 'regeneration' within a restricted discourse. It rests on an apparently expansive and diverse, if not contra-dictory, amalgam of spiritualities, psychologies and social organicisms. However, its blend of individualism, conservat-ism, liberalism and statism invites compliance with a policy agenda that excludes perspectives and questions that imply change for the whole 'body' in favour of an emphasis on its most obviously dysfunctional extremities. It is the excluded poor, the alarming 'underclass' who are assigned the fullest responsibility to be 'born again'.[49]

Some approaches to the urban Church

In the light of this discussion it is important to consider some voices that resist the bleak picture of the urban situation as represented in the tradition flowing from *Faith in the City* and so may also contest the need for resources such as *Patterns*. For example, Rod Garner asserts that 'there are unacknowledged "mission gains" in the inner city that elude the predictable parameters of success, yet nevertheless make a qualitative difference to local communities and the wider Church alike'.[50] One of his key assertions is that 'the Church is capable of being perceived by outsiders as an inclusive institution of indeterminate membership that is still prepared to blur the distinction between the household of faith and the wider community'.[51] An interesting question to pose to these assertions relates to specifically liturgical concerns, for while churches in various ways at the service of local communities might through their social provision regard themselves as 'porous' (in Garner's phrase) to inhabitants of their geographical setting, it does not seem to be commonly held that the Church's liturgy as a form of 'public service' is so inclusive.[52] Particular perceptions of exclusivity may attach to the Eucharist, perceived in the common memory as a rite of commitment and less readily identified as a celebration of hospitality.

The Methodist experience, upon which *The Cities: A Methodist Report* reflects, provides an instructive comparison to some of the Anglican approaches to liturgical questions that have been considered in earlier parts of this work. It made few references to worship, although at one point suggests:

> City churches are providing Christians everywhere with opportunities or new forms of devotion and prayer, worship, hymnody and meditation. Churches should encourage, and provide support for, such expressions of indigenous and rooted spirituality from and for the city.[53]

Experiments by the Urban Theology Unit (UTU) elaborate on the Methodist perspective. Yet, for a range of reasons, the

influence of the Urban Theology Unit on liturgical matters is
much less easy to trace than *Faith in the City* in the counterpart Anglican situation. It makes no claim to be systematic, but
develops a style that collects and reflects on stories that allow
inner-city dwellers to speak for themselves about the experience
of inner-city churches. Of course, some of this experience necessarily concerns worship, though the UTU literature above all
else provides examples of the kinds of struggles urban churches
face as well as signs of what John Vincent calls 'manifestations
of the kingdom', and they are perhaps best regarded as pen-
portraits and illustrations, often vivid ones. So, as one example,
Jane Grinonneau tells the story of a congregation battling with
a group of older children who gather outside their chapel. Having decided to set up a club for them, the congregation encountered all kinds of difficulties, but found the will to persevere
through encounters like that of one senior member of the congregation collecting from door to door in Christian Aid week:
she was greeted on one doorstep by the shout of one of the children known to gather outside the chapel, who on this occasion
called her mother to announce that 'her friend is at the door!'.[54]
From this unexpected sense of amiable connection, the woman
helped the church realize that the child had found an accept-
ance they had never appreciated, and so on. Here is an instance
of porosity (in Rod Garner's phrase), as well as an illustration
of a modest means of alleviating a vulnerable child's 'tenuous
connections'. Similarly, Duncan Wilson writes of working with
children who inflict damage in the church building and 'snatch
handbags from unwary elders on their way to church' and who
'later in the same week in junior club [will be] apparently happy
to accept the company, love and tolerance of the same people
whose church they made their target . . .'. Yet the hope of the
church is that, as he puts it, 'by some little miracle they become
puzzled by their acceptance among those they have already
wronged'.[55] In ways such as these, UTU books allow writers to
give specific, focused, lived examples of fragments of transformation. Indeed, the publications by the Urban Theology Unit have
sometimes provided the brightest assessments of the urban

Church[56] which might be related to *Faith in the City*'s vision of 'local, outward looking and participating churches'.[57] Of particular relevance to the quest for an urban liturgical theology and practice is the recognition that the Methodist background of the UTU may have meant that many of those influenced by the unit have not been expected to minister within the same liturgical confines as Anglicans preoccupied with 'common prayer'. Where writings of the UTU discuss liturgical matters, most of the references suggest highly participative, informal gatherings, using little liturgical text, though the project has generated a series of hymns, *Hymns of the City*, the best of which – associated with the Iona Community – have since appeared in mainstream hymnbooks and have enjoyed very wide use.[58]

Congregations associated with the UTU sometimes meet in pubs or social clubs rather than traditional ecclesiastical buildings. The Furnival is one such example, a public house on the Manors estate in Sheffield, converted into a worship space which resembles other facilities used by local people, traditional churches and chapels being reckoned to be alien to their experience. Where traditional church buildings have been employed, they may have been quite radically altered, made to resemble for instance a café, with people gathering around tables and chairs and meeting perhaps over food, or arranged more like domestic living space, with arrangements of sofas and seats rather than pews or chairs. The spatial focus of worship in such settings is much more diffuse than various inherited ways of arranging worship space, arguably stripped of the transcendent dimensions sometimes suggested by the traditional arrangement of liturgical areas and liturgical furniture, though it should be underlined that such assemblies often remain highly focused on the Eucharist – indeed explicitly celebrating some facets of the Eucharist muted in more traditional settings, such as its roots in the table-fellowship of Jesus. To understand the importance of these features of UTU congregations, some consideration is necessary of the possibility of a distinct urban subjectivity and its special needs.

Towards understanding of urban subjectivity

Steve Pile's comment, cited above, that 'living in cities has consequences for peoples' way of life' suggests the possibility of the
reality of distinct urban subjectivities and that, as Philip Sheldrake suggests, 'cities reflect and affect the quality of human
life'.[59] One aspect of the former dimension might be the ways
in which, in UPAs, enmeshment in 'the cycle of deprivation'
leads in turn to involvement in 'the benefits culture', itself a
major product of the welfare state, but with a shadow side.
One aspect of this shadow side to the benefits culture is that
dependence upon public services arguably in many cases inhibits initiative on the part of participants within that culture. As
a simple instance, the occupant of a council property or other
social housing may find part of the property broken and in need
of repair but may deal with this structurally only by referring
the 'problem' to the local authority rather than taking personal
initiative to undertake the work. Although minor in itself, a
lifetime's worth of such simple instances is not perhaps such a
trivial matter, as material poverty may be seen as being com-
pounded by a social system that permits referral of problems
but discourages and may penalize personal agency. A recognition of the range of factors which foster passivity of the kind just
mentioned need not entail the dangerous arrogance of 'blaming
the poor'[60] as such passivity may instead be seen as itself a form
of social exclusion. However, alongside examples of the inhibi-
tion of initiative, the theological claim might also be made that
such lack of initiative diminishes human beings when measured
against the Christian tradition's best notions of human capabilities, including self-governance,[61] which play their part in the
possibility of fuller life.

   One point that should be underscored as having special reference to the central concerns of this work is that envisioning a
church comprised by those living within the benefits culture as
'local, outward-looking and participative', as in the vision of
Faith in the City – indeed envisioning such a church celebrating 'full, conscious and active participation' in the liturgy (as in

Sacrosanctum concilium 14) – is likely to be a more demanding task than the application of the same principles in a liturgical church in circumstances outside that culture. At the same time, the liberative potential of such a liturgy in a culture marked pervasively by dependence on benefit may also be very great, capable of encouraging flourishing human being. In such a context, the liturgy itself may be one of few available resources offering a kind of opposition to limits imposed by the culture, and encouraging instead an expansion of human capacities.

Acknowledgement of the difficulties of overcoming cultural factors that inhibit initiative need not stand alone without any sense of how cultures might be changed. Richard Sennett's influential 1990s text in urban planning, *The Uses of Disorder*, is aware both of the problems that may so readily be encountered in the urban environment, as well as identifying structural aspects which good urban planning might change for the better. Sennett catalogues many ways in which 'ordinary lives' may be 'lived in disorder' in cities, though he is anxious to highlight the potential as well as the dangers of an 'anarchic urban milieu'. A powerful extract imagining the progress of an 'intelligent young girl' suggests a range of situations she will need to contest as she grows, simply by virtue of living in the dense, multi-ethnic environment of a city square rather than in the midst of a separated, stable and homogeneous community. Her life, as Sennett imagines it, is likely to involve: play on unclean and littered lawns, if lawns exist; constantly shifting neighbours, among whom 'everyone is in some way different'; and her school is likely to be a 'focus of conflict and conciliation for the parents' in that it needs to accommodate a great range of cultures. While elements of difference in the girl's experience may bear some benefits, working life (should it come) is likely, as Sennett imagines it, to present its own stretch of difficulties: gender-related inequalities in the workplace and 'two equally unacceptable alternatives of isolation: either a professional life where opportunities of social encounters are limited to colleagues who feel competitive and men who want possession, or the more usual housewifely and community routines, which offer no field for intellect'. Sennett seeks greater structural 'disorder' in the city in order to free the women he imagines from the cultural constructs and constraints that may inhibit them.

Likewise, in Sennett's view, more 'anarchic' cities would have some other boons, and for a wide range of people – not least those effectively marginalized by some ways of organizing urban geography. Among the benefits imagined by Sennett are, in relation to issues gathered around multi-ethnic identities, that 'enemies [may] lose their clear image, because every day one sees so many people who are alien but who are not all alien in the same way'. Furthermore, to aid 'the working class', the 'impersonal bureaucracy and faceless power' that can be 'used as the great weapon of the middle classes today over those who do routine labor' may be weakened through the reconfiguring of 'personal influence and personal alliance'. And this in turn would, he thinks, 'tone down feelings of shame about status and helplessness in the face of large bureaucracies'. For Sennett, what disorder promises is that 'men [*sic*] will become more in control of themselves and more aware of each other'.[62] In so far as Sennett's vision is realizable, the kinds of subjectivities possible within the urban environment entail liberative potential. Yet, just as in the different 'waves' of urban theology noted above, *Faith in the City* tempered the optimism of Cox's early texts, so it also might temper the assumptions that the creative disorder beloved by Sennett may be easy to achieve in any pervasive way.

Some reflections on urban religious sensibilities and urban liturgy

Perspectives on the potential of the city alongside those on the intractability of its problems yield a range of questions for liturgical theology. For example, how may liturgical texts and participation (whatever may be meant by that phrase) confirm identities that militate against and inhibit self-governance? Conversely, how may liturgical texts and participation expand capacities for creative disorder which allow identities to be enlarged and resourced, rather than liturgy functioning as a limited suspension of enmeshment in oppressive orders to which participants are subject? There is a need to be alert to Duncan Forrester's warning that 'even the Eucharist could perform the function of confirming the social order by periodically enacting its opposite'.[63]

Robert Orsi is helpful in approaching such questions in so far as he develops awareness of distinct urban subjectivities by considering their specifically religious dimensions, and so he mediates between the urban and the liturgical. He writes, 'The spaces of cities, their different topographies and demographics, are fundamental to the kinds of religious phenomena that emerge in them.'[64] Orsi endorses perspectives which might be imagined from attention to Sennett's work, such as that 'the arrangement of ethnic neighborhoods in relation to each other; the location of markets, schools, different sorts of recreational sites, and workplaces; the possibilities for and forms of intersections of neighborhoods; and the architectural details of different urban landscapes – including stoops, fire escapes, rooftops, and hallways' are geographical factors relevant to the formation of distinct perspectives – in Orsi's case, religious ones – in an urban setting. Indeed, Orsi uses the term 'architecture' to describe the limits and possibilities of 'urban religion':

> Specific features of the urban (and perhaps post-urban) landscape, which differ from city to city, are not simply the setting for religious experience and expression but become the very materials for such expression and experience. City folk do not live in their environments; they live through them. Who am I? What is possible in life? What is good? These are questions that are always asked, and their answers are discerned and enacted, in particular places. Specific places structure the questions, and as men and women cobble together responses, they act upon the spaces around them in transformative ways.[65]

In the light of this view, religion can be seen to help to envision and realize the potential of constructive proposals, such as

Sennett's prescription, for good life in cities. Specifically, the liturgical environment may be seen as itself a place of contest potentially enabling a range of questions and answers to questions such as those hinted at in the above extract from Orsi. Liturgical space may be regarded as a place of contest with the wider built environment – a liminal zone, in which the emergence of fresh identity may be possible as liturgical space makes its contribution to 'disorder' an otherwise more limited configuration of space which is lived in.

In the context of the UK, Laurie Green has offered some observations of his own on the topic of urban subjectivities (though he does not use the term as such) and his reflections, specifically on approaches to religion that seem to him to characterize UPA dwellers, are insightful pieces of testimony about the variety of particularities in the British context. Reflecting upon his own years of living as both a child and an adult, and then of working as a priest in a UPA, he concludes unsurprisingly that 'the Church does not seem to most inner-city people to be the appropriate vehicle of expression of their religious beliefs'. The Church, indeed, may be regarded by many as 'a foreign world', and the content of faith, in terms of Christian practices and doctrines, may well be unfamiliar to several generations – often all those living – within families. It is the various ad-hoc aspects of Green's personal reflections that are most interesting and valuable about his work, as few people have undertaken analysis of the kind on which he dares to venture, perhaps for fear of the danger which Green himself acknowledges of making 'the crass mistake of resounding generalization'. Yet believing that he is in as good a position as anyone to undertake the task, Green perseveres to attempt to discern 'some of the assumptions that make inner-city people feel that church religion is not for them'. These include the Church's seemingly 'fruitless hierarchy of values which, whilst being called "moral", do not convince them as worthwhile'. The perceived problem with so much of the Church's morality is that, according to Green, it is understood to 'denigrate . . . feelings of aggression, sexuality and other important survival instincts with the stigma of guilt'. But as well as questioning the morality which may be assumed as appropriate to human beings – and more fundamentally perhaps – 'there are problems about God's own morality too' for many in UPAs. For 'it would be easier for inner-city folk to accept a God who is above right and wrong – one who simply demands assent and obedience. But, as Fred would say, "God gives you a load of crap and then you're supposed to believe he loves you"'.[66]

The Church's seeming desire to 'wrap God up in abstraction' is seen by Green as a further factor in the Church's alienation from the dominant order of the UPA context: 'So the assumption of inner-city people is that they trust the truth of their senses whereas the Christian faith is so often presented in terms of metaphysical and subjective experience.' Another dimension is the common sense, which conflicts with perceptions of the Church, that 'it is not necessary to find ultimate meanings':

> So when the Christian theologian sees the faith as a way of finding answers to questions, searching for meanings, and making causal connections, they are working against the language system of UPA life. That system seems to prefer to focus in detail on the things at hand and define it rather than to place it in relationship with other things.[67]

Related to this, 'working-class language emphasises belonging' while 'the middle-class focus upon exclusive, private, subjective experience as the locus for encounter with God is often reflected in the language of the Church, and Christian professionals may thereby alienate the people of the inner-city'.

The major factor, however, apparently relates to spontaneity, which is related in turn to prayer, and therefore to liturgy:

> Living for today and never minding about the consequences for tomorrow is spawned of having a tomorrow which is so untrustworthy and beyond control that the discipline of long-term strategy proves always to be a nonsense. To save for such a precarious future is not a strong element in the culture! Many will lower their sights, feel happy with the life they lead now and 'have a laugh', whereas they see church people

saying goodbye to the fun of today in order to participate in a
life hereafter which doesn't sound much fun and, as with any
future, may not exist anyway.[68]

Drawing together various threads of his reflections, Laurie
Green concludes, 'Urban Priority Area inhabitants have every
reason to mistrust authorities and the Church has often not
served them well. Class, literacy, ethos and hierarchy have all
taken turns to promote an alienation' which the people of the
inner-city feel from the institutional Church. Yet, notwithstanding his critique, Green also notes a religious sense among UPA
inhabitants, albeit at a distance from institutional expressions.
Factors of this religious sense which touch on the life of the
institutional Church – although not in ways in which they might
be most welcomed by the institution and its representatives –
include, he senses, that 'the constant help and availability of the
Church, especially its clergy, is taken for granted not as charity
but a right'; that there is a representative quality about church
attendance; that buildings are sacrosanct; and that 'in general
the presence of clergy is counted as a blessing'. In the context of
both his critique of institutional Christianity and his awareness
of 'folk-religion', Green asserts,

> Worship's task is to affirm the continuing importance of the
> transcendence in the midst. Candles, smell, movement and
> music are all shared ways to touch on the numinous, whereas
> words seem to be less universal as a vehicle. It is difficult to
> know what a more working-class liturgy would be but I sus-
> pect that it would have to be similar to the temple worship
> in a Raiders of the Lost Ark movie. The atmosphere is all
> important, with the right mixture of emotion and toughness.
> Medieval plain chant from a heady choir or the gentle strum-
> ming of guitars do equally as well, but it must be direct, mov-
> ing and challenging.[69]

To respond to the range of issues identified by Green, worship
would need to embrace spontaneity and fight against abstraction in expression to a greater degree than may be the case in

much of what the UPA church inherits from the wider institutional Church. But other factors perceived by Green may
prove more difficult to accommodate, such as amendment of
the 'hierarchy of values' to which he refers, it being one thing to
adjust such a hierarchy and another to dispense with a thoughtful ordering of virtues, which may be implied by trends within
UPAs and elsewhere. The 'tribalism' that may be a part of some
ideas that could be associated with Green's comments on 'belonging' may yet be the most fundamental of difficulties attending any attempt to make worship more amenable to the kind
of culture with which Green is concerned.[70] And yet Green's
proposals do overlap in significant ways with the views of other
respected urban commentators, such as Kenneth Leech, whose
recent articulation of an 'agenda for urban spirituality' centres
on the importance of the material, conflict, wonder, the strange
and 'unknowing', among its central concepts.[71]

In addition to the challenges that emerge from Green's reflection on the structurally insignificant in the emerging urban
scene, the UPA dwellers, Graham Ward's studies in his *Cities
of God* explore another range of subjectivities in urban life
at the moment more accessible to those who find themselves
as the more powerful inhabitants of cities. The point of considering such a perspective alongside one that focuses on the
poor is obvious if Furbey's critique is to be taken seriously, or
Sheldrake's 'whole city' focus is to be appropriated adequately.
Ward's burden is precisely with the advances associated with
the New Economy, that is, the dual trend towards globalization
and towards atomization (one example of which is the urban
fenced community noted above), but both of which are represented particularly by the post-industrial new technologies such
as the Internet. As a piece of urban theology firmly located in
the third wave of literature, Ward strongly dismisses *Faith in
the City* – at least as relevant to the rapidly changing contemporary scene. His concern with 'the redemption of cyberspace'
represents one attempt to interpret the present fragmentation –
in Sennett's word, disorder – of urban forms of life as a means
of beginning to reclaim the ancient Christian concept stretching

back at least as far as Augustine of cities as settings for 'eternal aspiration'. Ward's argument is so complex as to be hardly digestible in brief reference, but from short citations we can learn at least that as he begins to conclude his explorations he expresses an understanding of the redemptive aspect of cyber technologies:

> Power today, the power to change human behaviours, the power to change minds, lies in the dissemination of information, the use and abuse of modes of representation by various forms of media. Theology is not either without access to this power or free of its problems. Theology can speak.[72]

One of the ways in which Ward wants theology to speak is to critique cyberspace for its tendency to diminish materiality, spatiality and temporality – the first of these three being very much part of Leech's key to a viable 'urban spirituality'. Ward's own attempt to do what he suggests is needed constitutes one of the first major theological engagements with the new technologies, and is also one of the first – and to date few – theological attempts to weigh its advances. Ward also thinks that theology

> can argue for the establishment of an analogical world-view in which the materiality of bodies is maintained and sustained by a theological construal of creation. It can amplify and transform what other, non-theological discourses are announcing as the direction in which we are heading. Analogically contextualised, the internet and the virtual communities it establishes, could then supplement our social relatedness and we would employ the computer prosthetically. This vision would constitute the theological response, and interjection, to the culture of virtual reality which is the non-foundational foundation of the contemporary city.[73]

Ward's proposals, for all their complexity, are undoubtedly important. His insistence that the redemptive elements of cyberspace are to be found in its capacity to promote and celebrate difference might be seen as essentially continuous with other perspectives in that he transfers some of the potential identified in the geographical space of the modern city to the virtual 'world'.[74] However, Ward's theological twist, distinguishing his view from the promotion of difference in non-theological contexts, is a push for a further possibility: that theology's vocation in such a context is – beyond its role as critic – to 'announ[ce] to the postmodern city its own vision of universal justice, peace and beauty'[75] that reclaims the materiality and so on that are currently 'being lost'.[76] So he begins to do some of the envisioning work called for by Sheldrake, the OU team, and others, when they ask questions such as 'why cities – what are cities for?'. For Ward, one practical consequence of this recovery is the 'recognition that I belong to myself only insofar as I belong to everyone else',[77] hardly a novel theological statement, despite the postmodern concerns of Ward's thought. Yet it is this note that keeps Ward's work free from the accusation that attention to the heart of the New Economy overlooks those excluded by it, a criticism which has been levelled at many celebrations of the New Economy, including those of Richard Rogers, as noted above.

Gathering fragments from Chapter 3

Perhaps, *taken together*, Green and Ward's reflections represent the beginnings of a comprehensive theological perspective on the modern city, however difficult the two kinds of realities with which they are respectively concerned might be to integrate. Such is the fragmentation of the city. Yet, as Sheldrake insists, the redemption of the city must be comprehensive, demanding as it may be to appreciate what holistic salvation may involve. Ward and Green's different understandings of what this will entail are at least two poles to which urban liturgy and liturgical theology might seek to be related and relevant. Urban liturgy needs to carry and communicate the tradition's best vision of flourishing human being, with its various attendant demands on participants from their diverse perspectives. Because *accommodation* to a culture – either excluded or atomized – may diminish the vision of fully human life, a crucial question to emerge for liturgical theology is how it might contest the virtual atomization of a technophile, or diminution in other modes, and come instead to function as an energizing and critical source of encouragement for appropriate self-governance, interdependence and indeed dependence upon God and others. An urban liturgy celebrated in any specific urban situation needs to promote a theological anthropology which enables personal freedom from manipulation and oppression in the manifold forms that these threats occur, and so offer a broader and better 'traditioning' than various cultural accommodations could possibly represent. In order to do this faithfully, urban liturgy needs to give expression to the concerns of the second wave of urban theology with its central emphasis on poverty and its resultant diminution of human potential, and which still remains crucial as a forceful critique of contemporary cities.[78] But urban liturgy certainly also needs to be educated in the school of the third wave of urban theology, in which stress also falls on relating various kinds of difference in a comprehensive approach to the city.

This raises questions about the possibility of 'common prayer', for common prayer in any particular context might represent the possibility of at least some kind of minimal relationship with persons of different contexts. The very possibility of this relationship might be one of liturgy's 'saving works',[79] enlarging worshippers' world of reference beyond that of their proximate culture. The third wave of urban theology's emphasis on the need for attention to the 'whole city', rather than either its most problematic or privileged parts, might encourage an appreciation of common prayer which resists liturgy becoming a reflection of the experience of the immediate locality or culture in such a way that prevents congregations closing down into mono-cultural enclaves that absorb the problems generated by urban conditions, and then sustaining those divisions. Awareness of the second and third waves could help to challenge urban divisions by embracing and expressing diversity, even as this is represented by 'common prayer' constituted by widely shared liturgical forms.

In our next chapter, we set alongside these reflections on developments in urban theology considerations relating to children in the churches, the other of *Patterns for Worship*'s major concerns.

Notes

1. Antonio Skarmeta, *Il Postino*, London: Bloomsbury, 1987, pp. 77–8.
2. Charles H. Kraft, 'Contextual Theology', Rodney Hunter, John Patton et al., eds, *Dictionary of Pastoral Care and Counseling*, Nashville: Abingdon, 1991, pp. 604–6, p. 604.
3. Vincent Donovan, *Christianity Rediscovered: An Epistle from the Masai*, London: SCM Press, 1982.
4. Margaret Craven, *I Heard the Owl Call My Name*, London: Picador, 1967.
5. Archbishop of Canterbury's Commission on Urban Priority Areas, *Faith in the City*, London: Church House Publishing, 1985, p. 67.
6. Lopez Vigil, *Oscar Romero: Memories in Mosaic*, London: DLT/CAFOD, 2000, pp. 136–7: '"Monseñor, [d]o you believe in God?" "Of course I believe in God." "And do you also believe in the Gospel?" "Yes. I also believe in the Gospel." "We're tied then! Because I believe in God and in the Gospel. We both say the same thing, but it's different! So guess my riddle, I've got a pain in my middle! Guess, your Magnificence, what is the difference?" Polín was going strong now, having fun with his gibberish.
'"I have no idea Polín. You'll have to tell me." Monseñor was laughing.
'"You believe in the Gospel because it's your job. You study it, you read it and you preach it. Your thing is being a bishop! And me . . . I can hardly read, and I haven't studied all the 'indiology' in the Gospel, but I do believe it. You believe in it as an occupation, and I believe in it because I need to. Because God says that He doesn't want there to be rich and poor. And I'm poor! See the difference? Do you get it? We have the same faith, but we're carrying it around in different containers."
'Monseñor looked at this man Polín who was all spark. And from that day on, they became the greatest of friends.'
7. Robert Schreiter, *Constructing Local Theologies*, London: SCM Press, 1985), pp. 16–17.
8. John Vincent, 'An Urban Hearing for the Church', John Vincent and Chris Rowland, eds, *Gospel from the City*, Sheffield: Urban

Theology Unit, 1997, pp. 105–16, p. 115. See also: John Vincent, 'Developing Contextual Theologies', *Epworth Review* 27 (2000), pp. 62–77.

9. John Vincent, 'Liberation Theology in Britain 1975–1995', John Vincent and Christopher Rowland, eds, *Liberation Theology UK*, Sheffield: Urban Theology Unit, 1995, pp. 10–20, p. 18.

10. Gustavo Gutiérrez, 'Toward a Theology of Liberation', James Nickeloff, ed., *Gustavo Gutiérrez: Essential Writings*, London: SCM Press, 1997, p. 24.

11. Christopher Rowland, 'Introduction', Christopher Rowland, ed., *Cambridge Companion to Liberation Theology*, Cambridge: Cambridge University Press, 1998, p. 2.

12. Quoted in Duncan Forrester, *On Human Worth: A Christian Vindication of Equality*, London: SCM Press, 2001, p. 157.

13. Ann Loades, ed., *Feminist Theology: A Reader*, London: SPCK, 1990, p. 1.

14. Janet Martin Soskice, 'Just Women's Problems?', Ann Loades, ed., *Spiritual Classics from the Late Twentieth Century*, London: Church House Publishing, 1994, pp. 55–8.

15. John Patton, *From Ministry to Theology: Pastoral Action and Reflection*, Nashville: Abingdon, 1990.

16. Some helpful recent remarks on the theological character of urban theology may be found in Kenneth Leech, *Through Our Long Exile: Contextual Theology and the Urban Experience*, London: DLT, 2001, chapter 7: 'The Captivity and Liberation of Theology'.

17. See Daniel W. Hardy, 'The Future of Theology in a Complex World', *God's Ways with the World: Thinking and Practising Christian Faith*, Edinburgh: T&T Clark, 1997, pp. 31–50, p. 32.

18. These themes have only very recently been incorporated into urban theologies: see, for example, Andrew Davey, *Urban Christianity and Global Order: Theological Resources for an Urban Future*, London: SPCK, 2001, Part I, 'Understanding the Urban'.

19. Steve Pile, 'What Is a City?', Doreen Massey, John Allen and Steve Pile, eds, *City Worlds*, London: Routledge, 1999, pp. 3–53.

20. John Allen, 'Worlds within Cities', Massey, Allen and Pile, eds, *City Worlds*, pp. 53–95.

21. Michael Pacione, 'Urban Restructuring and the Reproduction of Inequality in Britain's Cities: An Overview', Michael Pacione, ed., *Britain's Cities: Geographies of Division in Urban Britain*, London: Routledge, 1997, pp. 7–60, esp. p. 42.

22. John Vincent, *Hope from the City*, Peterborough: Epworth, 2000, p. 15.

23. Archbishop of Canterbury's Commission on Urban Priority Areas, *Faith in the City*, p. xv.

24. Anthony Harvey, 'Introduction', Anthony Harvey, ed., *Theology in the City*, London: SPCK, 1989, pp. 1–14, pp. 12–13.

25. Harvey Cox, *The Secular City*, London: SCM Press, 1967, p. 47.

26. Cox, *Secular City*, p. 48.

27. Cox, *Secular City*, p. 49. It should, however, be noted that Cox's own later writings recognize that 'instead of contributing to the liberative process, many cities have become sprawling concentrations of human misery, wracked with racial, religious, and class animosity', among many other comments that are less positive than his earlier assessments of urban life. It should also be noted that latterly he makes special references to the liberative contributions of new theologies emerging since the 1970s, especially liberation, feminist and black. Cf. 'The Secular City 25 Years Later', *The Christian Century* 1990 (7 November), pp. 1025–9.

28. Notably, David Ford, 'Faith in the Cities: Corinth and the Modern City', Colin Gunton and Daniel W. Hardy, eds., *On Being the Church: Essays on the Christian Community*, Edinburgh: T&T Clark, 1989, pp. 225–56.

29. Philip Sheldrake, *Spaces for the Sacred*, London: SCM Press, 2001, p. 166.

30. Sheldrake, *Spaces for the Sacred*, pp. 166–7; cf. Richard Rogers, *Cities for a Small Planet*, London: Faber and Faber, 1997, pp. 167–8, where these qualities are summarized; also, Massey et al., *Unruly Cities?*, eds Steve Pile, Christopher Brook and Gerry Mooney, London: Routledge/Open University, 1999, p. 367.

31. Ash Amin, Doreen Massey and Nigel Thrift, *Cities for the Many Not for the Few*, Bristol: Policy Press, 2000, p. v.

32. Sheldrake, *Spaces for the Sacred*, p. 163.

33. Sheldrake, *Spaces for the Sacred*, p. 148.

34. See David Byrne, *Social Exclusion*, Milton Keynes: Open University Press, 1999.

35. *Faith in the City*, 9.4.

36. Pile, 'What Is a City?', p. 49.

37. Pile, 'What Is a City?', p. 48.

38. Pile, 'What Is a City?', p. 49.

39. Amin et al., *Cities for the Many*, p. 4.

40. Forrester, *On Human Worth*, p. 14.

41. Amin et al., *Cities for the Many*, pp. 1–2.

42. Pacione, 'Urban Restructuring in Britain's Cities', p. 43.

43. Pamela Couture, *Blessed Are the Poor: Women's Poverty, Family Policy and Practical Theology*, Nashville: Abingdon, 1991, and *Seeing Children, Seeing God: A Practical Theology of Children and Poverty*, Nashville: Abingdon, 2000. Ann Loades's paper for the Centre for Theology and Public Issues (CTPI), 'Feminist Reflections

on the Morality of the New Right', is an exception to the British dearth: found in Michael Northcott, ed., *Vision and Prophecy: The Tasks of Social Theology Today*, Edinburgh: CTPI, 1991, pp. 49–61.

44. Couture, *Seeing Children, Seeing God*, p. 24. Interestingly, she draws attention to the remarkable, multinational consensus around the Convention on the Rights of the Child, 'the treaty that has created more international consensus than any treaty in history', as a means for assessing children's poverties. For consideration of some of the same issues from a British setting, see Michael Northcott, 'Children', Peter Sedgwick, ed., *God in the City: Essays and Reflections from the Archbishop of Canterbury's Urban Theology Group*, London: Mowbray, 1995, pp. 139–52.

45. The plight of asylum seekers is a topic that has as yet received almost no attention from theologians in the UK. The very sparse resources include: Helen Kimble, *Desperately Seeking Asylum*, Glasgow: Wild Goose Publications, 1998. An important contribution from another perspective is Michael Dummett, *On Immigration and Asylum*, Oxford: Oxford University Press, 2000. A modest contribution to the discussion is also Stephen Burns, *Welcoming Asylum Seekers*, Cambridge: Grove Books, 2004.

46. Inger Hermann, *Born into Violence: Children in the Shadows*, London: SCM Press, 2001, pp. 11–12.

47. Amin et al., *Cities for the Many*, p. 41.

48. Sheldrake, *Spaces for the Sacred*, p. 166.

49. Robert Furbey, 'Faith in Urban "Regeneration"?', *Modern Believing* 42.4 (2001), pp. 5–15, p. 13; and see also Robert Furbey, 'Urban "Regeneration": Reflections on a Metaphor', *Critical Social Policy* 19 (1999), pp. 419–45.

50. Rex Garner, 'Affirming the Urban Church', *Theology* 53 (2000), pp. 266–72, p. 267.

51. Garner, 'Affirming the Urban Church', p. 268.

52. Odo Casel defines 'liturgy' as 'public service' in *The Mystery of Christian Worship*, cited in a key extract, Odo Casel, 'Mystery and Liturgy', Dwight W. Vogel, ed., *Primary Sources of Liturgical Theology*, Collegeville: Liturgical, 2000, pp. 29–35, p. 30.

53. John Vincent and Helen Dent, eds, *The Cities: A Methodist Report*, London: NCH Action for Children, 1997, p. 125.

54. Jane Grinonneau, 'City Kids as Signs of the Kingdom', Vincent and Rowland, eds, *Gospel from the City*, pp. 12–29, p. 28.

55. Duncan Wilson, 'Gospel Values in the Urban Church', Vincent and Rowland, eds, *Gospel from the City*, pp. 86–104, p. 94.

56. A good example of which is Wilson, 'Gospel Values in the Urban Church'.

57. Wilson, 'Gospel Values', *passim*. Compare the echoes of emphasis on story in the urban church in Janet Walton and Eleanor Scott Meyers, 'Ritual Expression in the Urban Church', Eleanor Scott Meyers, ed., *Envisioning the New City*, Louisville: Westminister John Knox Press, 1992, pp. 156–67, p. 157.

58. Examples include 'Will you come and follow me?', 'Jesus Christ is waiting' and 'Inspired by love and anger'. Music books from the Iona Community include *Love from Below*, Glasgow: Wild Goose Publications, 1989, among many others. A number of hymns from the Iona Community have recently been incorporated into 'mainstream' hymnbooks.

59. Sheldrake, *Spaces for the Sacred*, p. 153.

60. See: Byrne, *Social Exclusion*, chapter 1.

61. On 'self-governance', see Ann Loades, *Feminist Theology: Voices from the Past*, Oxford: Polity, 2001, chapter 1.

62. All references to Richard Sennett, *The Uses of Disorder* are from Doreen Massey et al., eds, *Unruly Cities*, pp. 364–6.

63. Forrester, *On Human Worth*, p. 119.

64. Robert Orsi, *Gods of the City: Religion and the American Urban Landscape*, Bloomington, Indiana: Indiana University Press, 2000, p. 43.

65. Orsi, ed., *Gods of the City*, pp. 43–4.

66. Laurie Green, 'Blowing Bubbles: Poplar', Sedgwick, ed., *God in the City*, pp. 72–92, p. 82. Perhaps in a similar vein, a piece of graffiti on a wall near my home in Gateshead read 'God is a shit'.

67. Green, 'Blowing Bubbles', pp. 82–3.

68. Green, 'Blowing Bubbles', p. 83.

69. Green, 'Blowing Bubbles', pp. 84–5.

70. On 'belonging before believing' as a pattern of finding faith, see Grace Davie, 'Believing and Belonging', Geoffrey Ahern and Grace Davie, *Inner-City God: The Nature of Belief in the Inner City*, London: Hodder and Stoughton, 1987, pp. 71–4. For the general context of discussion about the relationship between belonging and belief, see John Finney, *Finding Faith Today: How Does It Happen?*, Swindon: Bible Society, 1992, and, for some helpful reflections on the potential danger of exclusivity, see Peter Selby, *Be-Longing: Challenge to the Tribal Church*, London: SPCK, 1991.

71. Kenneth Leech, *Through our Long Exile: Contextual Theology and the Urban Experience*, London: DLT, 2001, pp. 206–9.

72. Graham Ward, *Cities of God*, London: Routledge, 2000, p. 256.

73. Ward, *Cities of God*, p. 256.

74. Ward, *Cities of God*, p. 224.

75. Ward, *Cities of God*, p. 70.

76. Ward, *Cities of God*, p. 224.

77. Ward, *Cities of God*, 260.
78. Thus far, in the UK, such empathy and condemnation has been voiced in the likes of John Vincent's edited collection, *Hymns of the City*, Sheffield: Urban Theology Unit, no date) and in the occasional urban references within the Iona Community prayer texts.
79. Rebecca Chopp, *Saving Work: Feminist Practices of Theological Education*, Louisville: Westminster John Knox Press, 1995, develops the phrase 'saving work' to elaborate upon the task of theology.

4

CHILDREN IN THE CHURCH

This chapter develops the second core concern of *Patterns for Worship*, looking at the present situation of children in the Church. It begins by noting the strange absence of reflection on children's lives in a great deal of Christian theology, not least in relation to liturgy. It then turns to the Gospels in search of perspectives to inform a theology of children and childhood, before turning to the present opportunity for hospitality to children in the Christian community presented by recent moves towards their 'sacramental belonging' expressed in their participation in the Eucharist. Some of the developments in Anglican practice concerning children's involvement in worship are outlined, and some of the lessons that others might learn from Roman Catholic approaches to children's liturgy are outlined. In drawing on the experience and precedents of Catholic practice, the conversation stays connected to the principle of participation so clearly articulated at the Second Vatican Council, where this study began.

A theological oversight

Children are a neglected topic in Christian theology, as is evidenced by reference to almost any dictionary or standard text book in any of the various subject areas of theology's related disciplines – biblical studies, systematics, ethics, pastoral theology, or liturgy, for example. In such dictionaries, whole articles devoted to topics such as 'child', 'childhood', or 'children' are extremely rare, and, indeed, passing references to children in relation to other topics are also strangely infrequent.

An example of this phenomenon in the field of liturgical studies can be found in the widely used standard reference work *The Study of Liturgy*, edited by a team of leading liturgical scholars – in its initial edition by the Anglican Cheslyn Jones, Methodist Geoffrey Wainwright and Roman Catholic Edward Yarnold – and representing a variety of Christian traditions, as well as being republished and updated in 1992 (having originally appeared in 1978). The first edition includes no references to children in the headings of its 65 articles, and no subject heading exists in the index to suggest any substantial references to children. Nor do the 14 years between editions of the book seem to have generated fresh reflection about children in liturgy (itself an indicator of the very newness of concern with children's participation in the Eucharist, which began to come into a world-wide Anglican focus only in 1985).[1] One of the major parts of the book is given to topics relating to 'initiation', in which the historical shift from adult to infant baptism is delineated in the sketchiest terms. However, consideration of children as worshippers is entirely absent from other major parts of the book concerned with 'theology', 'setting' and 'pastoral orientation'.

Notwithstanding the book's achievements, this oversight of children in what is a basic orientation to important concerns in liturgical studies must count as one of its limitations (alongside the fact that although some of its authors have experience of life and worship in other cultures, they all write from their particular setting in either the USA or a limited area of Europe – all but one of the Europeans from the UK, all but two are ordained in their respective denominations, and all but one are men). The absence of thinking about children in such standard reference works may therefore be partially determined by the reality that theology in both its academic and ecclesial contexts remains dominated by men 'privileged' by post-Enlightenment versions of patriarchy. A recent book – possibly the first of its kind – about 'the child in Christian thought', edited by Marcia Bunge, includes only 4 (of 18) chapters about theologians writing since 'the birth of modern theology' – Friedrich Schleiermacher, Karl Barth and Karl Rahner, and then a collection of some recent Christian feminist writers who are considered together in one chapter. Of the three figures deemed major enough to receive a chapter to themselves, only Rahner devotes very focused attention to thinking about childhood – even then amounting only to a few articles in the enormous corpus of his work.[2] This notwithstanding, among contemporary theologians, Hans Urs von Balthasar and Stanley Hauerwas deserve some recognition alongside Rahner, for their consideration of children or childhood.[3] Had *The Child in Christian Thought* been more comprehensive, their perspectives might well also have been included in a survey of recent writings in theology devoted to 'the child'. However, as Bonnie McClemore-Miller points out in *The Child in Christian Thought*, it has been feminist theologians who have begun to make the most significant contributions to modern Christian thought about children, and in their case this has happened only very recently as the arguments of feminist theology have become established enough in broader theological discourse not to risk dissolving primary concern about women's self-determination by diverting attention to other matters, however important these might also be. In an environment that is ignorant of its patriarchal assumptions, feminists have needed to be particularly careful about not undermining their initial concerns in their emerging quest for justice for the young.

If children are mentioned in liturgical studies in reference to infant baptism, but in few if any other contexts, a similar neglect across the theological disciplines is observed in Ann Loades's remark that children are virtually absent from consideration in theological ethics from the stage of embryonic life through to adolescence, when in any case questions of sexuality are usually the narrow focus of concern.[4] Very gradually, sexuality is being considered as a linking theme between these periods of pre-natality and post-pubescence, and this is especially the case with forms of sexuality that have been grievously distorted by harmful adult–child relationships. The emerging concern of some theologians (again, often feminists) with the abuse of children testifies powerfully to these phenomena. Likewise, a limited amount of pastoral theology, such as that developed by Charles Gerkin and others who adopt developmental-psychological insights from 'life-cycle' perspectives such as those of Erik Erikson,[5] may do something to widen theological horizons and attend to some other needs of the young. However, pastoral-theological consideration of the young often remains strongly related to questions of well-being for childrens' primary carers. It is another feminist theologian, namely Pamela Couture, who has made some important connections between different theological subject areas, addressing the 'feminization of poverty' in her book *Blessed Are the Poor*,[6] and considering some of the implications of this for children's lives, alongside other matters, in a following work *Seeing Children, Seeing God*.

Retrieving the tradition

It may be significant that the widespread dearth of thinking about children is mirrored in the silence of the canonical Gospels' stories of Jesus. Mark and John make no reference to Jesus' years prior to his public ministry as a grown man, while only Matthew and Luke include some infancy narratives, the historicity of which is highly debated. The historically disputable status of the infancy narratives has itself become the subject of some thinking about children by pastoral theologian Donald Capps. In *The Child's Song*, he posits that the infancy narratives' 'theory' that Jesus was born of a virgin may function as a religious source of very real trauma, in so far as it may 'keep what really happened in Jesus' case from coming to light' and ally dynamics inherent in child abuse and children's struggles to free themselves from it.[7] Elaborating upon Jane Schaberg's studies of the illegitimacy of Jesus, Capps understands Jesus' view of himself as 'son of Abba' to be a means of keenly internalizing what was for him a secure means of self-affirmation, challenging the stigma of being the biological son of the Roman who sexually assaulted his mother, resulting in his birth.[8] Jesus' charisma and his capacity to infuse others with power and strength, which characterize his later ministry, are grown, according to Capps, from Jesus' understanding of his own childhood struggles with his fate and his own emerging sense of God, together galvanizing his conviction that 'dramatic changes occur when we view ourselves and others as persons of inherent worth, celebrating one another's expressions of self-affirmation as a most "beautiful thing" ' – a cross-reference to one of the women who anointed Jesus' feet.[9] Noting the 'verbal shaming' conducted by some academics in response to Schaberg's work, Capps invites those sceptical of Schaberg's work to offer some imaginative alternatives of their own, that might suggest links between Jesus' unknown childhood and the Gospels' presentations of his adulthood.[10]

Chapter 2 of Luke skips from Jesus' babyhood to a single incident (which only he records) about Jesus as a 12-year old boy, and then shifts quickly to the advent of his public ministry. Elaborations on Jesus' 'hidden years' are found in some of the extra-canonical gospels, such as *Thomas*,[11] and despite their strongly 'magical' tone – degrees beyond the canonical infancy stories – it is possible that their exclusion from the canon may reflect in part the kind of discussions that were evidently taking place in the early Church about the theological significance of children. Nestorius' incredulous, and notorious, comment that 'God is not a baby two or three months old . . .'[12] brought him into conflict with the orthodoxy of his day, although records of any great improvement on the part of the orthodox to assert the theological significance of children or of the meaning of the incarnation for children do not seem to be very apparent.

If the historicity of the canonical infancy narratives is disputable, the historical basis of the evangelist's reports of Jesus' ministry among children is less problematic, and the survival of at least a *construct* of Jesus' ministry among the young is itself significant, whatever it reflects of various historical occasions and conversations. It is this material, which is relatively untouched in any form of contemporary theology, which may provide a central aspect of what might be imagined as the potential 'blessedness' of children or childhood. And perhaps now, more than ever, an understanding of flourishing in the childhood years is needed to set against emerging perceptions of abuse-related pathologies, which will begin to fill the gaping space in most theological discussion about children as human beings meriting consideration alongside men and, latterly, women, in a fully inclusive theological anthropology.

Gospel traditions

The Gospels contain records of Jesus eating with children (for example, Matthew 14.21), though not specifically among children alone.[13] Yet it is clear that Jesus' ministry was directed to children, as it was directed to sinners, tax-collectors and others. Significantly, the Gospels portray Jesus' understanding of children as distinctive from the Jewish and Gentile cultures of the early Mediterranean world,[14] so that in a context where children were seen as 'essentially adults in the making . . . [and] contrasted with adulthood . . . weak in mind, deficient in "logos" . . . non-participants in the adult rational world',[15] Jesus' openness to children appears to have been not principally for their *potential*, but rather to their *present state*.[16] So when Gospel stories record disciples attempting to prevent children being brought to Jesus for blessing, they may well be reflecting the widespread perception of children as 'non-participants' in the 'adult' world that they themselves shared:

> People were bringing little children to him in order that he might touch them; and the disciples spoke sternly to them. But when Jesus saw this, he was indignant and said to them, 'Let the little children come to me; do not stop them; for it is to such as these that the kingdom of God belongs. Truly I tell you, whoever does not receive the kingdom of God as a little child will never enter it.' And he took them up in his arms, laid his hands on them, and blessed them. (Mark 10.13–16)

According to Mark's account of this incident, Jesus defied the disciples' attempt to prevent the children, conveying his indignation (the only time this emotion is ascribed to Jesus in the Gospels) to his circle of friends, and setting his blessing upon the 'little ones'. The symbolic significance of this gesture of tenderness towards children may have held a range of reson-ance for the Gospel's early hearers. It mirrors two contempor-aneous traditions, in Plutarch and Diodorus, who tell similar stories of women embracing children. The Gospel's underlin-ing of the responsibility of all disciples, men included, for the service of children introduces a new element of responsibility into patriarchally conceived social relationships.[17] It also would allow hearers of the Gospels to recall the scene in which Simeon took up the child Jesus in his arms (Luke 2.28) as well as the image, from Jesus' story of the forgiving father of the two sons, of the father's running to embrace and kiss the prodigal who had returned home (Luke 15.20). Among the Gospels' Jewish hearers, it may also have resonated with a rabbinic treatise in which 'the resurrection of the people of Israel was portrayed as an event in which "God embraces them, presses them to his heart and kisses them, thus bringing them into the life of the world to come"',[18] further underlining Jesus' challenge to his unwelcoming peers who did not wish him to convey to children the blessing for which they themselves hoped.

As well as recognizing the children and blessing them – as a gesture affirming their worth in God's sight – Jesus turned attention to children to speak of his understanding of God's new order. In his teaching, children become teachers of how the divine reign is to be received ('Truly I tell you, whoever does not receive the kingdom of God as a little child will never enter it'). Commentators tend to stress either the humility or trust of which children are capable as the marks of 'childlikeness', though a perhaps less sentimental interpretation is also emerg-ing, as developed by Bruce Chilton: 'children are the image of the confusing, grabby, unruly way in which the kingdom is to be greeted . . . the purity required by the kingdom is a purity of response, of being like children at rough play in grasping at the kingdom.'[19] Further, a more historically conscious view is also now being postulated, which relates the command to embrace 'child-like' humility or trust to Jesus' own relationship to the Torah, and the attitude to Torah he encouraged in others. Children were not expected to keep the Law, so child-likeness may refer to being neither obedient to, nor obligated to, the Law,[20] with the stress instead on direct dependence on God's mercy.

Further, in the Gospels' presentations of Jesus and children, children demonstrate what it means to aspire to please God (to be 'first' in God's reign), so that Jesus' setting of a child in the midst of his disciples suggests children's role as an example to others: for Jesus, children are models of discipleship who challenge disciples to turn from false values:[21]

> They came to Capernaum; and when Jesus was in the house he asked them, 'What were you arguing about on the way?' But they were silent, for on the way they had argued with one another who was the greatest. He sat down, called the twelve, and said to them, 'Whoever wants to be first must be last of all and servant of all.' Then he took a little child and put it among them; and taking it in his arms, he said to them, 'Whoever welcomes one such child in my name welcomes me, and whoever welcomes me welcomes not me but the one who sent me.' (Mark 9.33–7)

Matthew records a related but non-identical tradition to Mark's version:

> He called a child, whom he put among them, and said, 'Truly I tell you, unless you change and become like children, you will never enter the kingdom of heaven. Whoever becomes humble like this child is the greatest in the kingdom of heaven. Whoever welcomes one such child in my name welcomes me. If any of you put a stumbling block before one of these little ones who believe in me, it would be better for you if a great millstone were fastened around your neck and you were drowned in the depth of the sea.' (Matthew 18.1–6)

Indeed, children provide a test of the disciples' acceptance of 'kingdom values'. A capacity – or otherwise – to welcome children suggests a capacity – or otherwise – to welcome the saviour himself: how disciples respond to children indicates how they re-spond to Jesus (for further parallels on this theme, see Matthew 25.31–46): as Judith Gundy-Volf suggests, 'Welcoming children . . . has the greatest significance. It is a way of serving Jesus and thus also the God who sent him. Conversely, failing to welcome children is a way of rejecting Jesus and God.'[22]

The brutality to which children were sometimes subject in the ancient world is a further key to Gundry-Volf's interpretation of the significance of children, in that the experience of unfortu-nate children in the ancient world is seen by her as providing a way of alluding to the suffering of Jesus: Jesus' 'betrayal into human hands by one of his own' parallels the various forms of infanticide and acute dangers faced by children in his day. So 'we can construe both the little child and the Son-of-man as suffering figures and explain Jesus' self-identification with the little child in the light of this parallel'.[23] Donald Capps provides a point that relates to this approach to Jesus' suffering in that his understanding of Jesus' response to his illegitimacy supports his view of Jesus' 'protective approach to children' in that 'as one who knew what it meant to be a "despised" little one, Jesus' charge to his followers here is more than a moral injunction. It is a powerful act of personal self-affirmation . . .'.[24]

In so far as this set of Jesus' gestures, and their background, and the many possible interpretations of them – beginning with the Gospel texts themselves – can be condensed, it is evident at least that in Jesus' teaching God's new order belongs to chil-dren and the childlike. So learning from children and caring for them become key tasks for his disciples. That such themes have received relatively little attention in the Christian tradition is a matter of some puzzlement. Such teaching may well have been at the forefront of the concerns of many of those Christians who have galvanized practical action to protect or improve children's lives in different times and places, but it has attracted little concentrated theological focus.

The beginnings of an adequate theology of children might be found in the kind of fragmentary hints offered by feminist theologians, whose attention to children has been recognized in the above. For instance, contrary to Nestorius' statement cited above, Sara Maitland bluntly asserts the orthodox conviction that 'the neo-natal baby in Bethlehem is where "the fullness of God was pleased to dwell..."',[25] while other feminists propose that children might be regarded, in Ann Loades's phrase, as 'living prayers', or in Helen Oppenheimer's word, as 'epiphanies'.[26] An expanded theology of children and childhood is not what is attempted in what follows, though such a theology is most certainly reckoned to be needed. Rather, in what follows, the more limited task of a theologically alert discussion of children in the worship of the Church is undertaken.

'Sacramental belonging'

As suggested above, questions about children's participation in the Eucharist have been on the agenda of the Anglican Communion at least since 1985, when members of the International Anglican Liturgical Commission met in Boston, USA, to prepare the document *Walking in Newness of Life*. This recommended a whole-scale reconsideration of practices of initiation, not least as these related to children. Fresh attention was given the intiatory patterns of other Christian traditions, perhaps especially the Roman Catholic Church, which had in the reforms resulting from the Second Vatican Council produced its *Rite of Christian Initiation of Adults*.[27] In the UK, churches in several other traditions had also begun to admit children to participation in the Eucharist, notably the growing charismatic-evangelical churches, which had, knowingly or unknowingly, come in some respects to align their patterns of initiation and Communion to churches in the Frontier tradition of American Protestantism. In this American tradition, infant baptism is uncommon but children's place at the Eucharist is often assured – although Eucharist is characteristically celebrated less often than in those traditions touched by the liturgical renewal of the twentieth century. At the same time, Anglicanism in its land of origin began to recognize acute falls in numbers of participants in worship, most especially among children and young people, a trend which has not abated.

These factors suggest some of the background to a major shift that is presently taking place in the Anglican Communion, among other Christian traditions, relating to the inclusion of children in the central sacrament of the Eucharist. Across the world-wide Anglican scene many provinces now practise Communion before – or without – confirmation, and without always following the Roman Catholic tradition of a formal first Communion, which in a different though related way involves children in sacramental practices. Usually these Anglican provinces, following other churches, have based the policy of Communion before or without confirmation primarily within a theological retrieval of some early Church practices.[28] A bedrock of this retrieval is the discovery that children received Communion at least in some places by the early third century; for instance, Cyprian's witness to children taking 'the Lord's bread and cup' from 'the very beginning of their nativity' is consonant with other patristic elders. Moreover, the practice of infant Communion to which they testify was clearly well known in the medieval west and is still followed today in the eastern Orthodox tradition's pattern of sacramental initiation. In the east, 'confirmation' has never been practised and, in the west, 'confirmation' was not recognized as a separate rite until the thirteenth century – shortly before Communion, at least 'in both kinds', was withdrawn from all laypeople, child and adult, following certain developments in Eucharistic theology.

It is this history of baptism and confirmation to which the International Anglican Liturgical Consultation (IALC)[29] were referring when they recommended 'That since baptism is the sacramental sign of full incorporation into the church, all baptized persons be admitted to communion': as in the Church's earliest known practice, and its aspiration, if not always practice through most of Christian history, Communion should be open to all the baptized. Historic practice also lies behind their request 'That each province clearly affirm that confirmation is not a rite of admission to communion', in which they simply followed a principle affirmed by the world-wide bishops meeting at Lambeth in 1968.[30] Since that Lambeth conference nearly forty years ago, several important Anglican consultations and studies have been undertaken, with a clear trend emerging for change to inherited Anglican theology so that baptism, not confirmation, is now coming to be seen as the rite of initiation which admits to Communion. At the heart of another IALC document is this theological conviction:

> We wish to affirm on theological grounds that children of all ages are included among those for whom Christ died, that children of all ages are recipients of his love, that children of all ages are equally persons in the people of God, and that children of all ages have an active ministry in Christ among his people and in the world. We see no dogmatic or other credible basis for regarding some who are baptized as eligible to receive communion while others are not. We believe this is to run contrary to the inclusive character of the Gospel . . .[31]

It is now widespread for the implications of such convictions to be stated as a priority for future practice. For example, the 'first principle and recommendation' of the important IALC document on the Eucharist affirmed that 'in the celebration of the Eucharist, all the baptized are called to participate in the great sign of our common identity as the people of God, the body of Christ, and the community of the Holy Spirit. No baptized person should be excluded from participating in the eucharistic assembly on such grounds as age, race, gender, economic circumstance or mental capacity.'[32] Yet in the implementation of this principle, the Church of England has proved more resistant to reform than many of its related churches,[33] so that in response to the words at the fraction in the Church of England's *ASB* Rite A or *Common Worship* Order One, 'We break this bread to share in the body of Christ . . .', it has been noted that children might retort, 'No! We don't . . .'.[34] As the Church of England is beginning to embrace the notion of the 'sacramental belonging' of children, a new risk arises: that of attending to traditions and practice about Eucharist, yet failing to recover and enlarge the Church's tradition and practice of concern for children. Decisions about whether or not to allow children to partake in bread and wine at one particular point in the Eucharistic celebration, in isolation from considerations about what their involvement may mean for the whole Eucharistic assembly, miss many of the opportunities presented by present considerations of sacramental belonging. The debate about children and Communion needs to be connected at least to those elements in the gospel that preserve the tradition of Jesus' approach to children, along with his apparent understanding of their particular merits.

Roman Catholic perspectives

The period in which the Roman Catholic Church has produced its *Rite of Christian Initiation of Adults* has also seen the publication of the *Directory of Masses for Children* and some texts of Eucharistic prayer proposed for celebration with children. As Joan Patano Vos notes, the *Directory* represents the very highest level of concern about the inclusion of children in the worship of Roman Catholic communities, though its import has by no means always been appropriated in local congregations.[35] The *Directory* opens with the following strong statement:

> Today the circumstances in which children grow up are not favourable to their spiritual progress. In addition, parents sometimes scarcely fulfil the obligations of Christian formation they accepted at the baptism of their children . . . Although the vernacular may now be used at Mass, still the words and signs have not been sufficiently adapted to the capacity of children . . . We may fear spiritual harm if over the years children repeatedly experience things in the church that are scarcely comprehensible to them . . . The Church follows its Master, who 'put his arms around the children . . . and blessed them' (Mark 10.16). It cannot leave children in the condition described.

Insisting that adults can 'benefit spiritually' from their experience of sharing liturgy with children, and children's contributions to such liturgy, the *Directory* stresses the need for a gathering of 'a single assembly', inclusive of different generations and ages, as opposed to the splitting of the assembly into different age-related groupings. Proposing a variety of means of children's participation, from thoughtful bodily posture and gestures to engagement in reverent silence, the text outlines some contours of a participative worshipping community, including both adults and children engaged in public ministries.

It is attention to the kinds of issues taken up by the *Directory*, such as how children may not only partake of 'elements' of bread and wine but also share in worship as fully participative members of the assembly, which is characteristically lacking in much English Anglican discussion of sacramental belonging. Much of that latter discussion is apparently fixated with concern about the potential of children to receive Eucharistized elements 'unworthily', as in Paul's phrase in 1 Corinthians 11, or at least upon notions of children's proper reception which renders Jesus' apparently positive view of children naive. Mention of the word 'reception' raises the spectre of Eucharistic theologies particular to the Protestant traditions, which, at least on not always fully acknowledged levels, may effectively require the 'protection' of Eucharistized elements from the 'unworthy'. This has resulted in a tradition which is still practised among some Plymouth Brethren of 'table fencing' in which only the (s)elect are welcome to participate. The tradition of confirmation in the Anglican tradition has functioned in a less acute but nevertheless destructive way, dividing those who 'belong' at the Eucharistic celebration from those who do not, which is more than problematic when allied to the twentieth-century liturgical reform making the Eucharist central to congregations' patterns of worship, rather than some form of 'word' service which is believed, and is apparently widely experienced, to be more inclusive.[36] If this sense of exclusion at the Eucharist were to be diminished, a more concerted effort to root Eucharistic theology in the Gospel traditions of Jesus' table-fellowship, rather than the Pauline texts just alluded to, would need be made at a popular level. The Roman Catholic tradition has (perhaps in view of its Eucharistic theology that incorporates a very strong sense of divine presence in the Eucharistized elements, apart from their reception) been perceived to be less anxious about questions of 'worthy reception', though it has 'fenced the table' in manifold other ways. Nonetheless, from a perspective within the Roman Catholic tradition, Joan Patano Vos is one among a number of authors who take up the vision of the *Directory for Masses with Children* so as to make a series of practical proposals about how children might be made fully participative members of Eucharistic worship.

Suggesting that music included in children's masses needs to be of a kind which relates to that used in assemblies incorporating adults, and uncompromising about the need for children to be exposed to and increasing their comprehension of Scripture which will animate participation in the Eucharist, the heart of her concern is that children are incorporated into a genuinely participative assembly. Similarly, Mark Searle makes a range of proposals, representing some of the best thinking in North American Roman Catholic circles. As he begins his reflections, he magnifies the emphasis of the *Directory* to stress the 'ideal' of the liturgical assembly as 'a gathering of all God's people in a given place: men, women, children, the elderly, the sick, representatives of every social group and social stratum' and adds that this is important in order to make manifest the Church's share in Christ's work of 'gathering the scattered children of God into one'.[37]

Conscious of the absence of children in treatments of liturgical history, Searle seeks to redress this in so far as it may be possible by underlining the 'significant, indeed often prominent' role that young boys if not girls have performed in liturgical worship. He cites fourth-century practice which ordained boys to reading and singing in liturgy. He notes from the fifth century onwards training for such liturgical roles within the context of general education offered by the Church to youngsters, and the gradual expansion of children's ordination, including those as young as four or five, to lector, psalmist and acolyte, among other things.[38]

More importantly, however, Searle probes the symbolic meaning of children's participation in the liturgy. Expanding the understanding of children as 'defective adults', Searle traces the view that children were regarded in their supposedly diminished humanity as being closer to the 'non-human . . . invisible . . . supernatural world',[39] and therefore valued precisely for this. Examples of this 'unworldliness' which make their mark in the Christian tradition are the shout of the child in Milan who was heard to voice 'Ambrose for bishop!', and the sound of the child's encouraging Augustine to 'Take up and read' the New Testament.[40] Consequently, children's place in liturgy was based upon the view of them as 'standing closer to the veil that divides the visible from the invisible, the temporal order from the eternal'.[41] Nevertheless, despite the remarkable medieval tradition of 'role-reversal' in the liturgy for Holy Innocents' Day, when children would preside as 'bishop', preach and so on while senior clergy were demoted as choristers, acolytes and the like,[42] it remains that children's participation was for their symbolic significance for adults, still subservient to adults, as the exception to the rule itself demonstrates, for all its extraordinariness.

This notwithstanding, Searle is fully alert to the symbolic significance of children in contemporary assemblies, and he cites three kinds of symbolism which attach to children latterly. First, they may mark the exclusivity of a worshipping 'community' and in fact expose its antithetical relationship with Searle's ideal of 'gathering the scattered children of God'. Sound-proof 'cry rooms, for example, are highly ambivalent in this regard', for as well as providing 'a genuine service to parents with restless children', they may also be used to communicate that children are unwelcome in an assembly which is hostile to them.[43] Second, children may be 'paraded' in child-centred liturgies, and for various reasons, one of which may be to attempt to make worship accessible to unchurched adults unfamiliar with traditional practices of worship, without exposing them to the embarrassment or unease of more demanding forms. At its worst, this may be a 'concession to our enormous cultural appetite for entertainment',[44] which ultimately subverts authentic worship. More dangerously again perhaps, children may be paraded 'for the entertainment or ego-building of adults' as youngsters are pushed into 'vicarious' roles 'because if they succeed, that is marvellous and reflects glory on the parents; whereas if they make a mistake, well, they are only children'. These may simply be adults' means of 'pursu[ing] the glory of public roles, while minimalizing the risks of losing face'.[45]

Such insightful reflections give way to Searle's vision of 'children as members of the assembly'.[46] At the heart of this is the conviction that 'we should make no accommodation to our children. Rather than bringing the liturgy down to their level, I believe them better served by being surrounded by adult Christians celebrating an adult faith in adult way.'[47] This is not, however, a simple call to leave the status quo unquestioned. It entails recognition that 'radical equality in the Christian community . . . is betrayed – and the children know it – when we condescend to them', while the active care that children call forth from adults demands that those adults 'work for the conversion of children, the deliberate effort to help them recover from the harmful influences to which they have been exposed'[48] so enabling them to be free in their 'natural affinity to God'[49] as is suggested by all those early liturgical roles.

Searle's last point here, about the harm that may be done to children, is one that resonates with another strong voice in Roman Catholic consideration of children at worship, that of Mary Collins, who argues that the rejection of children is culturally pervasive.[50] Like Searle, she does not wish simply to 'accommodate' children:

On the basis of the evidence in published resource books on Christian celebration for the young it seems that those who are presently exploring children's liturgies have a romantic view of childhood and youth. Such a view actually denies their experience and ours. It also denies access to the mystery of our faith, namely that life's terrors and dangers are real, but our God gives life even in the face of cruelty and death. The children of the Hebrews have regularly cultivated the memory of suffering, hostility, and death. Why not the children of the church?[51]

She recognizes that such accommodation may be more for the supposed benefit of adults than for children themselves, and furthermore may in fact represent a form of the harm that may be done to children – in this respect by shielding them from the realities of the world in which faith may be found and may flourish, even in the midst of difficulties. Collins regards the Passover Haggadah is one means by which children in the Jewish tradition are introduced to the memory of suffering, with Purim being another example, and with Christians able to learn from both. As Collins develops her convictions, she suggests that all children's liturgy should be 'implicitly paschal' for 'anything less than a profound liturgical ministry for the young is a betrayal of trust, another form of exploitation of the young at their expense'.[52] The issue at stake, as Collins sees it, is whether children are presented with the 'euchatastrophy' of the gospel – by which she refers to the gospel's demanding story, but nevertheless 'a story with a happy ending', which is true, and worthy of a lifetime's dedication; or whether they are not, and offered in its place an altogether less durable 'resource'. As she elaborates, she insists that strictly upbeat celebrations create illusions, lacking both tension and ambiguity, and mimicking the 'simplistic situation comedies of prime-time TV'. By contrast, she asserts, 'the mystery proclaimed in Jesus is that the forces of diminishment and destruction are very real indeed, but the power and purpose of God will ultimately prevail'. Finally, Collins observes that 'liturgists for the young, like all of us in a consumer culture, tend to want to create novelty, not depth of significance'. Yet she insists as she continues, 'ritual redundancy and repetition are not of themselves inherently boring unless they are the activities of boring people who lack both memory and imagination'.

Anglican appropriation

David Holeton is one of very few Anglicans who have begun to appropriate the kinds of thinking articulated by Roman Catholic liturgists reflecting upon the implementation of the *Directory for Masses with Children*, and the possibilities it represents for more genuinely inclusive worship within their Roman Catholic tradition. As convener and chair of the conference of Anglican liturgists gathering in Boston and Toronto to make their powerful joint statements about baptism and Eucharist respectively, he is as able as anyone to assess movements to incorporate children in worship across the Anglican Communion more fully, in so far as such a task is possible at all. Holeton is well aware, for instance, of developments in New Zealand, where children's Communion is now among the most clearly established of all the Anglican provinces. The late New Zealand archbishop Brian Davies, who with Holeton has widely encouraged the world-wide Anglican Church to offer children Communion, includes in his notes and evaluation of its consequences for congregations that: many have introduced weekday 'Sunday schools' (then called 'church school') to give children their own time for learning and free them to attend worship on Sundays with those of all ages; some provide 'church school' during the ministry of the word in Communion, in order to offer age-appropriate learning for adults and children separately, but gathering together for sharing in the sacrament; and some provide liturgy with sections directed in turn towards children and then adults. Furthermore, Davies notes that, practically, the presence of children has also 'encouraged a re-thinking of church design and furnishings', demanding more carpeted areas for children's play, more use of free-standing chairs and less of traditional pews, banners, drama, dance, new music and liturgical roles for children and young people.[53]

Also writing from the Australasian context, though from Australia itself, Elizabeth Smith imagines changes that the full inclusion of children in worship will bring to churches who

have sidelined them into Sunday Schools, made children wait
for sacramental participation and so on:

> Renewed worship that happens as a result of children's inclu-
> sion will mean some changes in practice. It will also mean
> a shift in the spiritual orientation of the adult worshippers.
> Over time, some of the children's naïve confidence will rub
> off, and it will smooth down some of the adults' doctrinal
> hackles. Some of the children's hunger for physical connec-
> tion and bodily movement, for touch and caress, for eye-
> contact and direct verbal addresses, will rub off, and it will
> awaken some of the adults' dormant awareness of their own
> bodies in prayer. Some of the children's questions will stay
> around, and create a climate in which some of the adults feel
> free to ask questions too . . . . Those who seek the renewal of
> eucharistic worship will do well to pay close attention to the
> children whom the Spirit is giving to the church.[54]

Her views are not simply naive hopes, but reflect her experience
of participation in North American Episcopal Church life.

It is with similar convictions that Holeton develops his own
proposals and assertions, which are perhaps flavoured by a willingness to push further than are his Roman Catholic counterparts Collins and Searle are about just what children may
demand of adults in the Church, and what kinds of possibilities
may emerge from more inclusive worship:

> Once the right of presence in the eucharistic assembly and,
> consequently, admission to communion is guaranteed, we
> need to ask some serious questions about what children will
> find in the midst of that assembly. It is here that the most
> serious work will need to be done because this will involve
> the reconstruction of ourselves and our attitudes towards
> worship.[55]

Like Searle and Collins, however, Holeton does not wish to
advocate the preparation of children's liturgies which are then
celebrated by children alone. These would, he thinks, at best
counterbalance worship encountered at other times. Rather

there must be a 'serious evaluation of what most Anglican communities present as their regular fare of Sunday worship' and questions must be explored about how this could be opened up and made more generally and genuinely inclusive. At the very least, this will mean amending the Anglican tradition of its emphasis on the 'generally cerebral', the 'visually and emotionally unengaged' – 'book-bound, logocentric, clerical and male-oriented' – which, while it may very well nourish the intellect, may be regarded as deficient in other respects. A constructive critic, Holeton looks for clues and helpful insights in both Orthodox and oriental traditions which he recognizes to be 'indisputably liturgical yet formed on premises that are quite different from those of Anglicanism in the waning years of the twentieth century'[56] and in which he finds 'children . . . expected to be present and welcomed when they are' whereas 'Anglican worship is, in most parishes, basically seen as an adult activity in which children are allowed to participate as long as they conform to adult patterns of worship and follow adult rules'. Orthodox worship, as Holeton expounds it, combines both 'highly complex rites and [a] dense symbol system of allegories' with open liturgical space, filled with movement, light from candles and colour from icons, into which children find themselves welcomed and, moreover, integrated.[57] Holeton locates the possibilities he praises in Anglican contexts like the well-known St Gregory of Nyssa, San Francisco, and Portsmouth Cathedral, and calls for more patronal concern for the arts and artisans who in their turn may vivify the notion of 'play' as a key to participation in liturgy.

If and as such changes are embraced, Holeton is not naive about the 'revolutionary' consequences not only for children but also much more widely, and so he sees that the 'rightful claim of children to eucharistic communion challenges value systems, and can cause discomfort'. There is, however, a long way to go to complete the tasks he articulates as 'the significant consequences of welcoming children in our midst have yet to be incorporated into the liturgical life of most parishes'. Yet, he insists, the distance remaining should not deter Anglicans from a 'serious revisioning so that [Anglican worship] will become more holistic, truly inclusive, and less cerebral'.[58] His comments can be aligned to the assertion of *Youth a Part* that 'The primary frontier which needs to be crossed in mission to young people is not so much a generation gap as a profound change in the overall culture' of the Church.[59]

Gathering fragments from Chapter 4

What we can see from this brief survey is a range of practices from Roman Catholic, Anglican and Orthodox approaches to the involvement of children in the liturgy,[60] with each tradition formed by its particular history which has itself celebrated or marginalized the presence of children in a variety of ways. To press in the narrower Anglican context of the Church of England the kind of issues that David Holeton brings to light, we may note the work of the Church of England Doctrine Commission on sacramental initiation in which they stress baptism as analogous to 'adoption',[61] and all the suggestive related imagery of process, and ask what such gradualism will imply for a congregation concerned to include the children in its midst. We may also note, however, that the most sustained thinking about issues overlapping with David Holeton's concerns has in the Church of England been conducted by the arm of the Board of Education responsible for the report *Youth a Part*. Among many recommendations, that report urged that 'Young people must be taken seriously if they are to stay within the Church, or if the Church wants to attract young people into its work and mission . . . they *are* the Church of today . . .',[62] suggesting first, that young people's alienation from Church culture and, second, that the churches' worship patterns and styles may be significant factors in the decline of those from the younger generations in touch with Church life or participating in worship.[63] Related material apparently suggests that this possibility is perhaps most relevant to churches designated as being 'traditional' or 'liturgical', from which, it appears, young people are most likely to leave at transition points (such as confirmation(!), school-leaving, going to college etc.) as they progress through their teens.[64] However, the perspectives of liturgical theologians are absent from the work of the report, and debate with the kinds of perspectives articulated by those cited in the course of this chapter has not been incorporated into the report. This chapter, then, is an attempt to call attention to the merit of learning from this literature.

Part Two of this work has developed perspectives on the key issues that led to the production of *Patterns for Worship*, bringing up to date discussion of urban theology and of various churches' attempts to incorporate children. The 'gentrification' of at least some parts of some British cities, and the possibilities arising from fresh concern with the 'sacramental belonging' of children are issues of major importance that neither *Patterns for Worship* nor *Faith in the City* and *Children in the Way* (and their related documents) fully anticipated in their day. Indeed, in the case of key issues in what I have labelled a 'third wave' in urban theology the issues were barely imagined.

Such developments require that liturgical theology and the resources it attempts and is able to produce are reconceived in their light. And it is to voices in our conversation that I think can assist this to which we now turn.

Notes

1. Ruth Meyers, ed., *Children at the Table: A Collection of Essays on Children and the Eucharist*, New York: Church Publishing, 1995.
2. And interestingly, a 'Rahner Reader' includes none of his reflections upon children in what might be supposed to be his most significant work (Gerald A. McCool, ed., *A Rahner Reader*, London: DLT, 1975).
3. See John Saward, 'Youthful unto Death: The Spirit of Childhood', Bede McGregor OP and Thomas Norris, eds, *The Beauty of Christ: An Introduction to the Theology of Hans Urs von Balthasar*, Edinburgh: T&T Clark, 1994, pp. 140–60, and Samuel Wells, *Transforming Fate into Destiny*, Carlisle: Paternoster Press, 1998.
4. Ann Loades, *Thinking about Child Sexual Abuse: The John Coffin Memorial Lecture 1994*, London: University of London, 1994.

5. E.g. Charles V. Gerkin, *Introduction to Pastoral Care*, Nashville: Abingdon, 1997.

6. Pamela Couture, *Blessed Are the Poor: Women's Poverty, Family Policy and Practical Theology* (Nashville: Abingdon, 1991); Pamela Couture, *Seeing Children, Seeing God: A Practical Theology of Children and Poverty* (Nashville: Abingdon, 2000).

7. Donald Capps, *The Child's Song*, Minneapolis: Fortress Press, 1995, pp. 54–5, 99.

8. Capps, *The Child's Song*, p. 114.

9. Capps, *The Child's Song*, p. 115.

10. Although making no reference to Capps's *The Child's Song*, nor to Capps's challenge just cited (indeed one predates *The Child's Song*), two interesting and imaginative reconstructions of Jesus' 'hidden years' are Margaret Magdalen, *The Hidden Face of Jesus: Reflections on the Emotional Life of Christ*, London: DLT, 1994, pp. 3–40, and Jack Dominian, *One like Us: A Psychological Interpretation of Jesus*, London: DLT, 1998, pp. 57–71.

11. *The Infancy Gospel of Thomas*, Ron Cameron, ed., *The Other Gospels: Non-Canonical Gospel Texts*, Philadelphia: Westminster Press, 1982, pp. 122–31.

12. Cited in Henry Chadwick, *The Early Church*, Harmondsworth: Penguin, 1967, p. 192; also Frances Young, *From Nicea to Chalcedon*, London: SCM Press, 1985, p. 234.

13. See Stephen C. Barton, 'Child, Children', Joel B. Green, Scot McKnight and I. Howard Marshall, eds, *Dictionary of Jesus and the Gospels: A Compendium of Contemporary Biblical Scholarship*, Leicester: IVP, 1992, pp. 100–4.

14. See William A. Strange, *Children in the Early Church; Children in the Ancient World, the New Testament and the Early Church*, Carlisle: Paternoster, 1996, chapters 1 and 2.

15. James Francis, 'Children and Childhood in the New Testament', Stephen C. Barton, ed., *The Family in Theological Perspective*, Edinburgh, T&T Clark, 1996, pp. 65–85, 70.

16. Strange, *Children in the Early Church*, p. 50.

17. Judith Gundry-Volf, '"To Such as These Belongs the Reign of God": Jesus and Children', *Theology Today* 56 (4) (2000), pp. 469–80, p. 473.

18. Hans-Ruedi Weber, *Jesus and the Children: Biblical Resources for Study and Preaching*, Geneva: World Council of Churches, 1979, p. 19, quoting *Seder Elijahu Rabba*, 17.

19. Bruce Chilton, *Pure Kingdom: Jesus' Vision of God*, London: SPCK, 1996, p. 85.

20. Gundry-Volf, '"To Such as These"', pp. 473–4.

21. See Bruce Chilton and J. I. H. MacDonald, *Jesus and the Ethics of the Kingdom*, London, SPCK, 1987, p. 82.

22. Cf. Gundry-Volf, '"To Such as These"', p. 476.

23. Gundry-Volf, '"To Such as These"', p. 477.

24. Capps, *The Child's Song*, p. 57.

25. Sara Maitland, 'Ways of Relating', Ann Loades, ed., *Feminist Theology: A Reader*, London: SPCK, 1990, pp. 148–57, p. 155.

26. Ann Loades, 'Death and Disvalue: Some Reflections on Sick Children', *Hospital Chaplain* (1985): pp. 5–11; Helen Oppenheimer, 'Blessing', Daniel W. Hardy and Peter Sedgwick, eds, *The Weight of Glory: The Future of Liberal Theology: Essays in Honour of Peter Baelz*, Edinburgh: T&T Clark, 1991, pp. 221–9.

27. See Aidan Kavanagh, *The Shape of Baptism*, Collegeville: Liturgical Press, 1978, for perhaps the most authoritative interpretative guide.

28. David Holeton, 'Children and the Eucharist in the Tradition of the Church' and 'The Communion of All the Baptized in the Anglican Tradition', Ruth Meyers, ed., *Children at the Table*, New York: Church Publishing, 1995, pp. 11–18 and 19–41. Among the prayer books from the churches of the Anglican Communion, the *Book of Common Prayer* (1979) of the Episcopal Church in the United States and the *Book of Alternative Services* (1985) of the Anglican Church in Canada do not require confirmation before Communion and permit children to receive the sacrament at their baptism and thereafter.

29. The International Anglican Liturgical Commission (IALC) is a body of bishops and scholars who oversee the writing, compiling and theology of the prayer books of the Anglican Communion. For a list of its members see the signatures attached to the 'Dublin Statement' in David Holeton, ed., *Our Thanks and Praise: The Eucharist in Anglicanism Today*, Toronto: Anglican Book Centre, 1998.

30. See David Holeton, ed., *Christian Initiation in the Anglican Communion: The Toronto Statement 'Walk in Newness of Life'*, Findings of the Fourth International Anglican Liturgical Consultation, Toronto, 1991, Nottingham: Grove, 1991.

31. 'Children and Communion: An International Anglican Liturgical Consultation held in Boston, USA, 29–31 July 1985', Meyers, ed., *Children at the Table*, p. 132.

32. David Holeton, ed., *Renewing the Anglican Eucharist*, Findings of the Fifth International Anglican Liturgical Consultation, Dublin, Eire, 1995, Cambridge: Grove, 1996, p. 7. It is not only in Anglican churches that appeal to these historic foundations has been made: *Baptism, Eucharist and Ministry* challenged 'those churches which baptize children but refuse them a share in the Eucharist before

such a rite [as confirmation]' to 'ponder whether they have fully accepted the consequences of baptism'.

33. Donald Gray, 'Pushing the Door: (i) The Church of England', Meyers, ed., *Children at the Table*, pp. 99–106, compared with the reports in the same volume of changing practice in other churches in the Anglican Communion.

34. See John Leach, *Visionary Leadership in the Local Church*, Cambridge: Grove, 1997, p. 1.

35. Joan Patano Vos, 'Unpacking the Directory for Masses with Children', Eleanor Bernstein and John Brooks-Leonard, eds, *Children in the Assembly of the Church*, Chicago: Liturgy Training Publications, 1992, pp. 81–99, p. 81.

36. On the Parish Communion Movement see Horton Davies, *Worship and Theology in England: The Ecumenical Century*, Grand Rapids: Eerdmans, 2nd edn 1996.

37. Mark Searle, 'Children in the Assembly of the Church', Bernstein and Brooks-Leonard, eds, *Children in the Assembly of the Church*, pp. 30–50, p. 32.

38. See also: Susan Buynton, 'The Liturgical Role of Children in Monastic Communities from the Central Middle Ages', *Studia Liturgica* 28 (1998): pp. 194–209.

39. Searle, 'Children in the Assembly', p. 35.

40. Searle, 'Children in the Assembly', p. 37.

41. Searle, 'Children in the Assembly', p. 38.

42. Searle, 'Children in the Assembly', p. 37.

43. Searle, 'Children in the Assembly', p. 41.

44. Searle, 'Children in the Assembly', p. 42.

45. Searle, 'Children in the Assembly', p. 42.

46. Searle, 'Children in the Assembly', p. 42.

47. Searle, 'Children in the Assembly', p. 43.

48. Searle, 'Children in the Assembly', p. 44.

49. Searle, 'Children in the Assembly', p. 43.

50. Mary Collins, 'Is the Adult Church Ready for Worship with Young Christians?', *Worship: Renewal to Practice*, Washington DC: Pastoral Press, 1987, pp. 277–95, p. 279.

51. Collins, 'Is the Adult Church Ready?', pp. 280–1.

52. Collins, 'Is the Adult Church Ready?', pp. 283.

53. Brian Davies, 'New Zealand Initiation Experience: (i) Changing Initiatory Patterns', Meyers, ed., *Children at the Table*, pp. 85–93, especially pp. 91–2.

54. Elizabeth J. Smith, 'Whose Prayer Will Make the Difference? Eucharistic Renewal and Liturgical Education', David Holeton, ed., *Our Thanks and Praise: The Eucharist in Anglicanism Today*, Toronto: Anglican Book Centre, 1998, pp. 99–114, p. 104.

55. David Holeton, 'Welcome Children, Welcome Me', *Anglican Theological Review* 51 (1999), pp. 93–111, p. 105.

56. Holeton, 'Welcome Children', p. 107.

57. Holeton, 'Welcome Children', pp. 107, 109.

58. Holeton, 'Welcome Children', p. 111.

59. *Youth a Part*, 2.11. While arguments for age-streamed congregations, such as 'youth congregations', are often vigorously resisted, and for some good reasons as may emerge from appropriation of some of the concerns expressed by Lathrop, Saliers and White in relation to American Megachurches, among other reasons, the fragmentation of the North American Roman Catholic scene into congregations catering for the special needs and preferences of a range of ethnic groups may offer models for how age-streamed congregations may be established. On ethnic parishes, see Mark R. Francis, *Shape a Circle Ever Wider: Liturgical Inculturation in the United States*, Chicago: Liturgy Training Publications, 2000, pp. 100–4. Reserve in the British context about the appropriateness or need of ethnic congregations might well be educated by Kenneth Leech, 'Racism and the Proclamation of the Gospel', Kenneth Leech, *Struggle in Babylon: Racism in the Cities and Churches in Britain*, London: SPCK, 1988.

60. Of major importance for addressing questions about the inclusion of children in worship from a British Methodist perspective is Mike Bossingham, *Building Family Friendly Churches*, Peterborough: Inspire, 2004, which merits close attention. It is, however, excluded from study in this chapter because it does not directly engage with liturgical tradition in the way that other perspectives considered in this context do so.

61. See [David W. Brown], 'Spirit, Sacraments and Structures', Doctrine Commission of the Church of England, *We Believe in the Holy Spirit*, London: Church House Publishing, 1991, Chapter 5.

62. *Youth a Part*, 76. Emphasis in original.

63. *Youth a Part*, 95. See also Bob Mayo, *Gospel Exploded: Reaching the Unreached*, London: Triangle/SPCK, 1996.

64. Patrick Angier, *Changing Youth Worship*, London: Church House Publishing, 1996, p. 73. Traditional worship is 'characterized by beauty in building, music, liturgy, drawing on the historical resources of choral music and hymnody accompanied by organ and choir . . .', p. 57. For analysis of recent statistics, see Leslie J. Francis and David Lankshear, *Continuing in the Way: Children, Young People and the Church*, London: National Society, 1991, and *In the Catholic Way; Children, Young People and the Church in Catholic Parishes of the Church of England*, London: National

Society/Church Union, 1995, and *In the Evangelical Way: Children, Young People and the Church in Evangelical Parishes of the Church of England*, London: National Society, 1995.

Part Three

Exploring Liturgical Theology:

Body, Heart and Home

Body, heart and home are keywords – but not comprehensive descriptions – that I use to provide some clues to the central features of the illuminating contributions to liturgical theology made by the three thinkers who are the focus of this part of this work, James White, Don Saliers and Gordon Lathrop. Without ever referring to it, each one of these authors takes themes that emerge in *Patterns for Worship* and offers considerable direction to the debates in which Patterns engages.

Gordon Lathrop's contributions to our liturgical-theological conversation centre on one of his keywords, 'body'. He is concerned with people gathered together as 'the body of Christ' as the primary symbol of liturgy: consequently, *Holy People* is the title of his 'liturgical ecclesiology'. At least equally significantly, however, Lathrop gives unrivalled attention to what we may think of as the 'bones' of Christian worship: its essential skeletal elements from which the body lives and which bring order and structure to the praise, doctrine and practice of faithful people.

Lathrop's emphasis on aspects of the humanity of worshipping human beings finds a complementary voice in the work of Don Saliers. Consideration of the 'heart' is Saliers's most significant contribution to liturgical theology, and consistently, and quite distinctively, he encourages worshippers to bring their human 'pathos', the full stretch of their humanity – from sorrow to joy – and all their senses to the 'ethos' of God, in order to be made more fully alive.

James White makes a crucial counterpoint to perspectives expressed by both Lathrop and Saliers, in his reminder (that neither of the others would deny, but do not express with the same force as White) that the faithful are to be found not only in churches known as 'liturgical', for the 'non-liturgical' traditions (a misnomer, but commonly applied to many of the more recent Protestant churches) also produce their saints. His key contribution to liturgical theology is to explore these traditions as 'homes' that nurture Christian people, despite the fact that they may have been almost entirely overlooked by the vast majority of other liturgical scholars. White's contribution can be seen as encouraging a wider sense of hospitality in the discipline of liturgical theology, while an important ancillary concern of his work relates to the theme of hospitality in another way, giving detailed attention to the architecture of the Church's buildings. And so 'home' relates also to the 'house of the Church' and a range of environmental factors relevant to the Church's gatherings.

All of these themes, with others, will emerge in the explorations of Part Three of this work, as Lathrop, Saliers and White's writings are explored in order to educate the kind of conversation that is in my view needed in urban-deprived and child-inclusive assemblies in the British context. In each of the chapters about their work some organizing categories are identified in the writing of the three theologians, around which I group their insights. I believe that these organizing categories cover the main themes in their own work, yet, in order to attempt to ensure that I do not misrepresent them, my presentation of their distinctive contributions has not here been standardized by use of overlapping terminology, except where this occurs in their own work. By attempting to allow the distinctiveness of their own perspectives to emerge, it will more readily be seen that they are sometimes in contradistinction, and even contradiction, as well as at times in harmony with one another. Read together they offer a fascinating and fruitful dialogue relevant to my concerns.

5

EXERCISING THE 'BODY':
Gordon W. Lathrop

Introduction

Gordon W. Lathrop is a leading North American liturgical scholar, active in both his own denomination, the Evangelical Lutheran Church in America, and in a number of ecumenical, scholarly bodies, such as Societas Liturgica and the North American Academy of Liturgy, of which he was vice-president in 1984.

Lathrop was ordained as a Lutheran pastor in 1969, going on to serve pastorates in Washington State and Wisconsin, though for most of his career he has taught candidates for ministry at the Lutheran Theological Seminary at Philadelphia, where he is Charles A. Schieren Emeritus Professor of Practical Theology and Chaplain. Beyond that particular institution, his main local ecclesial connection is the Episcopal Cathedral, Philadelphia, where he took up an appointment as Lutheran Pastor, an initiative that followed the recognition of full communion between the Evangelical Lutheran Church in America and the Episcopal Church of the USA.

That Lathrop's professorial chair is in the discipline of practical theology is of interest, as his doctoral studies were not liturgical in any strict sense either, but rather in the biblical field, on the 'tradition and redaction of Mark 6.1–6'. Consequently, concern about the biblical roots of liturgy, and the use of the Bible in the liturgy, as well as practical aspects of liturgical celebration all feature strongly in Lathrop's writings.

Lathrop's PhD was undertaken at the Catholic University of

Nijmegen in the Netherlands towards the end of the 1960s. This context for his studies assured Lathrop's contact with a particular kind of Roman Catholicism emerging in the wake of the Second Vatican Council, and which was fostered in Nijmegen by characters such as Edward Schillebeeckx, who had at the time recently published influential material, controversial in the wider Catholic world, on sacramentality. (The alternative approach to Eucharistic transubstantiation, transignification, is widely attributed to Schillebeeckx's *The Eucharist* and *Christ the Sacrament of Encounter with God*).[1] Nijmegen in the 1960s was a context in which both Scripture and sacrament were able to become focal for Lathrop, and these twin themes – which have been consistently held in tension or, in his characteristic phrase, in juxtaposition throughout his life's work – can be traced back to this time.

Lathrop has himself been deeply involved in the reform of prayer books in the ELCA in the period after the production of new Roman books after Vatican Two. Central sections of the *Lutheran Book of Worship*,[2] on baptism, Eucharist and holy week are contributed by Lathrop. Lathrop has also been involved in the production of liturgical texts of a less authoritative status, and much of his work has been concerned with providing resources for good use of the lectionary, not least his *Psalter for the Christian People*, *Lectionary for the Christian People* and a series of *Readings for the Assembly*[3] for the three-year lectionary cycle. This Psalter and these cycles of readings were undertaken in collaboration with his wife, Gail Ramshaw, who had earlier compiled a single-volume book of readings for liturgical use, *Richer Fare for the Christian People*,[4] among other notable texts in the liturgical field. That Lathrop is married to another highly regarded figure in North American liturgical 'circles' is significant, especially given that they have undertaken a number of joint projects, and focused their writings on the same areas – notably, baptism and Eucharist, as may be seen from Ramshaw's popular books for Liturgy Training Publications, *Words around the Font*[5] and *Words around the Table*[6] – apart from developing their particular academic interests. (Ramshaw's most acclaimed independent writings tend to focus on liturgical language, as represented recently in her *Reviving Sacred Speech*,[7] updating her thinking about an earlier, very influential book, *Christ in Sacred Speech*.)

Lathrop himself has been publishing in academic journals, notably *Worship* (of which he is now an associate editor), since the early 1980s. One particularly important contribution was his essay 'A Rebirth of Images',[8] published in 1984, which was a version of his vice-presidential address at the North American Academy of Liturgy. Joyce Ann Zimmermann claims that this essay/address was 'a blueprint for academic and pastoral activity that has been carried out by liturgists for the two decades since',[9] and its concerns have quite evidently remained central in Lathrop's own writings. It was, however, in the 1990s that Lathrop developed a reputation as a most significant liturgical scholar, particularly for his companion books *Holy Things: A Liturgical Theology*,[10] *Holy People: A Liturgical Ecclesiology*,[11] and *Holy Ground: A Liturgical Cosmology*.[12] The first of these books in particular received great acclaim almost instantly, and is constantly cited – perhaps more than any other contemporary text – in works of liturgical theology to date. *Holy Things*, *Holy People* and *Holy Ground* were published by the Lutheran publishing house in the US, Fortress Press, but more than that they relate to and develop academically Lathrop's work in a body with a clear official Lutheran status, the World Lutheran Federation, of which he was a leading member in a study group preparing the document *Worship and Culture in Dialogue*,[13] which in turn shaped a series of official statements and 'declarations' about the Lutheran Church in relationship to contemporary culture. Lathrop has also recently edited and introduced a series of influential short pamphlets, *Open Questions in Worship*,[14] which are aimed at a more popular dissemination of the approach represented in his companion books and in the Lutheran World Federation materials, and which draw in a series of scholars and pastors to comment and reflect upon eight aspects of contemporary experience of worship, such as changing sacramental practice, and the ethical and evangelistic potential of liturgy. Most recently, Lathrop has produced *Central Things*,[15] another more popular attempt to bring his major concerns to wider attention. He has also recently been honoured with the North American Academy of Liturgy's 2006 Berakah Award, and a collection of essays in his honour: *Ordo: Bath, Word, Prayer, Table*.[16]

It is not only the titles of *Holy Things* and *Holy People* that relate to the invitation to Communion cited in Cyril of Jerusalem's *Mystical Catechesis* (5.19–20): 'Holy things for the holy people: one is holy, one is Lord, Jesus Christ. O taste and see that the Lord is good.' The focus of the books concerns the kinds of transformation, both personal and communal, which may be possible as worshippers yield to the flow of the liturgy, open to its influence upon them. To this end, *Holy Things* and *Holy People* are an attempt to identify the central 'essentials of Christian worship' and to develop a theology specifically from the various possible juxtapositions of liturgy's primary symbols – baptism, Bible, Eucharist and assembly – as they are involved in the enactment of liturgy. Lathrop locates these four elements of liturgy as the heart of a common ecumenical inheritance, more or less constant through the various centuries. But in order to promote fresh inquiry about their meaning and significance he strips layers of accumulated interpretations from them by characteristically identifying them by the simple designations 'bath', 'book', 'meal' and 'people'.[17] Fundamentally basic to his inquiry is this question: 'why is it that people assemble, that biblical texts are read, that people are sometimes washed, that the fragment of a meal is held, and that these things are done side by side?',[18] especially amidst a 'flood of modern conditions' – wealth and decay, new knowledge and ignorance, pluralistic democracies and fierce new xenophobias, among many other ills – all of which might seem to threaten the survival of the ritual patterns which constitute Christian worship.[19] This question is key to 'liturgical theology', which

> inquires into the meaning of the liturgy, to use the ancient name of the assembly for worship and its actions. As theology,

as word-about-God, it does so especially by asking how the Christian meeting, in all its signs and words, says something authentic and reliable about God, and so says something true about ourselves and about our world as they are understood before God.[20]

Liturgical theology is, then, at least for Lathrop, a particular stream of liturgical studies that is not content to limit its orbit to historical reconstruction. Practices of retrieval have contemporary import in shaping 'a new public symbolism . . . able to hold and reorient, in material and social realities, our experience and our lives . . .', and capable of yielding fresh 'bearings for both public thought and personal hope'.[21]

Lathrop develops his liturgical theology in three modes – primary, secondary and pastoral. Combined, these modes make the task of liturgical theology one of 'critical classicism', meaning that it is 'marked by the willing reception of traditional patterns and archaic symbols, in the belief that these classics bear authority among us . . . [yet] at the same time . . . marked by the willing elaboration of a contemporary critique of received tradition'.[22] Following Aidan Kavanagh, Lathrop asserts that primary theology is the liturgy itself, and then not the texts for the rite, but such texts alongside action in which persons participate. In its primary mode, liturgical theology is the 'communal meaning of the liturgy exercised by the gathering itself'. In its secondary mode, it is 'written and spoken discourse that attempts to find words for the experience of the liturgy and to illuminate its structures, intending to enable a more profound participation in those structures by the members of the assembly'.[23] In doing so, 'it speaks of God as it speaks about the ways the assembly speaks of God', but it is not simply descriptive and must also have a 'critical, reforming edge'.[24] That edge, when 'turned toward specific problems of our time', is what Lathrop refers to 'pastoral liturgical theology'. In this respect, Lathrop adds to the tasks of liturgical theology as seminally identified by Alexander Schmemann (to whom *Holy Things* 'is meant as a homage of thanks' for *Introduction to Liturgical*

Theology),[25] by placing weight on the critical – 'pastoral' – aspect of the task, akin to the model of Geoffrey Wainwright's *Doxology*,[26] at least as that very influential text is understood by Maxwell Johnston.[27]

Several key features of Lathrop's work will be outlined in what follows: the juxtaposition of Scripture and sacrament, word and action; people in the place of worship – his concern with the primary symbols in liturgy in their environment; and liturgy and cultural criticism – liturgy's tasks in relation to experience of the modern world.

Scripture and sacrament

As might be expected from Lathrop's expertise in biblical studies, the Bible is a major feature of his theology. 'Patterns of reading and preaching the parts of the book, of praying the language of the book, of doing the signs of the book – these are the principal patterns of Christian worship', and yet 'the biblical foundations of Christian liturgy are more subtle than the obvious presence of the Bible',[28] as the 'old book' is juxtaposed with people present, situated as they must be, amidst their 'flood of modern conditions'. Not only are the Scriptures present within the liturgy – read and preached, perhaps also processed, sensed, kissed – they create an 'environment' of memory for worship and, in their juxtaposition with contemporary readers and hearers, say 'a new thing', 'greater than they have contained'.[29] They also set patterns of sacramental action within the worshipping assembly, narrating stories and interpretations of baptisms and Eucharists, suggesting alignments of words (for example, Jesus' name or a naming of the Trinity; or fragments of a narrative) against actions (for example, pouring water; or wine), while fixing these juxtapositions in a particular history – that of Israel and the early Church. This, too, creates fresh meanings in present contexts, while following a pattern which is itself what might be called intra-biblical, interpreting new practices in relation to old stories, so that old traditions are freed up to infuse freshness and depth into the present. This is what Lathrop means by 'the rebirth of images', the title of his seminal article. Echoing that earlier work in *Holy Things*, he writes,

> Christian corporate worship is made up of chains of images: our gathering, our washing, our meal are held next to biblical stories, themselves read in interpretative chains, and this whole rebirth of images is itself biblical.[30]

It is forms of this biblical pattern that Lathrop finds amplified in the Christian practice of assembly for worship from earliest times. Noting the description of worship which Justin Martyr provided in his *Apologies* for Emperor Antoninus Pius (*c.* AD 150), Lathrop suggests that Justin's reference to several readings – perhaps from what became portions of the Old and New Testaments, the 'writings of the prophets' and the 'memoirs of the apostles' – itself testifies to a dynamic of juxtaposition, as 'old words are caused to speak the new'.[31] Justin wrote,

> On the day named after the sun all, whether they live in the city or the countryside, are gathered together in unity. Then the records of the apostles or the writings of the prophets are read for as long as there is time. When the reader has concluded, the presider in a discourse admonishes and invites us into the pattern of these good things. Then we all stand together and offer prayer. And, as we said before, when we have concluded the prayer, bread is set out to eat, together with wine and water. The presider likewise offers up prayer and thanksgiving, as much as he can, and the people sing out their assent saying the amen. There is a distribution of the things over which thanks have been said and each person participates, and these things are sent by the deacons to those who are not present. Those who are prosperous and who desire to do so, give what they wish, according to each one's own choice, and the collection is deposited with the presider. He aids orphans and widows, those who are in want through disease or through another cause, those who are in prison, and foreigners who are sojourning here. In short, the presider is a guardian to all those who are in need. (1 *Apology* 67)[32]

This extract is of the utmost importance to Lathrop, shaping his vision of worship, and providing contours for his critique of contemporary worship practice. Just as Justin recounts the practice of a presider in the early assemblies inviting hearers into 'the pattern of these beautiful things', so Lathrop understands preaching and sacramental action, indeed 'all the liturgy',[33] as a graced pattern of experience that promises transformation for those who yield themselves to it.

Lathrop's perspective builds also on the view he expressed in an early article 'At Least Two Words' which was more recently reprinted in *The Landscape of Praise: Readings in Liturgical Renewal*, a collection of the best contributions to *Liturgy*, the journal of the Liturgical Conference, and which remains salient. In it, Lathrop outlines some key aspects of the understanding of juxtaposition that would later become so central to his work: proclamation of

> the truth about God . . . takes at least two words . . . In this world speaking about God with just one 'word' – one connected and logical discourse for example – will almost inevitably mean speaking a distortion, even a lie. It will suggest that God is a consequent idea, not a burning fire and a mysterious presence . . . for us the mystery of God, for all that it may indeed be graciously present in human speech, must be proposed by triangulation. Words, even such contradictory words as 'now' and 'not yet' or 'judgment' and 'mercy' or 'absence' and 'presence' or 'death' and 'life' or 'one' and 'many', will necessarily be put side by side, like two candles near the altar or the two cherubim on the ark of the covenant . . .'[34]

So it is that lectionary readings stand in juxtaposition to one another, speaking 'different – even wildly contrasting – views',[35] and the ministry of the word is juxtaposed to the 'visible word' of the table, and central sacramental symbols are themselves set in a context which juxtaposes sign or movement and dominical or deeply traditional words.[36] And 'Christians believe that among these pairs God is encountered in worship, not just talked about.'[37]

For Lathrop, this juxtaposition of word and word, and word and sacramental action, is basic to the way in which elements of Christian worship are patterned with meaning, and with grace. Such patterns constitute the 'shape of the liturgy', or, in the phrase which Lathrop adopts from Alexander Schmemann, the *ordo* of Christian worship. However, unlike Schmemann, for whom the *ordo* was defined by a very particular version of the Eastern Orthodox rite and its rubrics, Lathrop adopts an understanding of the *ordo* in harmony with many other liturgical scholars of the twentieth century, influenced by the Liturgical Movement and in turn by the Second Vatican Council. In so doing, he focuses upon some core elements of activity in worship and their interpretation, and although noting awareness of 'cautions about . . . too-easy harmonizations', particularly as articulated by Paul Bradshaw (but represented in this work by James White), he asserts 'that there is a core Christian pattern which, in its largest outline, can be explored in early sources'.[38] This ecumenically conscious *ordo*'s 'root elements' include gathering on Sunday, daily prayer, praise and intercession, Scripture, meal, teaching to inquirers and bathing,[39] though not all of these find full or equal expression in his own Lutheran tradition, formal forms of daily office being a case in point. Another set of elements constitutive of the *ordo*, which lie 'only a little behind [the root elements] in importance for Christian meaning',[40] are another set of juxtapositions: praise and beseeching, teaching and bath, and pascha and year.[41]

Yet from early times – at least perhaps in Lukan communities, or those reconstructed, if not reported, in the writing of the Acts of the Apostles (20.7–12; 2.42; and the Emmaus story [Luke 23.13–35]) – Lathrop proposes that the elements of 'word' and 'table' appear to have gained place as governing the range of authentic patterns for worship, as the early Church effectively appended a shared meal to a synaxis related in style to the synagogue meeting. This pattern, grounded in two poles, had certainly become embedded in at least some places by the end of the second century as it is represented in the first available descriptive writings about Christian worship, beyond the very sketchy possible allusions within Scripture, provided by Justin Martyr in the late second century. In addition to Justin's description of worship as he perhaps knew it, Lathrop gives precedence in his contemporary articulation of the meanings of worship to Justin's interpretation of the pattern as 'thanksgiving', and to its outcome, evoking from participants a collection for the poor. However, it is the basic two-fold pattern of word and table which Lathrop holds as not only ancient but also historically continuous, at least to a considerable measure, in that it

> has been called by a variety of names in the Christian East and West, but it has been universal. Even when the *ordo* has decayed, as in the loss of preaching or of vernacular scripture reading among Roman Catholics and the Orthodox, or as in the disappearance of the weekly meal among Western Protestants, the resultant liturgical practice has often been accompanied by a memory that the full twofold action was the classic Christian norm for Sunday.[42]

While Lathrop is more confident than some others about the centrality of this *ordo* and its elements, his stress upon it stands in continuity with many forebears, mentors and peers. It is his accent upon juxtaposition in the *ordo* which is distinctive and refreshing, and not only that, for if he is correct to stress them, 'a loss of these juxtapositions carries with it a diminishment in the clarity of the faith'.[43]

People in the place of worship

Lathrop's stress on Scripture and sacrament in the pattern of the *ordo* represents a particular construct of what he would himself recognize as secondary liturgical theology. Other major themes of Lathrop's work emerge in Part Two of *Holy Things*, concerned with 'things', and in *Holy People*, the second of his related major works. These attempt to shift the focus to primary theology, the discernable, material elements which are needed for the *ordo*, and which secondary liturgical theology interprets. Following the emphasis of Robert Hovda's influential presider's manual, *Strong, Loving and Wise*, Lathrop argues that the key 'thing' is people, and *Holy People* is dedicated to the exploration of human beings gathered in one place as the first and dominating symbol of worship: 'People are primary',[44] but 'to "have church" you do need some things',[45] such as bread and wine, Bible and chalice, whether those used are simple or elaborate, and whatever the setting for their use (frugal home or dazzling basilica, indoor or outdoor and so on). Lathrop draws on a seventh-century Byzantine tradition in which Peter counsels one of his converts, Pancratius, about the necessary equipment for the establishment of a church: 'two gospel books, two books of Acts composed by the divine apostle Paul, two sets of silver paten-and-chalice, two crosses made of cedar boards, and two volumes of the divine picture stories containing the decoration of the church . . .'[46] Whatever the historical foundation of this tradition, it represents both the continuity of aspects of the *ordo*, as understood by Lathrop, and some embellishments around its core. Although Lathrop does not use the term 'sacramentality' to describe these items, the notion is implied and of importance: 'for the great Christian tradition, the spiritual is intimately involved with the material, the truth about God inseparable from the ordinary', which in a reference from Luther is said to act as 'ford, bridge, door, ship, and stretcher', helping humans find access to the divine.[47] So a variety of 'sacred objects' is considered – bread, wine, water and also cup, plate and tub – all of which have both practical usefulness and symbolic significance, though with the former in the list containing more symbolic significance than the latter. For instance, 'Bread suggests a larger order. Wine gives festivity, leaving troubles behind. Water comes from a source away from here.' And all three are ambiguous: 'All three give life. All three suggest death.'[48]

Lathrop refers to a definition of symbol as 'a complex of gestures, sounds, images, and/or words that evoke, invite, and persuade participation in that to which they refer',[49] and underlines the polyvalence of things in so far as what they may symbolize. Given that the central symbols are themselves polyvalent, Lathrop underlines the danger that the 'lesser symbols' of plate and cup, tub, and less so again in his view things such as fire, oil, incense and garments, may obscure the *ordo* if special care is not taken that they are used only to enrich the key things and their core symbolism.

This distinction between central and lesser symbols, though now ecumenically recognized, is a strong Lutheran theme, and the focus of Lathrop's thought on 'Lutheran liturgical hermeneutics', in another place: 'In his "Treatise on the New Testament, that is the Holy Mass" of 1520, Martin Luther proposes that the ability to distinguish what is central and constitutive in the Eucharist from what is additional and secondary in its celebration is "the greatest and most useful art".'[50] Essential to the range of meanings which emerge for the central and lesser objects is, for Lathrop, their juxtaposition to the word and the symbolism that the word either excites or inhibits. Yet the word, signalled by the book of Scripture is also 'a kind of vessel',[51] infused with significance in its own turn by other elements in its environment. Place and time, the ordering of space and the taking of shape (circles, ranks, open, facing) all form part of this wider environment.

Particular fragments of Lathrop's writing have concerned one of these lesser symbols which is often central in many liturgies – money. Lathrop links this to notions of offering and sacrifice, with a very clear desire to reform the way in which many churches perform the likes of their 'offertory processions' and the gathering and giving of finances in liturgical contexts. Unlike other Lutherans, Lathrop is not primarily concerned about what such processions may do to ally ideas of humans being able to 'give to God', but rather with the ways in which they distort, by diffusing, or perhaps diluting, notions of sacrifice. Lathrop recognizes that 'at the heart of genuine offering there is always killing',[52] if only of the flowers on the altar, and yet it remains that contemporary cultures continue to be fascinated with sacrifice in its grossest extremes, as evidenced in the crowds attending viewings of the frozen bodies of 'Juanita', a child once sacrificed on Nevado Ampato, or various redis-covered 'Bogmen'. Lathrop seeks a reorientation of Christian liturgical practice along the lines of the ancient and occasionally revived practice of giving money or food away as an integral action of assembled worshippers, and so he wants to invigor-ate the accent on a less familiar 'offertory procession' – that of 'going into the world to serve' at the end of liturgy. Precedents for his convictions are found in Paul, Chrysostom, Luther and above all in Justin Martyr (whose record of the collection for the poor is cited above). A contemporary expression of this tra-dition is also located, in the practice of the Episcopal Parish of St Gregory of Nyssa, San Francisco. The kind of involved and costly giving that the maintaining of such a tradition is likely to entail would, for Lathrop, incorporate this lesser symbol into a liturgical framework more clearly governed by its central word and sacrament, together magnifying the costly sacrifice of Christ. And so this concern with money serves as an example of how Lathrop wishes all lesser symbols and secondary liturgical elements to operate.[53]

Lathrop's final point about 'things' is that people, the pri-mary symbol, shape the pattern of things in their environment. And people, assembled, are also polyvalent. Knowing that their assembly will certainly be prone to 'self-selecting characteris-tics', Lathrop holds that the *ordo* is a corrective to exclusivity, in that

> it will continually propose that this gathering is too small, too narrowly conceived. The holy circle is not holy enough, the sacred assembly not wide enough . . . After all, the center of this circle and the meaning of the *ordo* is Jesus Christ, the one who is always identified with the outsider.[54]

In his contribution to the Don Saliers festschrift, *Liturgy and the Moral Self*, Lathrop intensifies this conviction by reference to a 'remarkable dictum': 'Draw a line that includes us and excludes many others, and Jesus Christ is always on the other side of the line.'[55] However, another possibility is that people, assembled, may – as they hold things dear to them in common – bear marks of community, which Lathrop envisions as a particular kind of assembly, with some depth:

> So, go into church. Before you, in some form, are some things: a pool, a book, bread, and wine. Around you are some people, the primary thing. In this place, at an appointed time, these all will interact. If you let them, they will interact with you, inviting you to the breaking, surrounding you with the faith, engaging you in sending portions.[56]

Culture and liturgical criticism

Part Three of *Holy Things* shifts the focus to 'pastoral liturgical theology' and a number of 'applications', concerned with local embodiment of the *ordo*, leadership in the assembly and the relationship between liturgy and society. The first of these three concerns is expanded in the essays collected in the 'Open Questions in Worship' series edited by Lathrop, with each volume introduced and concluded by him. Indeed, in many senses, the seventh chapter of *Holy Things*, 'Liturgical Criticism', can be seen as setting the very questions that the pastors and scholars featured in 'Open Questions' address. Some characteristic examples are:

> Is the Sunday meeting clearly people gathered graciously and peacefully around the two events of word and table? There is an order to the assembly, even when the group calls itself non-liturgical; is the order this ancient one of scripture and meal? Is that what a visitor would say was going on? Is that what the children would portray if they play-acted this meeting? . . .[57]

To begin with, evidence of concern with such questions can be seen in the titles of the 'Open Questions' series – *What Are the Essentials of Christian Worship?*, *What Is Contemporary*

Worship?, How Does Worship Evangelise?, What Is Changing in Baptismal Practice?, What Is Changing in Eucharistic Practice?, What Are the Ethical Implications of Worship?, What Does Multicultural Worship Look Like?, And How Does the Liturgy Speak of God?. They can also be seen in a collection of essays by Lathrop's peers as liturgy teachers in American Lutheran seminaries, *Inside Out: Worship in an Age of Mission,* to which Lathrop contributes an endnote piece.[58] As well as sharing Lathrop's questions, all of these separate publications promote the central emphasis of 'Liturgical Criticism' on the need to 'call attention to the major oppositions of the *ordo* and to encourage their lively presence in the local assembly'.[59]

It is also in the same chapter of *Holy Things* that Lathrop's thinking finds a strong Christological focus: 'The fullness of the central signs is to be accentuated not for their own sake, but in order to communicate the meaning of Jesus Christ to present human need. Assembly, Sunday, bath, word, meal, prayers and ministries are called upon to "speak and drive Christ"', a quote from Luther. For,

> Jesus Christ, his death and resurrection and the faith that is through him, juxtaposed to these pre-existent rituals, is the institution and consecration of sacraments. He was baptized; he read the scriptures; he ate with sinners. His death was a baptism and the meaning of baptisms. Risen, he opens to us all the scriptures. He is known as risen in the bread. His death was a cup that he gives us to drink. The patterns of the liturgy root in Jesus Christ.[60]

And Lathrop's grasp of the need for the centrality of liturgy for understanding Jesus Christ emerges in his essay 'Liturgy and Mission in the North American Context' in *Inside Out*:

> There is much talk about God and about Jesus in North America. In many ways, our cultures are soaked in religion and spirituality. But without the stories of the scriptures, without 'this is my body, given for you,' without the living water of baptism, this talk can be hazy, unhelpful, perhaps

Gnostic, often simply code words for the self. The life-giving presence of God is actually given in word and sacrament.[61]

Lathrop's criticism of North American churches' accommodations to their cultures are particularly striking. He notes the ways in which Roman Catholic communities 'often experience the temptation to obscure the *ordo missae* with secondary matters', though the fact that they are not authorized to do so encourages restraint, for which Lathrop is grateful. Yet he is clearly more troubled by the state of much contemporary Protestantism:

> North American Protestant churches – and churches of the world which are influenced by their choices – have been drawn toward patterns of worship which accentuate those words and music which move the individual Self toward conversion, or to use more modern language, engage in the 'marketing' of personal 'happiness' and the 'meeting of needs'. Such religion, for all of its Christian vocabulary, is easily tempted to Gnosticism.[62]

It is this collapse towards merely 'meeting needs' to which Protestants may become prone which also may drive Roman Catholics to accentuate elements that obscure word and sacrament. Yet the greatest threat to the *ordo* shaped around word and sacrament is readily identified as the apparently thriving 'seeker services' of Megachurches. Contrary to the stress on 'participation' arising from the Liturgical Movement and crystallized in Paragraph 14 of *Sacrosanctum concilium*,[63] the alternative embodied by the Megachurch minimalizes participation; reduces music to easily singable and oft-repeated choruses; operates screens and TV monitors as a mode of easing passive observation, often using such technology to beam out images of staged drama which often precedes a 'message' of some kind. The message itself may be introduced or concluded with a few verses of Scripture, but this is likely to be the limit of explicit biblical content. Such services tend often to close abruptly after the message, and may often feature a period of time in which people are asked to give some visible signal of response to the message, such as the raising of a hand to indicate a decision of commitment to Christ as proclaimed. Although money may be collected at some point in the proceedings, there is no sacrament to which this 'offering' might be juxtaposed in order to enhance its depth and meaning. Indeed, sacraments are entirely absent, while the form of the word is radically reshaped, as is implied in the rejection of the terms 'preaching' and 'sermon', and as is openly indicated in the virtual absence of Bibles or biblical reading.[64] Although this pattern and style of worship can be traced through the evolution of 'frontier' worship in North America, it is acutely at odds with the ecumenical consensus celebrated in liturgical renewal. The critical point of disagreement between liturgical churches and Megachurches is identified by Lathrop as

> the question of means . . . Is the church centred on individuals and their processes of decision-making? Or is it centred on – indeed, created by – certain concrete and communal means which God has given . . . ? From the classic Christian point of view, if decision-making is the central matter, the meeting will not really be around God, no matter how orthodox or trinitarian a theology may be in the mind of the 'speaker'.[65]

While Lathrop's criticisms are acid and strong, he is fully aware of the attractiveness of the kind of assembly that seeker-services represent in a culture to which such services are attuned. His response centres on the need for churches in liturgical traditions 'to work on a kind of participation which is lively – in singing, praying, bathing, eating and drinking – but which does not exclude. The participants are not insiders. All of us . . . are seekers. . . All of our Eucharists must be "seeker services".'[66] But this will not mean for him any compromise of the 'strong center' of the *ordo*, which by virtue of its relationship to Jesus Christ is held to promise deep and genuine inclusivity. Finally, it is Lathrop's understanding of Lutheran liturgical hermeneutics that ensures both open welcome and some borders to hospitality towards expressions of contemporary cultures in liturgy. For Lathrop, at all times, the centre of word and sacrament must be clear, while the assembly is also porous to 'the gifts of many cultures of the world: their languages, their music, their patterns of festivity and solemnity, their manners of gathering, their structures of meaning'.[67] Yet cultural patterns, not least western or northern cultural forms, may never 'usurp the place of the center'.[68] Rather,

> They must come into the 'city' to gather around the 'Lamb' (Revelation 21.22–7); they must be broken to the purpose of the Gospel of Christ. Cultural patterns of all sorts – southern and northern, western and eastern, rural and urban, specifically local and increasingly worldwide – are welcome here. But they are not to take the place of the Lamb. They are not welcome to obscure the gift of Christ in the Scripture read and preached, in the water used in his name, and in the thanksgiving meal.[69]

Engaging the debate about Patterns for Worship

Establishing a dialogue between the work of Gordon Lathrop and the issues considered in earlier parts of this work might find a focus in a number of areas:

It is obvious to state that the *ordo* that is so clearly valued by Lathrop is simply not considered as a 'treasure' in many of the urban assemblies or those with children that have been the concerns of Part Two of this work. This can be seen in the common, somewhat laissez-faire approach to the presentation of the kind of services that have come in many places to be known as 'family services'.[70] These may often involve a simplification of the *ordo*'s juxtapositions if not a jettisoning of much of its content, perhaps especially its sacramental heart.

In relation to such practices, Lathrop's appreciation of the *ordo* has a great deal to contribute to the consideration of the shape of Christian worship, even when the young or barely literate are present. Given the concern of many proponents of 'family services' with evangelism, Lathrop's critique of worship that decimates the *ordo* offers an important challenge to assumptions about the kind of truth and the characteristics of the community into which the evangelized are to be invited. More mundanely, though also important, wider knowledge of the views that Lathrop promotes would cast much discussion about rules and rubrics for worship in a new light. Even when rubrics offer unprecedented freedoms, as in *Patterns for Worship* in the English Anglican tradition, their being set in a much broader context by cross-reference to the seriousness with which Lathrop approaches the topic of essentials for Christian worship might enable rubrics – perhaps especially minimal ones – to be valued to a greater extent than is often apparent.

Lathrop raises very important concerns about juxtaposition as a key means by which theology is learned. These concerns need to be brought into conversation with those responsible for worship with children and in urban contexts, and they merit careful attention by those who plan and lead worship, or create resources for worship. For instance, if children are to be recognized as constituent of the primary symbol of Christian worship, the assembly itself, then facilitating children's understanding of theological juxtapositions is a crucial task of Christian catechesis, as is drawing out and celebrating children's own contributions to the juxtapositions by which the Church articulates its seeking and praise of the divine. Here, Gail Ramshaw's work to make liturgy accessible to children may be a leading light for many more contributions towards the same end. And accessible 'abecedaries' of the kind of which Ramshaw has developed – for instance, *Letters for God's Name*, revised as *A Metaphorical God*[71] – may also be significant among urban Christians resistant to the temptation to which theologians are apparently often regarded as being prone – to that which Green labels as 'wrapping God up in abstraction'.

If children are to encounter the juxtapositions of the liturgy, and so to become conversant with at least enough theology to enable a relationship with God, it is clear that children need above all to be present as participants in liturgical celebration.

And yet this point is by no means uncontentious. The presence of children at all in many British churches is unusual enough, though even where they are present they are very often subject to congregational practices that remove them from most if not all parts of the liturgy. Their removal – even with 'blessing' mediated by appropriate adults (among others, the vicar's 'let's pray for the children before they leave for Sunday School') – may be largely for the convenience of the adults present, while, conversely, the presence of children may also be largely for the benefit of adults seeking or requiring simple presentations of aspects of the faith, a reality of which Mark Searle was aware, as we saw in citations from his work in Chapter 4 above.

The practice of children departing from worship may communicate very much about perceptions of children – if, for instance, it is considered appropriate for children to be present for a confession of sin but not for reflection on Scripture or for reception of the Eucharist, a particular view of children may be operative, even if acknowledgement that this is the case is difficult to elicit. Even in congregations in which children's 'sacramental belonging' is accepted, and in which children participate in Communion, particular views of children may be operative if liturgical roles open to lay adults are not also open to children. And yet resistance to children's involvement in the proclamation of Scripture or in the distribution of the sacrament is sometimes quite vigorously resisted, and even legislated against: bishops' licences to lay Eucharistic ministers may be restricted to the over 16s.

In the case of these two particular examples – Scripture reading and handling the sacrament – echoing the expectation of a psalmist that 'out of the mouths of babes Yahweh ordains his praise'[72] does not seem to be easy, while neither does facilitating the embodiment in public roles of the status of children as created in the divine image and so capable of serving as sacramental channels of divine grace. The apparent resistance to children's involvement in handling of the Eucharist at least reveals the paucity or discomfort attending images of God as child – compare 'father' and for some though not for all, 'mother' –

and this at least suggests an image beginning with 'c' that might fruitfully emerge in an abecedary.[73] Children's participation in liturgy as an expression of their own capacity, and the capacity of aspects of their lives, to symbolize the divine is crucial, as is their own participation in symbol. And both their participation in symbol and the symbolism of their participation are desirable in the catechesis of the Church as an all-age community. The young's contribution to the Passover, not least their leading questions – 'Why is this night not like any other night?' and so on – suggest important cues and leads to the ways in which children may not only be involved in symbolic reality but also be valued in the role of leading others into participation in God's work according to Scripture and tradition.

Perhaps as problematically for both adults and children, the removal of children from the worshipping assembly in order for them to attend Sunday School may communicate that worship is an adult activity while learning is for children. This threatens to rupture the appropriate life-long association between discipleship and learning.[74] Many British churches have much to learn from the commonplace North American practice of Sunday School as an all-age activity, in which many members of congregations will be involved in some form of religious education, and most likely in a form distinct from the didactic style of sermons. The removal of children from the assembly in ways that are characteristic of many British churches may not only disenfranchise children from the traditions of worship which so many seem to find it impossible to (re-)engage on 'growing out' of Sunday School, and so leave – as they grow out of and leave other forms of schooling – it may also disenfranchise adult Christians from means of learning the Christian faith that are perhaps most appropriate to their own adult capacities and needs. Even the concession to adult learning represented by mid-week 'home-groups', popular in Britain in many evangelical and charismatic churches as a means of fellowship between Sundays, allows adult Christian learning to become the pursuit of a keen 'elite', whereas attempting to establish the normalcy of all-age Sunday School on Sundays would hold more potential for strengthening the ordinariness of the connection between 'disciple' and its etymological links to learning.

Even in assemblies where it is for whatever reasons considered appropriate for children to depart from parts of services of worship intended primarily to include adults, other lessons could be learned by many British churches from another commonplace North American practice by the Christian churches – that of provision of 'children's chapels'.[75] Children's chapels are perhaps the closest equivalent to the Sunday School as it is commonly practised in Britain, as they involve the church's children in activity limited to their own age range. However, in contrast to the mainstream British view of Sunday School, children's chapels typically offer liturgical experience, and are likely to use prayer-text and ritual performed in a specially designed liturgical environment. The environment may include a miniature scaled altar-table, ambo from which the Bible is read, pews if these are present in the sanctuary, and liturgical arts such as stained glass and religious images. The prayer-text and ritual will also typically be aligned to that which is used in the sanctuary. For instance, the 'Preschool Children's Worship Service' at St Philip's Cathedral, Atlanta, includes a procession involving some children as acolytes, the ritual lighting of candles, and dialogue between a liturgical leader and the children that incorporates among other things the Lord's Prayer, a lection for the day and both trinitarian greetings and the *sursum corda*. Song and intercession are clearly crafted with the aptitude and appetites of the under fives in mind, but the various elements of prayer appear in the children's liturgy in the same order as they are likely to do so in the Eucharist of the *Book of Common Prayer* (1979) of the Episcopal Church. Examples of text from the St Philip's order include, at the confession:

> **Forgive us, Lord, for things we've done**
> **that were not kind and good.**
> **Forgive us, Lord, and help us try**
> **to do things as we should.**

And, at the offertory, the following exchange, as not money but a cross and flowers are presented on the altar-table:

What does the cross mean?
God loves us.
What do the flowers mean?
We love God.[76]

This exchange is a prelude to the singing of 'All things bright and beautiful'. This latter example of liturgical dialogue may not be profound, but it is at least a crude juxtaposition of meaning revealed in the context of Christian liturgy, and in a clearly ritualized way that has few parallels in British Sunday Schools as they have typically operated. Notably, material that is much used in British Sunday schools among parallel age groups, for example, Susan Sayers's *Pebbles* and Scripture Union's *SALT*, may typically include a prayer (and Sayers's is likely to include a lection of the day, though both use Scripture), but neither assumes a ritual context such as the St Philip's preschool liturgy.

As understood by Lathrop, the *ordo* both in terms of its characteristic content and historic shape offers treasures to children in so far as it fosters capacity to manage and state theological juxtapositions and to participate in symbolic reality. Consequently, loss of the *ordo* may frustrate children's – as well as others' – progress towards 'full maturity' in Christ. Opting for, or being directed to, apparently 'simpler' forms of Christian worship may, perhaps despite claims to the contrary, in fact enlarge the 'hazy, unhelpful, gnostic, self-referential' forms of theology of which Lathrop is wary. In so far as Lathrop's hesitancy is prudent, he offers a sense of how the *ordo* may foster Christians in various counter-cultural perspectives, and so on the basis of Lathrop's work we may hold that participation in the *ordo* constitutes a radical alternative to removing children into Sunday School, as well as to entertaining adults in family services, seeker services, and a range of other possibilities.

As well as offering critical gifts for discipleship to children and those who worship alongside them, counter-cultural views encouraged by the liturgy may have a special poignancy in urban contexts. For churches meeting in geographical space which touches proximate but separate communities such as are characteristically found in cities may be challenged by their liturgy to abandon at least some of the selectivity which, unrestrained, might enable worship to centre on the narrowly perceived needs of one 'community of interest' or another. Embracing the *ordo* enjoyed or endured by the Christian people if not 'at all times and in all places' then in a good many of them may correct or resist any tendency to exclusive self-selectivity which is in Lathrop's estimation the inevitable consequence of the dark side of human polyvalency.

These comments relating Lathrop's perspectives to thinking about worship with children and urban congregations are meant to be suggestive rather than exhaustive, and they do, I believe, suggest the fruitfulness of attending to his insights.

In our next chapter, we consider the contribution of Don Saliers.

Notes

1. Edward Schillebeeckx, *The Eucharist*, trans. N. D. Smith, London: Sheed and Ward, 1968; Edward Schillebeeckx, *Christ the Sacrament of Encounter with God*, trans. Paul Barrett and N. D. Smith, London and New York: Sheed and Ward, 1963.
2. *Lutheran Book of Worship*, Minneapolis: Augsburg Publishing House, 1978.
3. Gordon W. Lathrop and Gail Ramshaw, *Psalter for the Christian People: An Inclusive-Language Revision of the Psalter of the Book of Common Prayer 1979*, Collegeville: Liturgical Press, 1993; Gordon W. Lathrop and Gail Ramshaw Schmidt, *Lectionary for the Christian People, Cycles A, B and C*, Collegeville: Liturgical Press, 1986–8; Gordon W. Lathrop and Gail Ramshaw, eds, *Readings for the Assembly*, three vols, Minneapolis: Fortress Press, 1996.
4. Gail Ramshaw, ed., *Richer Fare for the Christian People: Reflections on the Sunday Readings, Cycles A, B, C*, New York: Liturgical Press, 1990.

5. Gail Ramshaw, *Words around the Font*, Chicago: Liturgy Training Publications, 1994.
6. Gail Ramshaw, *Words around the Table*, Chicago: Liturgy Training Publications, 1991.
7. Gail Ramshaw, *Reviving Sacred Speech: The Meaning of Liturgical Language: Second Thoughts on 'Christ in Sacred Speech'*, Akron: Order of St Luke (OSL), 2000. This is a revised version of her *Christ in Sacred Speech*, Minneapolis: Fortress Press, 1986.
8. Gordon W. Lathrop, 'A Rebirth of Images', *Worship* 58, 1984, pp. 291–304.
9. Joyce Ann Zimmermann, 'Gordon W Lathrop: Word Meets Ritual', Dwight Vogel, ed., *Primary Sources of Liturgical Theology: A Reader*, Collegeville: Pueblo, 2001, pp. 213–4, p. 214.
10. Gordon W. Lathrop, *Holy Things: A Liturgical Theology*, Minneapolis: Fortress Press, 1993.
11. Gordon W. Lathrop, *Holy People: A Liturgical Ecclesiology*, Minneapolis: Fortress Press, 1999.
12. Gordon W. Lathrop, *Holy Ground: A Liturgical Cosmology*, Minneapolis: Fortress Press, 2003.
13. S. Anita Stauffer, ed., *Worship and Culture in Dialogue*, Geneva: Lutheran World Federation, 1994.
14. Gordon W. Lathrop, ed., *Open Questions in Worship*, 8 vols, Minneapolis: Fortress Press, 1995–6.
15. Gordon W. Lathrop, *Central Things*, Minneapolis: Augsburg Press, 2005.
16. Geoffrey Wainwright, *Doxology: The Praise of God in Worship, Doctrine and Life: A Systematic Theology*, London: Epworth Press, 1980.
17. Lathrop, *Holy Things*, pp. 10–11.
18. Lathrop, *Holy Things*, pp. 2–3.
19. Lathrop, *Holy Things*, p. 1.
20. Lathrop, *Holy Things*, p. 3.
21. Lathrop, *Holy Things*, pp. 3–4.
22. Lathrop, *Holy Things*, pp. 4–5.
23. Lathrop, *Holy Things*, p. 6.
24. Lathrop, *Holy Things*, p. 7.
25. Lathrop, *Holy Things*, p. x.
26. Dirk Lange and Dwight Wogel, eds, *Ordo: Bath, Word, Prayer, Table*, Akron: Order of St Luke, 2005.
27. Maxwell E. Johnston, 'Liturgy and Theology', Paul Bradshaw and Bryan Spinks, eds, *Liturgy in Dialogue: Essays in Memory of Ronald Jasper*, London: SPCK, 1991, pp. 202–25, which compares a number of contemporary liturgical theologies and theologies of

worship. Cf. also David Fagerberg's *What is Liturgical Theology? A Study in Methodology*, Collegeville: Liturgical Press, 1993.

28. Lathrop, *Holy Things*, p. 16.
29. Lathrop, *Holy Things*, pp. 19–20.
30. Lathrop, *Holy Things*, p. 24.
31. Lathrop, *Holy Things*, pp. 31–2.
32. Quoted in Lathrop, *Holy Things*, pp. 31–2.
33. Lathrop, *Holy Things*, p. 34.
34. Gordon W. Lathrop, 'At Least Two Words: The Liturgy as Proclamation', Blair Meeks, ed., *The Landscape of Praise: Readings in Liturgical Renewal*, Valley Forge: Trinity Press International, 1996, pp. 183–5, p. 183. On juxtaposition in *Holy Things*, see p. 10 for the first mention of 'intentional juxtaposition' and follow references in the index. Note also Geoffrey Wainwright's review in *Worship* 69 (1995), pp. 287–8, p. 288.
35. Lathrop, 'At Least Two Words', p. 183.
36. Lathrop, 'At Least Two Words', p. 184.
37. Gordon W. Lathrop, 'Afterword', Gordon W. Lathrop, ed., *What Is Contemporary Worship?*, Open Questions in Worship 2, Minneapolis: Fortress Press, 1995, pp. 31–2, p. 31.
38. Lathrop, *Holy Things*, p. 35, n. 9, with reference to Paul Bradshaw, *Search for the Origins of Christian Worship*, London: SPCK, 1991.
39. Lathrop, *Holy Things*, p. 34.
40. Lathrop, *Holy Things*, p. 55.
41. Lathrop, *Holy Things*, Chapter 3, *passim*.
42. Lathrop, *Holy Things*, p. 51.
43. Lathrop, *Holy Things*, p. 52.
44. Lathrop, *Holy Things*, p. 87, referring to Robert Hovda, *Strong, Loving and Wise: Presiding in Liturgy*, pp. 55–6.
45. Lathrop, *Holy Things*, p. 88.
46. Quoted in Lathrop, *Holy Things*, p. 88.
47. Lathrop, *Holy Things*, p. 89.
48. Lathrop, *Holy Things*, p. 95.
49. Lathrop, *Holy Things*, p. 92, n. 6, referring to Stephen Happel, 'Symbol', Peter E. Fink, ed., *New Dictionary of Sacramental Worship*, Washington DC: Liturgical Press, 1991, pp. 1237–45, p. 1238.
50. Gordon W. Lathrop, 'A Contemporary Lutheran Approach to Worship and Culture: Sorting Out the Critical Principles', Anita Stauffer, ed., *Worship and Culture in Dialogue*, Geneva: Lutheran World Federation, 1994, pp. 137–51, p. 137.
51. Lathrop, *Holy Things*, p. 97.
52. Gordon W. Lathrop, 'The Bodies on Nevado Ampato: A Further Note on Offering and Offertory', *Worship* 71 (1997): pp. 546–54, p. 552.

53. For a related critique turned on Catholic liturgy's propensity to obscure a 'sense of solidarity with the hungry' in the acts of offering, see Gordon W. Lathrop, 'The Revised Sacramentary in Ecumenical Affirmation and Admonition', Mark R. Francis and Keith F. Pecklers, eds, *Liturgy for the New Millennium: A Commentary on the Revised Sacramentary: Essays in Honor of Anscar J. Chupungco*, Collegeville: Liturgical Press, 2000, pp. 129–41, p. 141.

54. Lathrop, *Holy Things*, p. 115.

55. Duane Priebe, quoted in Gordon W. Lathrop, '"O Taste and See": The Geography of Liturgical Ethics', E. Byron Anderson and Bruce T Morrill, eds, *Liturgy and the Moral Self: Humanity at Full Stretch before God: Essays in Honor of Don E. Saliers*, Collegeville: Liturgical Press, 1998, pp. 41–53, p. 51.

56. Lathrop, *Holy Things*, p. 115. See also Gordon W. Lathrop, 'Koinonia and the Shape of the Liturgy', *Studia Liturgica* 26 (1996), pp. 65–81.

57. Lathrop, *Holy Things*, p. 167.

58. Gordon W. Lathrop, 'Liturgy and Mission in the North American Context', Thomas H. Shattauer, ed., *Inside Out: Worship in an Age of Mission*, Minneapolis: Fortress Press, 1999, 201–12.

59. Lathrop, *Holy Things*, p. 179.

60. Lathrop, *Holy Things*, p. 173.

61. Lathrop, 'Liturgy and Mission', p. 208.

62. Lathrop, 'Revised Sacramentary', p. 137.

63. Gordon W. Lathrop, 'Strong Center, Open Door: A Vision of Continuing Liturgical Renewal', *Worship* 75 (2001), pp. 35–45, pp. 35–6.

64. Gordon W. Lathrop, 'New Pentecost or Joseph's Britches? Reflections on the History and Meaning of the Worship Ordo in the Megachurches', *Worship* 72 (1998), pp. 521–38, pp. 523–4.

65. Lathrop, 'New Pentecost', p. 537.

66. Lathrop, 'Strong Center', pp. 42–3.

67. Lathrop, 'Contemporary Lutheran Approach', p. 138.

68. Lathrop, 'Contemporary Lutheran Approach', p. 138.

69. Lathrop, 'Contemporary Lutheran Approach', pp. 138–9.

70. See: *Patterns for Worship*, pp. 2–5; also, Michael Vasey, 'The Family and the Liturgy', Stephen C. Barton, ed., *The Family in Theological Perspective*, Edinburgh: T&T Clark, 1996, pp. 169–85.

71. *A Metaphorical God: An Abecedery of Images for God*, Chicago: Liturgy Training Publications, 1995. This is a revised version of *Letters for God's Name*, Minneapolis: Seabury Press, 1984.

72. Psalm 8.2 (International Consultation on English in the Liturgy [ICEL]).

73. Janet Pais considers the metaphor of God as child in *Suffer the*

Children: A Theology of Liberation by a Victim of Child Abuse, New York: Paulist, 1991.

74. 'Learner' is a meaning of μαθητής.

75. Disappointingly, children's chapels receive little attention in books about the creation and design of liturgical architecture and environment: note, for example, lack of reference in James F. White and Susan J. White, *Church Architecture: Building and Renovating for Christian Worship*, Akron: Order of St Luke, 2nd edn 1998, in which the omission is not rectified in the second edition, even in a chapter on 'subsidiary spaces'. It is to be hoped that children's chapels are designed on very similar principles as space for all-age assembly, and that this is the reason for the failure to mention them in texts.

76. I am grateful to the Very Revd Samuel Candler, Dean of St Philip's Cathedral, Atlanta, for permission to use texts from children's liturgies at the cathedral. The text 'Forgive us, Lord . . .' was crafted by Sam Candler himself; credit for the offertory exchange beginning 'What does the cross mean?' belongs to former Canon of Children's Ministries, Bobbie Williamson.

6

EXPRESSING THE 'HEART':
Don E. Saliers

Introduction

Don E. Saliers is William R. Cannon Distinguished Professor of Theology and Worship at the Candler School of Theology and the Graduate Division of Religion at Emory University, Atlanta, Georgia, USA. Prior to joining the Candler faculty in 1974, he worked at Yale Divinity School, after completing his PhD at Yale University. Previous studies were undertaken at Cambridge University, England, and Ohio Wesleyan University.

Saliers is himself an ordained United Methodist, and has indeed crafted some of the United Methodist Church's liturgical resources – most notably, the seasonal material for Advent and Christmas, 'From Hope to Joy', and for Lent and Easter, 'From Ashes to Fire'.[1] Yet more significant perhaps is the fact that he was involved, as both contributor and commentator, in the church's hymnbook, the *United Methodist Hymnal*, giving him extensive influence on the shaping of the American Methodist people's spirituality. Saliers's ecclesial and academic contexts merge in so far as Emory University is itself a Methodist foundation, and in so far as a body of his own writing reflects Methodist concerns quite directly.

Although occupying a significant place in the United Methodist Church, Saliers has wide ecumenical interests, having since the period of growing liturgical consensus in the 1970s – that he helped to foster and to promote[2] – occupied a major role in encouraging his denomination in ecumenical convergence. Saliers is an oblate of the Benedictine Order, with strong connections to St John's Abbey, Minnesota, the foundation of *Orate Fratres*, which became *Worship* (of which he is associate editor).

Apart from United Methodist Church liturgical resources, Saliers is the author of many articles and several monographs: notably, *The Soul in Paraphrase: Prayer and the Religious Affections*,[3] *Worship and Spirituality*,[4] *Worship as Theology: Foretaste of Glory Divine*[5] and *Worship Come to Its Senses*.[6] He is co-author with his Anglican colleague Charles Hackett of the presider's manual *The Lord Be with You*,[7] the (Revised) Common Lectionary resource book *(New) Handbook of the Christian Year*[8] and *The Conversation Matters*,[9] a treatise on the contemporary shape of United Methodism which he co-wrote with Henry Knight III, and most recently co-author of *A Song to Sing, a Life to Live: Reflections on Music as a Spiritual Practice*,[10] co-authored with his daughter Emily Saliers, a member of the popular folk-group Indigo Girls. Saliers is also co-editor of *Christian Spirituality III: Post-Reformation to Modern* in the 'World Spirituality' series,[11] contributing an endnote piece on 'Christian Spirituality in an Ecumenical Age', and of *Human Disability and the Service of God: Reassessing Religious Practice*, to which he adds a piece on the 'spirituality of inclusiveness'.[12] He is also the subject of a festschrift, *Liturgy and Moral Self: Humanity at Full Stretch before God*,[13] which gathers writings that reflect Saliers's concerns as expressed in his particularly influential article, 'Liturgy and Ethics: Some New Beginnings'. Contributions to the collection are written by former students, renowned Methodist scholars, colleagues at the Candler School of Theology and those in organizations such as the North American Academy of Liturgy, of which he was President in 1982, and from which he received its Berakah Award in 1992. An extraordinary, anonymously scripted tribute used on the occasion of his Berakah Award presentation hints at some of the marks of his work, and may act as a kind of preface to more thoroughgoing exploration:

> To . . . a fountain among us . . . From your pen flows philosophy for the learned, piety for the faithful, music for a thou-

sand tongues to sing. For us who are thirsty you pour out yourself, singing a spirit of praise, teaching a grammar for prayer, giving us words for our blessings. A blessing yourself, you have strangely warmed our hearts, and for you we give thanks.[14]

The editors of *Liturgy and Moral Self*, Ron Anderson and Bruce Morrill, identify some themes of Saliers's work in their introduction: 'prayer and belief', 'prayer and the Christian affections' and 'practicing a liturgical aesthetic'. These themes are reflected in their organization of the various honorary articles that follow, which are structured into three main parts under the headings: 'Liturgical theology: tradition, practice, and belief', 'Formation of character: person, practice, and affection' and 'Word and music: forming a liturgical aesthetic'. In their introduction, Morrill and Anderson write that 'Saliers consistently articulates a liturgical theology that unites prayer, belief and ethical action',[15] and in relation to their chosen themes they emphasize in turn: the prior and normative role of prayer in theology; liturgy as an arena in which Christian affections may be formed through practice; and liturgy well conceived and well celebrated as an enabling 'art'. In a dense foreword to the same book, Rebecca Chopp concentrates these themes further: 'the Christian pattern' encoded in worship is, she writes, for Saliers the beginning of theology, for theology 'gestures to God through the communal symbolic, ritual, and cultic acts of how Christians know God and world'.[16] Crucially, ecclesial practices 'order the fullness of life', and in the closest she allows to an example of how this might happen she suggests that 'shaped to stand before God, the body bows in prayer in the intimacy of partaking in liturgy. In this intimate partaking, the moral imagination of reverence and solidarity is nurtured.'[17]

Her use of 'reverence' relates to Anderson and Morrill's stress on prayer in Saliers's work, while 'solidarity' perhaps especially reflects particular concerns of her own with 'the praxis of suffering',[18] which she finds amply echoed in Saliers's writings. Reflecting again on these two themes, she writes that:

'the Christian pattern teaches one, shapes one, to have an attitude of awesome wonder and deep recognition of suffering and death'.[19] As Chopp sets these emphases in the wider context of contemporary theology, she finds interest with worship as primary theology and ethical guide 'quite startlingly antimodern and yet not quite postmodern'[20] – at least in Saliers's unfolding of such interests. Referring, I think, to Saliers's understanding of primary theology, she sees this as offering not 'a remaking of theology' but an opportunity for the 'refashioning of . . . the enduring spaces, full of character and memory, to invite vital forms of holy Christian dwelling'.[21]

While my own reflections on the central themes of Saliers's work will at times simply set out a different ordering of things already distilled by Chopp, Anderson and Morrill, I also want to underscore some points not drawn out by others. The three keys to Saliers's thought I wish to explore are: the range of the heart, the travail of liturgy and grace as an eschatological gift.

The range of the heart

Saliers is unabashed in his employment of some traditional – and popularly used – Christian terminology. While such language may – especially in its traditional and popular forms – invite the charge of vagueness, or even non-rationality, Saliers attempts to define a range of meaning for such terms as 'heart' and 'soul', without at the same time wishing to eschew the merits of poetic expression. For instance, his first book, *The Soul in Paraphrase* takes its title from George Herbert's sonnet 'Prayer', from *The Temple*, while focusing a particular spiritual tradition's use of the language of feeling in tension with some contemporary questions about character formation.

For Saliers, 'to characterise the heart is to say what a human being is by calling attention to how the world is experienced and regarded'.[22] The comprehensiveness of this quotation is a clue to the fact that, for Saliers, the concept of the heart acts as a point of convergence for the central foci of his earliest to latest writings. *The Soul in Paraphrase*, sets out many of his themes in a particular order, while many of his later works – as Rebecca Chopp may suggest – refashion their arrangement into different shapes, with each new writing pointing in a different direction, with fresh implications.

From the first, Saliers has been concerned to refuse the familiar dichotomy between the anti-doctrinal bias sometimes encountered among experientially oriented religious seekers and distrust of experience sometimes found among the theologically reflective.[23] In response to the former, he wishes to distinguish intense experience and deep emotion, which are not necessarily linked.[24] In response to the latter, he seeks to convince that 'there is . . . a pattern of particular affections which constitute and govern the life of the Christian': gratitude, awe, sorrow, joy and so on, and that 'to confess faith in God is to live a life characterized by these emotions'.[25]

Such emotions, he suggests, are essential to the meaning and practice of prayer, for prayer is the school or activity in which affective knowledge of God may be gained. With special reference to the Eucharistic prayer, Saliers writes:

> At the heart of Christian liturgical prayer and action is a pattern of thanksgiving and praise which – when addressed to its most fitting object, the God of all creation – opens a way of life and consequently a way of knowing God. Such a knowing is not simply doctrinal or cognitive; it is profoundly affectional.[26]

According to Saliers, prayer – at least when learned well (a standard for which his successive books provide evermore refined criteria) – enables encounter with both 'the mystery of God' and 'the ambiguous reality of our own humanity before God'. This 'double-journey', as he sometimes calls it, into divine and human mysteries, is another notion to which Saliers returns again and again; and for him the journey to get closer to God and to humanity is always coterminous, as it were.[27] Saliers's mature writing re-expresses this central conviction in terms of the relationship between 'human pathos and divine ethos' (a chapter title in *Worship as Theology*). When at once 'open to the world's sufferings . . . [and] also open to the grace of God', 'authentic liturgy lures us by grace into a new pathos, now directed to the passion of God at the heart of the gospel'.[28]

In Saliers's accounts, emotions may be 'lived into' through encounter with 'a wide range of life' expressive of such emotions (as mediated by, for example, literature, poetry, ritual, Scripture) and in this process a person's capacity for emotional dispositions is enlarged, just as such emotions may also be 'honed' to precision. Prayer, in partnership with the other means just mentioned, and focusing those other means, may 'evoke and educate', 'express and critique' a constantly expanding and sensitive emotional life.[29]

> Emotion-terms are part of a proper description of the life of prayer: thanksgiving, adoration, awe, remorse and sorrow, pity and compassion. These are features of the form of life in which praying has meaning and point. To take up a prayerful way of being in the world requires readiness; the language of prayer and worship not only expresses such emotions, it also forms and critiques, it shapes and refines these emotions in persons.[30]

Although Saliers admits that it is particularly in communal forms of prayer that emotions may be shaped, his earlier work focuses on resources more likely to be familiar in the 'holiness' tradition of Methodism which was his own context of nurture in younger life. (Only later are the shape and structural aspects of the classical *ordo* explored in depth – the preface and afterword to the second edition of *The Soul in Paraphrase* can disguise this fact, as they to some extent redress the emphases of the main text by including more references to 'ritual practices', 'common worship' and so on.)

At the early stages of his thinking and writing, a particular inspiration was the nineteenth-century revivalist Jonathan Edwards, whose writings clearly shape Saliers's own interest in and conception of emotions, and the Scriptures. It is apparent that themes which in later work like *Worship as Theology* are unfolded from their liturgical context and function are in the earlier *Soul in Paraphrase* rooted in their biblical 'soil'. Special attention is given to the Psalms, which have remained an abiding focus for Saliers, as may be seen in the manner in which the core of his article, 'David's Song in Our Land',[31] has found many later expressions. He calls the Psalms 'acoustic metaphors'.[32] Correspondingly, Saliers has set several of the Psalms to music for liturgical use, and many are included in the United Methodist Hymnal. What the psalter may have especially impressed upon Saliers is its 'full expressive range' of emotions that may school the heart in 'passional life before God'.[33] Psalm 104 reaches to the limits of beatitude at one 'pole' of the emotional range contained in the psalter: 'I will bless you, Lord my God! You fill the world with awe. You dress yourself in light, in rich, majestic light . . .'[34] Saliers is, however, characteristically keen to stress contrasts between, for example, the psalmists' sense of jubilation and despair, and between the sense of divine presence and divine absence. He also considers the ways in which such contrasts may be explored through acoustic harmony and dissonance in musical accompaniment and singing. He is clearly fond of the Methodist hymn writer Fred Pratt Green's piece 'When in Our Music God Is Glorified', which combines in music and song a range of contrasts:

And did not Jesus sing a psalm that night
when darkest evil fought against the light?
So let us sing, for whom he won the fight: Alleluia!

The potential of musical contrasts to widen and refine the emotions is another repeated theme in Saliers's work and one that helps to yield fresh insight into the range of the heart.[35] Further depth is also lent to these insights in his explorations of liturgical 'feasts and seasons' – the contrasts gathered into Advent, for instance, like desert and fiesta – and all that they may entail when entered into (for more on Advent, see below). And, to reiterate a point introduced earlier, the various activities – praising, invoking, confessing, interceding and so on – contained in the inherited patterns of the classical *ordo* may open divine grace to participants, at least those prepared to engage in 'authentic prayer', as distinguished from more simple willingness to recite prayer texts (the deeper engagement being marked by 'whole-hearted attentiveness and attunement to God in and through the utterances'):[36]

> The meaning of praying is not a simple matter of saying the words. To pray is to become a living text before God. In this sense, meaning what we say requires more than the onset of lively emotions. Meaning what we pray involves sharing a form of life in which the affections and dispositions are oriented towards God.[37]

Like the breadth of Psalms and the richness of seasons, the range of elements in classical liturgical structures may enact the full stretch of life and constitute 'primary theology' – forms of knowing God. So for Saliers, these three dynamics of liturgical worship – employing psalmody, observing fasts and feasts and keeping seasons, and following classical structures – are means by which the heart may learn its range. All may be means which invite discovery of, or offer resources for coping with, life 'at full stretch'.

Saliers's vivid image of life or humanity 'at full stretch' is one that Saliers puts to repeated use and which has come increasingly to characterize his writings, as its inclusion in the subtitle of the festschrift suggests. It acts as a kind of summary for his conviction that what he has come in his latest writings to call 'durable emotions'[38] yield abilities to recognize and respond to the 'fullness of life' in both its joyous and painful extremities.[39]

The travail of liturgy

By use of the word 'travail', Saliers means to engage several dimensions of the realities of worshipping communities. His explorations of humanity at full stretch relate the resources of Christian worship to ministries of pastoral care and their work of

aligning with those who in various ways may be embracing travail.[40] For instance, he suggests that attention to lament ensures
that liturgy is not irrelevant or insensitive to those experiencing
difficulties. Yet Saliers also seems to mean more than this, as
contemporary North American culture is understood by him to
set a context with which liturgy must wrestle to make known
divine grace. He regards that culture as an environment whose
diminution may be contrasted to that 'formation and expression
of God's grace in human form'[41] which practices of worship, at
their best, may display. Saliers's short book *Worship Come to
Its Senses* hints at some aspects of the ways in which contempor-
aries may be malformed. In it, he identifies four dimensions of
a related problem. He asserts that participants in North American culture are fast losing their capacity for awe, especially as
the culture becomes more distant from nature and domesticates
death. Further, they are confusing delight with entertainment
'or the frivolity of mere self-expression'. Additionally, they
are kept at a distance from other persons by failing to question social habits of polite niceties or the simplicities weaved
by 'spin', instead of seeking the 'social grace' which may yet
be a fruit of truth – for all its complexities. Finally, they are
too content to dissolve hope into hope's shadow, optimism, as
they lose their knowledge of the resources offered by Scripture's
'long memory'.[42]

'Liturgical Travail in Contemporary American Culture' (the
title of an unpublished manuscript, for which Saliers received
the Luce Fellowship in 1999–2000)[43] may then turn out to be
about the struggle for worship formed around classical patterns
to yield its sense of awe, delight, truth and hope (the subjects
of the central chapters of *Worship Come to Its Senses*) in the
face of pervasive societal malady. Saliers notes that, mercifully,
'none of these [cultural] captivities can separate us from the
grace of God',[44] but he is certainly to be counted among those
North-American liturgical theologians who are anxious to resist
captivities of these kinds, if they can.[45] And this struggle may
be especially acute in a new situation in which the muscles of
the Megachurches are pressed against the mainstream Christian

traditions and the latter are drawn increasingly into the 'culture war' between 'traditional' and 'contemporary' worship that now characterizes much of contemporary North American Christianity.[46] As Saliers has in his time exerted significant influence upon the United Methodist Church (UMC) to take on classical patterns of Christian worship, the pressure of Mega-churches' methods and forms – some of which are adopted from the Frontier and holiness traditions which had been integrated with other church styles in the UMC – may seem especially troubling. But perhaps the Megachurches represent only the sharp end of a longer-standing dilemma, and another aspect of 'liturgical travail' may be found closer to the heart of the liturgical mainstream in some of the less than encouraging findings of the consortium entitled *The Awakening Church*, which studied the appropriation of liturgical renewal in North American Roman Catholicism in the 25 years following the Second Vatican Council. This project, and Saliers's contribution in particular, revealed the paucity of 'the sense of transcendent mystery in the experience of the primary symbols' of liturgy,[47] such as light, water, bread, oil, wine, fire, gestures and touch. Saliers was, however, able to suggest some reasons and practical remedies for such malaise (for more on symbol, see below), though the new depth and direction that emerged from the acknowledgement of failures of connection are now again eclipsed by more contemporary challenges. For instance, distress is expressed in a recent edition of *Worship* by various authors who reflect on the North American liturgical scene in the 25 years to date and voice disappointment at trends towards 'new rubricism and absolute uniformity' and with attempts to reverse the mandates of Vatican Two. Although especially pertinent to the Roman Catholic situation, the ecumenical environment which liturgical renewal has ensured mean that these trends have gathered a wider range than one might have expected.[48]

Saliers's own response to at least those aspects of this travail which touch directly on United Methodism has been to underscore the 'rich diversity' which comprises the ethos of recent Methodist worship. In terms of the challenges presented by the

Megachurches, which generate the question of whether, in the attempt to 'target' the unchurched, Christian worship is possible without employment of central symbols from the tradition (even such basic ones as those employed in baptism and Eucharist), Saliers insists that exploration of 'the tradition in all its richness'[49] need not be 'boring' as commonly supposed, and will readily provide access to the kind of resources adequate to the demands of 'life at full stretch', whereas symbols, Scripture, sacramental actions, rituals and so on, when pared right down – or forgotten – will most probably not.

In some of his most recent writing, Saliers notes that 'Christian worship is always culturally embedded and embodied, although the theological and liturgical implications of this have come only recently to general awareness'.[50] Saliers traces the meaning of the statement through a patient study of the cultural situations in which various popular forms of American Methodist spirituality have emerged, each of which are constitutive of the tradition 'in all its richness'. The urban context gave rise especially to 'revivals', shaped after Frontier camp meetings, emphasizing free-forms and enthusiasm, within a simple liturgical structure: 'preliminaries', message and 'altar-call'. In other areas, a 'Sunday School' model pertained in which all, of whatever age, attended lay-led classes, and where faith was 'learned' in this way, in contrast to the revival model which often stressed sudden conversion. In yet other places, an 'Anglican aesthetic' permeated Methodist worship, especially in prosperous areas of cities. Texts played a more prominent part in proceedings than in the other spiritualities, and there was more emphasis both on the architectural environment and on beauty expressed in choral singing for instance. A fourth mode of spirituality arose in American Methodism at a later stage, after the Second Vatican Council, and in some measure in response to it. This mode sought a steady, shared pattern for worship and yet fostered pluralism, seeking to include diverse elements in a binding shape of worship. Saliers himself has been at the forefront of this fourth mode of Methodist worship, appropriating the historic and contemporary ecumenical corpus of worship for the

Methodist tradition, writing liturgical texts and contributing to its key hymnbook.

Reflecting on the legacy of these four modes of Methodist worship in the American history of the denomination, he poses three questions which are relevant to the British situation, and are indeed close to the surface in the thinking underlying *Patterns for Worship* and the understanding of Anglican worship which that prayer book represents.

First, 'how can we "liven up" our Sunday morning worship?' Saliers asserts that 'being more "alive"' may or may not involve dispensing with 'traditional' forms and styles. In line with criticisms noted above by White and Lathrop, Saliers states that 'captivity' by contemporary culture may invite 'lifelessness', inhibiting 'the sense of joining in the one church's praise and vulnerability to God "in all times and places"'.[51] He suggests that the best way to curtail 'boring worship' is to explore the tradition more deeply.

Second, 'how can worship form a deeper spirituality?' It is this question with which most of Saliers's work is in fact concerned, but in the context of his particular reflections on the four modes of American Methodist worship he underlines 'the formation of durable emotion' as the means to ensure spiritual depth. Also, the importance is stressed of the content of services cohering with the style of both leadership and congregational participation, for 'attention seeking leadership – either folksy or pompous' especially debilitates 'ownership by the assembly'. Exploring the necessity of congregational ownership and participation, Saliers expands on the 'content' of Christian worship in another piece of writing, identifying its 'heart' as 'a broken symbol . . . [so that] unless we break open the symbols by bringing our life to them, taking into account human pathos, they will remain inaccessible'. Liturgy must be 'of the real, the palpable, the incarnate'.[52]

Third, 'How can Christian worship "target" the unchurched?' According to Saliers, there is a great need to 'unburden the Lord's day of trying to do too many things at once, including evangelism', especially as he believes that more people are convinced that Christianity is real when they see the quality of concern, commitment and responsible facing of the complex issues of life and death than when they are given spiritual entertainment',[53] though the search for 'more honesty and joy' in worship is most certainly appropriate, and the subject of his book *Worship Come to Its Senses*. The point is that the kind of celebration which promotes the formation of durable emotion is the key connection 'between liturgy and life'. By insisting that 'what is done in our public worship of God rehearses what we are to be in our life relationships',[54] Saliers places evangelism a step away from worship events themselves, in the context of relationships which may emerge with those who worship.

On several occasions, Saliers quotes Joseph Gelineau: 'Only if we come to the liturgy without hopes and fears, without longings and hunger, will the rites symbolize nothing and remain indifferent or curious "objects". '[55] Therefore, for Saliers, the 'art of liturgy' is always of central importance. And he means by this language of art at least 'the quality of texts, gestures, movements, and the form of the symbols . . . [and a]ttention to each element and to their interrelation in the whole pattern of the liturgy . . .',[56] (on which, see more below). In one particularly luminous section of Saliers's *Worship and Spirituality* he suggests what may be missed by the jettisoning of tradition and reflection upon it.[57] Thinking about the Eucharistic action – 'take, bless, break, share' he argues that 'The pattern gives us the very shape of the life God calls us to live responsibly in this world . . .'. First, mirroring Jesus' taking of bread at table, in our celebration of the Eucharist, we are to 'offer ourselves . . . Giving ourselves over to the mercy and to the compassion of the One who created all things and called them good'. Second, mirroring Jesus' giving thanks at table, we are to pattern our lives on the Eucharistic prayer, for

The act of the great thanksgiving is what our lives are meant to be . . . We may follow in our lives the structure of the ancient eucharistic prayers: acknowledge God in praise for who God is, a mystery of being yet a furnace of compassion, our creator hidden in glory yet revealed in the whole created order . . . Then we acknowledge God's holiness . . . And, as the prayer of thanksgiving develops, so do our lives.

For the eucharistic prayer illumines not only the faithfulness of God but in remembering events on 'the night in which [Jesus] was betrayed', also illumines 'our alienation, our turning aside'. Third, as Jesus broke bread at table, so too 'our lives . . . must be broken in order to be shared', and fourth, just as Jesus gave bread at table, 'so we must be prepared to be given for others'. For Saliers, Eucharistic prayer links with life, embracing human hopes and fears, and giving shape to the life of Christian people:

> . . . and this is the most terrifying and beautiful matter – through this form of life we receive back our own lives . . . Grace is given in the Eucharist, but this is the grace we also encounter in offering, blessing, breaking open, and sharing our lives with all in this needy world. This is our lost identity; this is the secret hidden from the eyes of the detached and self-possessed world.[58]

Grace as an eschatological gift

A number of themes may be gathered from the corpus of Saliers's work that point towards grace as an eschatological gift. An obvious one is suggested by the woodcut, *Dancing Figures*, by Stephen Alcorn, an image of grace that Saliers uses to illustrate his thinking, not least as the cover-piece for *Worship as Theology*. Depicting a Shaker dance, it is expressive of Saliers's stress on undiminished celebration – at least on some occasions – as a characteristic of good liturgy, and the need for cultivation of practices such as 'delight-taking' in order to imbibe such occasions with appropriate joy. The woodcut of the Shaker dance also invites association with Saliers's wide-ranging explorations of what he calls 'the tradition in all its richness'. The appropriate subject of liturgical theology is, for him, not only the mainstream traditions with their now widely recognized classical patterns, as he also attends to marginal aspects of the tradition, being suspicious of excluding, which is sometimes 'disguised cultural imperialism' in liturgical 'aesthetics',[59] a point that is anticipated in the subtitle of *Worship as Theology* – 'foretaste of glory divine' – which takes up a quotation from a 'folksy' Frontier hymn.[60] So along with the Shakers (whose dancing, with others, 'is that part of the tradition that can best express God's wisdom – the playful, creative aspect of God's activity'),[61] the hymnody of African-American and Hispanic churches and – among some ancient examples – elements of non-canonical gospels are also considered in his work. A prime example of an early marginal tradition to which Saliers gives heed is the *Acts of St John*'s account of events on 'the night in which Christ was betrayed', which elaborates on Jesus' vigil on the Mount of Olives and pictures him engaging the disciples in a dance:

> Grace dances.
> 'I will pipe; dance, all of you.' –
> [And we circled around him and answered] 'Amen.'
> 'I will mourn; lament, all of you.' –
> [And we circled around him and answered] 'Amen.' . . .[62]

(Echoing Saliers's other key themes, as outlined above, here festivity and sorrow converge in a dance on the threshold of death, the movement and song embodying humanity at full stretch.) In respect of these marginal elements, Saliers insists that 'God regards the sincere gestures of the faithful, no matter how humble and how less culturally elaborate the form: here the widow's mite and the dance of David are not rejected'.[63] For he is adamant that it is not only in the 'folksy' but also in the 'overly formal', and not only in 'low' but also in 'high' traditions of worship that 'forms employed and the style of celebrating Christian liturgy may subvert the very saving mystery that resides in the incarnate action of God waiting to be realised in particular Christian assemblies'.[64] And so only the 'broken'[65] symbols of Christ at the heart of the liturgy may set ultimate standards for liturgical aesthetics, and liturgical symbols themselves must correspond to those central Christic symbols, by being 'real . . . palpable . . . incarnate . . .' in their turn. (And it is in this light that Saliers's problems with the Megachurches become clearer, as these, for him, cannot be categorized with the marginal elements of the tradition that he does explore – instead, they subvert it.)

It is in the context of discussion of apparently marginal aspects of the tradition that one of Saliers's more recent emphases is rightly considered. His latest work has given special attention to questions raised by interaction with feminist and liberationist perspectives, which may bring guidance to liturgical theology as to how marginal elements may not only come to be considered but also critique the mainstream. So marginal theologies have taught Saliers that 'naming liturgical "oppressions" . . . highlights the vulnerability of Christian worship to immoral and unethical captivities'[66] – just some of which he identifies as 'excessive clericalism, exclusion of women from primary roles, lack of hospitality, lack of vital preaching juxtaposed to the ritual actions, and the loss of participation in the bread and cup'.[67] At the same time, aware that consciously non-Western or gendered theologies employ a 'hermeneutics of suspicion' about the 'malestream' or dominant strand of tradition considered to be at least in part responsible for their 'problems', Saliers holds that the hermeneutics of suspicion may 'require some suspicion too'. Notwithstanding the force of criticism of the mainstream, it remains for him that authentic celebration of worship – that which is 'engaged in the struggle to show in life what is implied in the gathering' (another dimension of 'liturgical travail'?) – may yet permit the kind of vulnerability to grace which 'transforms not simply the inner life of feeling and desire but the social relationships that make us human in the sight of God'.[68] So it may be that as liberationists and feminists prioritize their praxis and amend their theology in its light, so Saliers underlines the priority of worship as primary theology expecting more truthful and refined secondary modes of theology to emerge from it.

According to Saliers, it is particularly in its eschatological references that worship may 'lure'[69] persons into transformed perspectives and behaviour, as 'what is seen and what is heard in Word and sacrament over time reveals what is not yet fully seen or heard in human life'.[70] As the Shakers founded their dancing on a confident realized eschatology, Stephen Alcorn's woodcut is a key to a crucial aspect of Saliers's work: his constant return to eschatological dimensions of worship, such as Advent and the image of 'the heavenly fiesta', as hinted at above. Whereas eschatologically weighted theological systems may often tend towards escapism, Saliers's approach 'implies a realism about life that confronts pain and anguish squarely but does not pronounce them to be victorious',[71] a strength blended in the meeting of this third central theme and the first, as discussed above, the 'range of the heart'.

Saliers relates a pastor's reflection on a fragment of conversation with a parishioner that vividly summarizes his hope that the eschatological impact of worship may be felt:

> It's like a dream . . . a vision . . . that people gather for prayer, worshipping, offering praise, thanksgiving, the music, the responding, singing. At some point they say 'we could stay here forever.' That's the kingdom.[72]

Good liturgy, then, may do more than critique bad liturgy and its captivities to cultural oppressions (apart from those forms of oppression that rest on the foundations of religious traditions) – 'good liturgy disturbs, breaks open, and discloses a new world'.[73] Using a string of olfactory images, Saliers suggests that worship may offer a taste of 'the complete palette of delight', 'a feast for all peoples', 'the heavenly fiesta'.[74] Sustaining his cultural critique, he admits that 'for us who already are too fat with our own consumption, this is an ambiguous picture',[75] and yet he can also re-conceive communal worship as a dance in the light of the eschatological vision:

> To redescribe coming to the sanctuary, greeting friends, sitting down, standing for singing and certain prayers, moving towards the altar for prayer and for Holy Communion, and movement out of the building as a slow, complex dance can

be revelatory. For in fact, this is a deep feature of the experience for many.[76]

So liturgy is, in his view, a 'revelatory' experience in which dancing and all worship's aesthetic dimensions – beauty in its manifold forms – may play a part. And it is not simply that the arts may be employed in worship, but rather that liturgy itself is an art form, and an art form with a distinctive eschatological bent: all living and dying is to be oriented to the heavenly feast.[77]

It is in this context – of consideration of art and taste and dance – that Saliers's stress on symbol is most pertinent. One of his key contributions to liturgical theology has been to stress the need for primary theology to get 'beyond words alone' and 'beyond the text', and by so doing give proper acknowledgement to the non-verbal aspects of liturgical celebration. The considerable significance of this theme in Saliers's work has been hinted at in much of the above, but it deserves to be made explicit. The consortium The Awakening Church in which Saliers was involved helped to force recognition of the lack of attention such dimensions had received in the reflection generated as a direct response to the renewal of Vatican Two:

> 'Full, conscious, and active participation' is only a receding slogan from paragraph 14 of the Constitution on the Sacred Liturgy if we do not attend to specific questions concerning resistance and vulnerability to the non-verbal and symbolic dimensions of liturgical celebration in specific social/cultural contexts.[78]

As might be imagined, those who engaged in reflection on reformed rites characteristically had neglected such questions more than even their Roman Catholic counterparts, making the study of non-verbal components of liturgy a kind of 'virgin territory', at least for theologians – it has of course been subject to social scientific thought, especially by anthropologists. Saliers's own mapping of the area has called for renewed attention to space and architectural shape, movement and gesture, sound and silence, and considerations about the quality and quantity of material used for sacramental purposes, among other things. Yet in relation to such neglected considerations, he has also wished to resist a 'biblical minimalism' that would run the risk of increasing 'subjective projection into the symbol (and, ironically onto the biblical texts themselves)'.[79] It is the alignment of word and gesture or matter, the convergence of symbolic and cognitive suggestion that together form the multivalent environment of liturgical celebration. And it is precisely the shifting juxtapositions and potential for ever fresh alignment of meanings that may unveil eschatological hope and propel participants on in their 'double-journey' into God and into their own human depths. So he can write that:

> the liturgy is not a static system or structure to which we bring our life experience; rather it is a crucible for meanings that, if entered into with our whole humanity, makes experience possible: deeper gratitude, deeper awe, a greater capacity for suffering, hope, and compassion.[80]

And through the imparting of such possibilities, liturgical formation constitutes for Saliers a 'rehearsal' of participation in the undiminished glory of God to be revealed in the social grace of a heavenly banquet and yet also prefigured in the paschal events. Engagement in such rehearsal may itself enable human beings, for all their frailties, at times to experience life as sublime and luminous. Yet the sense of frailty and the demand for continual conversion remain everpresent:

> Christian conversion points towards participation in the Messianic banquet that continually offers the grace of Christ to a lacerated, self-destructive world. Yet comprehending what the Eucharist gives and asks humankind takes continual practice over time. No one dares presume to claim the fullness of this mystery in language, much less claim to have made it fully manifest in all its spiritual and ethical dimensions. Yet it is the most radical meal, the most revolutionary symbolic action in which human beings can partake.[81]

As partakers yield to the symbols and imagery of the biblical and sacramental vision of the messianic banquet 'this relativizes all lesser human good, yet supplies the moral imagination with root images to sustain intention and action amidst the ambiguities of human existence'.[82]

Saliers's imagery of dancing invites associations with the notion of participation, that central undergirding principle of contemporary liturgical renewal, as inspired by paragraph 14 of *Sacrosanctum concilium*. Dancing will certainly also require rehearsal, which links in with the notion of practice, which, with others, Saliers has done much to rehabilitate in contemporary theological circles.[83] And, further, dancing may demand improvisation – as liturgy calls for enactment in ethics. Unlike less ambitious liturgical theologies, Saliers's is, he writes, concerned 'with the performed liturgy, the actual "lived" liturgy that throws together our lives and what we do in the assembly. It is the worship of God in cultic enactment and service of God in life that constitutes the "primary theology".'[84]

Engaging the debate about *Patterns for Worship*

Establishing a dialogue between the work of Don Saliers and the issues considered in chapters 1–4 might be focused on a number of themes.

Saliers, himself a musician, illustrates the way in which music and song are central to many Protestant spiritualities, and in various writings he is concerned with the capacity of song to evoke feeling, not least through notions which bolster Lathrop's insights gathered around his key concept of juxtaposition. Saliers's attention to the liturgical year's feasts and seasons offers another trajectory for uncovering and entering into juxtapositions. Here in Saliers's work, then, is another set of lenses for approaching liturgy that promises to enrich the discussion that has been focused in Britain by *Patterns for Worship* and the reasons for its publication. For music is experienced by many worshippers as a more readily mediating experience of the spiritual than they consider prayer-text to be.

How children's participation in both song and shifting time may be facilitated is perhaps a particularly crucial agenda for the Church's catechesis. The music included in St Philip's Cathedral preschool liturgy, which was considered in the closing section in the chapter on Lathrop, draws on both traditional hymnody and simple rhymes. This is markedly in contrast to so much music in age-grouped gatherings that does not, and this reality in itself may suggest that finding or creating music that allows styles of music to be 'blended' in single events is an art that deserves attention.[85] This at least is a generous interpretation of worshipping communities whose musical expression is restricted in one particular stream or style of music or another – a less generous interpretation being that music so easily colludes with self-selecting characteristics of congregations not alert enough to the inclusivity implied in the gospel of Christ. This notwithstanding, intelligent critique of both popular worship music and traditional hymnody is just one instance of the way in which 'worship wars' often fix on music. In Britain, Pete Ward's studies of the ways in which the musical styles of one generation prevail in the next suggest the influence gained, and cost of the losses, entailed in 'victory' in battles over music for the assembly's praise.[86] Saliers's own distinctive twist on the merit of maturing in musical juxtaposition focuses on the range of music's capacity to resonate with, accompany, and so nurture the potential transformation of many forms of the human pathos that is an ordinary part of growing through life.

Saliers also makes other important contributions that enlarge concern for inclusivity in liturgy. Generally, his convictions mediate between the positions of Lathrop and White, who of the three authors in the focus of this work represent poles of opinion about expressing either a central consensus or legitimate diversification in the celebration of worship. Saliers's willingness to search what he calls 'the tradition in all its richness' for precedents, correctives and influence of different kinds suggests an attitude to mediation in liturgical matters that helpfully challenges any temptation to settle prematurely at one pole. For instance, Saliers's approach might both question the sense that 'family services' and what they often seem to entail are a utilitarian necessity in the cause of evangelism and would resist pressure towards uniformity as that is represented by very powerful bodies such as the proponents of particular kinds of liturgical conservatism – or romanticism – in ascendancy in some Catholic circles. Saliers's mediating position encourages deep knowledge of the tradition, and yet is also aware that the edges of tradition may sharpen up options that may refocus the mainstream, or cut through the mainstream so as to broaden it out. Saliers's sensitivity to the contributions of revivalism to the revitalization of his own United Methodist Church, especially in many urban areas of his nation, is a case in point, and one that lays bare his sense of the subtle balances needed between generosity and defence in matters that involve the wielding of 'cultural imperialism', or suspicion of it.

As befits a stance so focused on 'the heart', the search for integrity in worship is one that Saliers illumines. His conviction that the first purpose of worship is praise of divine glory so that it ought not to be distorted so as, for example, primarily to 'target' persons evangelistically, reflects great confidence in worship's integrity as a worthy activity in itself.[87] And in Saliers's own configuration of the way in which worship does relate to evangelism, his insistence that the ethical quality of worshippers' lives must mediate between the work of worship and the work of evangelism itself demands integrity of all who would worship. Proponents of 'family services', and many others, would do well to explore the implications of his understanding.

Saliers's stress on the educative promise of liturgy also magnifies the links between discipleship and learning, as noted in the final section on Gordon Lathrop's work. This stress further questions assumptions that liturgy can offer any kind of 'quick-fix', instantaneous conversion perhaps especially included. His constant references to prayer as a 'school' and such like underline Saliers's understanding of worship as a forum and support for life-long learning, with his explorations of affectional knowing and ethical response expanding narrower doctrinal or cognitive approaches to conversion in the assumptions he wishes to question. Wisely, his own approach has time built into it.

Of particular relevance to his approach to time, Saliers's stress on eschatological themes and imagery underlines another distinctive feature of his work. Others might learn from this also. For his concern to appropriate eschatology represents a serious dialogue with theology in his liturgical construction, and Saliers's eschatological reflections offer a worked example of the potential of theological understanding to influence and deepen the meanings inherent in the celebration of worship. Yet it is perhaps around his eschatological focus that Saliers is also potentially most open to critique, for eschatology is notorious for its unhelpful potential to accommodate persons to intolerable versions of the status quo. For instance, the Holocaust survivor Tadeusz Borowski's charge against the Jewish tradition in which he was raised, that 'we were never taught how to give up hope, and this is why today we perish in gas chambers',[88] is one appalling commentary on the weakness of unchecked eschatology, while another son of Saliers's Atlanta, Martin Luther King Jr, in one of his sermons, offers a critique of eschatology as it sometimes appears in the Christian tradition:

> It's alright to talk about 'long white robes over yonder', in all of its symbolism. But ultimately people want some suits and dresses and shoes to wear down here. It's alright to talk about 'streets flowing with milk and honey', but God has commanded us to be concerned about the slums down here, and his children who can't eat three square meals a day. It's alright to talk about the new Jerusalem, but one day, God's preacher must talk about New York, the new Atlanta . . .[89]

Saliers's searching in his later work of liberationist and feminist theology is one guard against the risk to which he is perhaps most vulnerable, and such explorations have in turn bolstered his sense of the healthy way in which initially marginal elements of the tradition may generate friction in the mainstream. Through these searchings, Saliers offers the hope that preoccupation with liturgy need not necessarily lead to an evasion of necessary contest with injustice but rather resource the cause of the marginalized in the contest. Indeed, one of the things of which Saliers is most clear is the potential of liturgy to open out a vision of alternative possibilities among those who most need change in their circumstances. Comments about finding and choosing to live 'in the kingdom' as the divine reign is revealed in the liturgy hint at what he thinks is possible. These possibilities, of which Saliers is the principal champion in the context of this work, are vital in the divided arenas of cities, in parts of which life is crushed, and in a situation in both Church and nation in which children are neglected in thought and deed.

Our next chapter considers James White's perspectives on shared themes.

Notes

1. These resources were incorporated into the *United Methodist Worship Book*, Nashville: United Methodist Publishing House, 1989.
2. James F. White, 'Shaping the 1972 United Methodist Eucharistic Rite', *Christian Worship in North America 1955–1995: A Retrospective*, Collegeville: Liturgical Press, 1997, 143–54; and other essays in the same volume.
3. Don E. Saliers, *The Soul in Paraphrase: Prayer and the Religious Affections*, New York: Seabury, 1980; Akron: Order of St Luke, 2nd edn 1991.
4. Don E. Saliers, *Worship and Spirituality*, Philadelphia: Westminster Press, 1984; Akron: Order of St Luke, 2nd edn 1996.
5. Don E. Saliers, *Worship As Theology: Foretaste of Glory Divine*, Nashville: Abingdon Press, 1994.
6. Don E. Saliers, *Worship Come to Its Senses*, Nashville: Abingdon Press, 1996.
7. Charles Hackett and Don E. Saliers, *The Lord Be with You: A Visual Handbook for Presiding in Liturgy*, Akron: Order of St Luke, 1990.
8. Hoyt L. Hickman, Don E. Saliers, Laurence Hull Stookey and James F. White, *Handbook of the Christian Year*, Nashville: Abingdon Press, 1984; Hoyt L. Hickman, Don E. Saliers, Laurence Hull Stookey and James F. White, *New Handbook of the Christian Year*, Nashville: Abingdon Press, 1994). The new handbook accounts for the publication and use of the *Revised Common Lectionary*.

9. James Knight III and Don E. Saliers, *The Conversation Matters: Why United Methodists Should Talk with One Another*, Nashville: Abingdon Press, 1997.
10. Don E. Saliers and Emily Saliers, *A Song to Sing, a Life to Live: Reflections on Music as a Spiritual Practice*, San Francisco: Jossey-Bass, 2004.
11. Louis Dupré and Don E. Saliers, eds, *Christian Spirituality III: Post-Reformation to the Present*, London: SCM Press, 1991.
12. Don E. Saliers and Nancy Eisland, eds, *Human Disability and the Service of God: Reassessing Religious Practice*, Nashville: Abingdon Press, 1998.
13. E. Byron Anderson and Bruce T. Morrill, eds, *Liturgy and the Moral Self: Humanity at Full Stretch before God: Essays in Honor of Don E. Saliers*, Collegeville: Liturgical Press, 1998.
14. Editorial notice, *Worship* 66 (1992), pp. 184–5.
15. Anderson and Morrill, eds, *Liturgy and the Moral Self*, p. 12.
16. Rebecca Chopp, 'Foreword', Anderson and Morrill, eds, *Liturgy and the Moral Self*, pp. ix–xii, p. ix.
17. Chopp, 'Foreword', pp. x–xi.
18. See Rebecca Chopp, *The Praxis of Suffering*, Louisville: Westminster John Knox, 1987.
19. Chopp, 'Foreword', p. xi.
20. Chopp, 'Foreword', p. ix.
21. Chopp, 'Foreword', p. xii.
22. Saliers, *Soul in Paraphrase*, 2nd edn, p. v.
23. Saliers, *Soul in Paraphrase*, 2nd edn, p. 2.
24. Saliers, *Soul in Paraphrase*, 2nd edn, p. 4.
25. Saliers, *Soul in Paraphrase*, 2nd edn, pp. 6, 9.
26. Don E. Saliers, 'Liturgy Teaching Us to Pray', Eleanor Bernstein, ed., *Liturgy and Spirituality in Context: Perspectives on Prayer and Culture*, Collegeville: Liturgical Press, 1990, pp. 62–83, p. 74.
27. Saliers, *Soul in Paraphrase*, 2nd edn, p. 3; for hints at the continuity of these themes, see *Worship as Theology*, pp. 88–9 and *Worship Come to Its Senses*, p. 17.
28. Saliers, *Worship as Theology*, pp. 35, 38.
29. For instance, Saliers, *Soul in Paraphrase*, 2nd edn, pp. 23, 24. On the process of acquiring, refining and transforming emotions, see James R. Averill and Elma P. Nunley, *Voyages of the Heart: Living an Emotionally Creative Life*, New York: Free Press, 1992, which does not refer to Saliers's work, though it is broadly consonant with it, blending appreciation of the role which may be played by religious practices in the development of emotional life into its overarching psychological perspectives.
30. Saliers, *Soul in Paraphrase*, 2nd edn, p. 36.

31. Reprinted in the 'best of' collection of articles from the Liturgical Conference's journal *Liturgy*: Don E. Saliers, 'David's Song in Our Land', Blair Gilmer Meeks, ed., *The Landscape of Praise: Readings in Liturgical Renewal*, Valley Forge: Trinity Press International, 1997, pp. 235–41.

32. Saliers, *Worship as Theology*, p. 212.

33. Saliers, 'David's Song', pp. 236, 240.

34. Psalm 104.1–2a, *ICEL Psalter*, Chicago: Liturgy Training Publications, 1995.

35. See especially Don E. Saliers, 'Liturgical Musical Formation', Robert Leaver and Joyce Ann Zimmermann, eds, *Music and Liturgy: Lifelong Learning*, Collegeville: Liturgical Press, 1998, pp. 384–94; Don E. Saliers, 'Singing Our Lives', Dorothy C. Bass, ed., *Practicing Our Faith: A Way of Life for a Searching People*, San Francisco: Jossey-Bass, 1997.

36. Saliers, *Worship as Theology*, p. 87; cf. Saliers, 'Liturgy Teaching Us to Pray', p. 63.

37. Don E. Saliers, 'Liturgy and Ethics: Some New Beginnings', Anderson and Morrill, eds, *Liturgy and the Moral Self*, pp. 15–35, pp. 25–6.

38. Don E. Saliers, 'Divine Grace, Diverse Means: Sunday Worship in United Methodist Congregations', Karen Westerfield-Tucker, ed., *The Sunday Service of the Methodists: Twentieth-Century Worship in Worldwide Methodism: Studies in Honor of James F. White*, Nashville: Kingswood, 1996, pp. 137–56, 152.

39. Also illuminating on some of these neglected themes are three essays – John A. Bernsten, 'Christian Affections and the Catechumenate', pp. 229–43. Jeff Astley, 'The Role of Worship in Christian Learning', pp. 244–51, and Craig R. Dykstra, 'The Formative Power of the Congregation', pp. 253–65 – collected together in Jeff Astley, Leslie J. Francis and Colin Crowder, eds, *Theological Perspectives on Christian Formation: A Reader on Theology and Christian Education*, Leominster: Gracewing, 1996. Bernsten makes reference to Saliers's work on the emotions. See also Craig Dykstra, *Growing in the Life of Faith: Education and Christian Practices*, Louisville: Geneva, 1999, which includes 'Formative Power' and other related essays.

40. Among many examples, Saliers, *Worship as Theology*, pp. 28–9, 37–8, 147, 150.

41. Saliers, *Worship Come to Its Senses*, p. 81.

42. Saliers, *Worship Come to Its Senses*, pp. 20, 47, 54, 56, 67, 43; and also Don E. Saliers, 'Afterword: Liturgy and Ethics Revisited', Anderson and Morrill, eds, *Liturgy and the Moral Self*, pp. 209–24, pp. 216–18.

43. Abingdon Press have, however, released an audio-cassette of Saliers lecturing on 'Christian Worship in a Culture of Hype', on related themes: Don E. Saliers, *Christian Worship in a Culture of Hype*, Nashville: Abingdon Press, 2001 (audio).

44. Saliers, *Worship Come to Its Senses*, p. 91.

45. James White and Gordon Lathrop also express concern about these matters. Marva Dawn's recent companion books, *Reaching Out without Dumbing Down: A Theology of Worship for the Turn of the Century*, Grand Rapids: Eerdmans, 1995, and *A Royal 'Waste' of Time: The Splendor of Worshiping God and Being Church for the World*, Grand Rapids: Eerdmans, 1998, are significant, extended discussions of some these themes.

46. Saliers, 'Afterword: Liturgy and Ethics Revisited', p. 217. Carol Doran and Thomas Troger, *Trouble at the Table: Gathering the Tribes for Worship*, Nashville: Abingdon Press, 1992, is an excellent introduction to the nature of this 'war', written jointly by a Roman Catholic and an Anglican (Episcopalian) author.

47. Don E. Saliers, 'Symbol in Liturgy, Liturgy as Symbol: The Domestication of Liturgical Experience', Lawrence J. Madden, ed., *The Awakening Church: Twenty-Five Years of Liturgical Renewal*, Collegeville: Liturgical Press, 1992, pp. 69–82, 72.

48. See especially Rembert G. Weakland, 'Liturgy in the United States These Past Twenty-Five Years', *Worship* 75 (2001), pp. 5–12, and Robert F. Taft, 'A Generation of Liturgy in the Academy', *Worship* 75 pp. 46–58, (2001).

49. Saliers, 'Divine Grace, Diverse Means: Sunday Worship in United Methodist Congregations', Westerfield Tucker, ed., *Sunday Service of the Methodists*, pp. 137–56, p. 156.

50. Saliers, 'Divine Grace, Diverse Means', p. 138.

51. Saliers, 'Divine Grace, Diverse Means', p. 151.

52. Don E. Saliers, 'Toward a Spirituality of Inclusiveness', Eisland and Saliers, eds, *Human Disability and the Service of God*, p. 28.

53. Saliers, 'Divine Grace, Diverse Means', p. 153.

54. Saliers, 'Toward a Spirituality of Inclusiveness', p. 29.

55. For examples, *Worship and Spirituality*, p. 35; 'Symbol in Liturgy, Liturgy as Symbol', p. 70; *Worship as Theology*, p. 139.

56. Don E. Saliers, 'Aesthetics, Liturgical', Peter E. Fink, ed., *New Dictionary of Sacramental Theology*, Collegeville: Liturgical Press, 1991, pp. 30–9, p. 37.

57. Quotations relating to Saliers's reflections on Eucharistic prayer are drawn from his *Worship and Spirituality*, pp. 61, 67–8.

58. Saliers, *Worship and Spirituality*, p. 68.

59. Saliers, *Worship as Theology*, p. 194.

60. Saliers, *Worship as Theology*, p. 210.

61. Saliers, *Worship Come to Its Senses*, p. 44.

62. Saliers, *Worship as Theology*, p. 198; on the hymn from the *Acts of St John*, see also James Miller, *Measures of Wisdom: The Cosmic Dance in Classical and Christian Antiquity*, Toronto: University of Toronto Press, 1986, pp. 81–7, 98–110.

63. Saliers, *Worship as Theology*, pp. 195–6.

64. Saliers, *Worship as Theology*, p. 194; also, 'Afterword: Liturgy and Ethics Revisited', pp. 216–18.

65. On corresponding to broken symbols, see especially Saliers, 'Toward a Spirituality of Inclusiveness', p. 28; cf. Saliers, 'Symbol in Liturgy, Liturgy as Symbol', p. 82.

66. Saliers, 'Afterword: Liturgy and Ethics Revisited', p. 216.

67. Saliers, 'Afterword: Liturgy and Ethics Revisited', p. 222.

68. Saliers, 'Afterword: Liturgy and Ethics Revisited', pp. 223–4.

69. An image used, for example, in *Worship and Spirituality*, p. 89; *Worship as Theology*, pp. 38, 40.

70. Saliers, *Worship as Theology*, p. 17.

71. Laurence Hull Stookey, review of *Worship as Theology*, *Theology Today* 52 (1996), pp. 524–5, p. 524.

72. Saliers, *Worship as Theology*, p. 145.

73. Saliers, *Worship as Theology*, p. 213.

74. Saliers, *Worship Come to Its Senses*, pp. 44–7.

75. Saliers, *Worship and Spirituality*, p. 86.

76. Saliers, *Worship as Theology*, p. 164.

77. Saliers, *Worship and Spirituality*, p. 90.

78. Saliers, *Worship as Theology*, p. 141; cf. Saliers, 'Symbol in Liturgy, Liturgy as Symbol', p. 71.

79. Saliers, 'Symbol in Liturgy, Liturgy as Symbol', p. 75.

80. Saliers, 'Symbol in Liturgy, Liturgy as Symbol', p. 75.

81. Don E. Saliers, 'Pastoral Liturgy and Character Ethics: As We Worship So We Shall Be', Joanne M. Pierce and Michael Downey, eds, *Source and Summit: Commemorating Josef A. Jungmann, SJ*, Collegeville: Liturgical Press, 2000, pp. 183–94, p. 191.

82. Saliers, 'Pastoral Liturgy and Character Ethics', p. 193.

83. See Craig Dykstra and Dorothy C. Bass, 'Times of Yearning, Practices of Faith', Bass, ed., *Practicing Our Faith*, pp. 1–12.

84. Saliers, *Worship as Theology*, p. 16.

85. See Carol Doran and Thomas H. Troeger, *Trouble at the Table: Gathering the Tribes for Worship*, Nashville: Abingdon Press, 1992; Brian Wren, *Praying Twice: The Music and Words of Congregational Song*, Lousiville: Westmister John Knox, 2000.

86. Pete Ward, *Growing Up Evangelical*, London: SPCK, 1996; Pete Ward, *Selling Worship*, Carlisle: Paternoster Press, 2005.

87. Ann Loades, 'Why Worship?', *In Illo Tempore: Ushaw Library Bulletin and Liturgical Review* 16 (2000), pp. 34–42, notes the difficulties she and others encounter in attempting to answer the question. For Saliers's own posing of the question, see Don E. Saliers, 'The Nature of Worship: Community Lived in Praise of God', Robin Leaver and James H. Litton, eds, *Duty and Delight: Routley Remembered*, Norwich: Canterbury Press, 1985, pp. 35–46, p. 39.

88. Tadeusz Borowski, *This Way for the Gas, Ladies and Gentleman*, cited in Richard L. Rubenstein and John K. Roth, *Approaches to Auschwitz: The Legacy of the Holocaust*, London: SCM Press, 1987, p. 277. Compare Michael Downey's comments on Yaffa Eliach's account of Hanukkah in Bergen Belsen, as the faithful crafted artefacts from clogs and string, with shoe polish to serve as oil: Michael Downey, 'Worship between the Holocausts', *Worship at the Margins: Spirituality and Liturgy*, Washington DC: Pastoral, 1994, pp. 223–37, p. 224.

89. Martin Luther King Jr, 'I've Been to the Mountaintop', 3 April 1963, cited in Gabe Huck, Gail Ramshaw and Gordon Lathrop, *An Easter Sourcebook: The Fifty Days*, Chicago: Liturgy Training Publications (LTP), 1988, p. 41.

7

EXPANDING THE 'HOME':
James F. White

Introduction

James F. White worked in a number of academic appointments, most recently before his death on 31 October 2004 as Professor of Liturgical Studies at the University of Yale Divinity Faculty's Institute of Sacred Music. He moved there from a short-term post at Drew University as Bard Thompson Professor of Liturgical Studies. These recent short-term appointments are in marked contrast to the many years which Professor White spent as Professor of Theology 'with a primary specialization in Liturgical Studies' at the University of Notre Dame, South Bend, Indiana, where he taught for over thirty years. It was while at Notre Dame that he cemented his reputation as one of the most distinguished and longstanding academics working in the area of liturgical studies in the United States, having taught the subject for over four decades – before Notre Dame for seven or so years at Perkins School of Theology, Texas. White's distinction among liturgical scholars is recognized in his reception of the North American Academy of Liturgy's Berakah Award in 1983, among other notable achievements.

Like Saliers, White was an ordained Methodist presbyter, and had spent parts of his teaching career at United Methodist Church theological schools, such as Perkins School of Theology and Drew University. However, the vast majority of his career, based at University of Notre Dame, was in the context of a Roman Catholic foundation that has been a most important centre of renewal, liturgical and charismatic, in North American Roman Catholicism.

White's published work is extensive and diverse. He was one of the principal authors of the present Eucharistic rite of the United Methodist Church, the development of which he charted in an illuminating article gathered in a retrospective collection. Moreover, he penned over a dozen monographs covering a wide range of topics broadly related to the study of worship. A version of his Duke University PhD was published as *The Cambridge Movement: The Ecclesiologists and the Gothic Revival*,[1] and marked the beginning of a sustained interest in the historical study of Christian worship. Indeed, White regarded himself as 'first and foremost an historian'.[2] Other early works dealt especially with the relatively neglected theme of architecture appropriate to the celebration of worship, including *Protestant Worship and Church Architecture: Theological and Historical Considerations*, and this work marked out at an early stage another abiding concern in White's work, that 'not only does space form faith but it can, and frequently does, deform and distort faith'.[3]

White's first published work on the Cambridge Movement was perhaps his most specialized and technical work. Other writings have been deliberately designed to make accessible the field of liturgical study to a 'more general audience'. In his 'tribute' to White, Grant Sperry-White makes the comment that 'it is clear that White's writing in the 1980s reflected the pastoral and strategic concerns so central to his overall work',[4] and this is verified by books such as *Introduction to Christian Worship*,[5] *Documents of Christian Worship: Descriptive and Interpretive Sources*[6] and *A Brief History of Christian Worship*,[7] which have become some of the most influential textbooks in liturgical studies. The *Introduction* has been translated into several languages and has been used widely by seminarians and others across Christian confessional traditions.

That White's work has become ecumenically significant, used as a basic text across traditions, is appropriate to another major feature of the corpus of his work: his desire to attend to the particularities of various traditions. Three books are especially important in this regard: *Protestant Worship: Traditions in Transition*,[8] *Roman Catholic Worship: Trent to Today*[9] and *The Sacraments in Protestant Practice and Faith*.[10] These books suggest the broad sweep of his interests and expertise, reflecting lessons appropriated from both his ecclesial and academic contexts. While these books also embrace a broadly historical approach to his subjects, the ecumenical dimension of White's work is also apparent in the closest he has come to an attempt at systematic theology, *Sacraments as God's Self-Giving*,[11] which includes a response from a Roman Catholic colleague at the University of Notre Dame, Edward Kilmartin of the Society of Jesus.

In addition to these singly authored texts, White is also co-author of a number of books, notably *Church Architecture: Building and Renovating for Christian Worship*,[12] written with Susan J. White, to whom he was for a time married, and *The (New) Handbook of the Christian Year*,[13] with Hoyt L. Hickman, Don E. Saliers and Laurence Hull Stookey, colleagues on the United Methodist Church panel of worship.

Beyond this considerable corpus of major writings, White has written a large number of articles and shorter pieces on themes related and non-related to his key publications. Many of the most significant essays were collected together and published as *Christian Worship in North America, a Retrospective: 1955–1995*, which with *Protestant Worship: Traditions in Transition* especially reveals another key interest of White's – what may be thought of as the 'Americanization of Christian worship'. White is also celebrated by a book of essays in his honour, *The Sunday Service of the Methodists: Twentieth-Century Worship in Worldwide Methodism*, edited by Karen Westerfield-Tucker. However, rather than relating directly to White's work, the festschrift attempts a 'descriptive and analytical study of [Methodist] Sunday worship' across the globe and includes at its end a 'tribute' to White, followed by a complete bibliography of his writings. The studies in the book of Methodist worship in global perspective complement White's characteristic focus on the North American scene, though White himself lived and studied for a time abroad in Cambridge, England, in preparation for his PhD on the Cambridge Movement, in Rome just after the Second Vatican Council, and again in the British Isles, in Lincoln, when Susan J. White taught for a time at its Anglican theological college.

In what follows I draw attention to three particular features of White's writings: his situation as 'a scholar in the trenches', his developing understanding and critique of liturgical theology, and his stress on attention to the particularities of worshipping traditions in different ages, and the Americanization of Christian worship especially.

'Scholar in the trenches'

In his tribute to White in *The Sunday Service of the Methodists*, Grant Sperry-White describes White as 'a scholar in the trenches, a figure far removed from the ivory tower stereotype pilloried today by those with little understanding of academia'.[14] A most obvious example of the engaged nature of White's contribution is his work as a key author of the Service of Word and Table, the Eucharistic liturgy of the United Methodist Church. By his own admission, this was the most important work in which he participated.[15] Because of his involvement in the construction of the contemporary Eucharistic rite, White has had perhaps more influence on his denomination than Lathrop has had on his, and because of his involvement in the actual production of the text it is certainly notable that White can be regarded as having no direct Roman Catholic peers either. This is so in the sense that most of the persons who did most of the work of liturgical reform in the Roman tradition did so in the 1960s when White, with Saliers and Lathrop, was a student or teacher at the beginning of his career. The Roman Catholic equivalents of White (and to lesser extents Lathrop and Saliers) in his work on actual texts and the contents of prayer books were respective chairs and secretaries of the Central Preparatory Commission on the Liturgy, established by Pope John XXIII in anticipation of the

Second Vatican Council, and of the Conciliar Commission on the Liturgy.[16] So any direct parallels between these Roman revisionists and White and his North American counterparts are therefore quite strained. And White's contemporary Roman Catholic academic peers – Mary Collins, Aidan Kavanagh and David Power, for instance – have not had the opportunities to reshape and write the 'heartlands' of their liturgical tradition as White has had within United Methodism.

As well as shaping liturgical texts clearly indebted to these liturgical forebears, White took much of his inspiration from Wesley's *Hymns on the Lord's Supper*, in order to introduce a sacrificial tone to his Protestant Eucharistic prayer that would find at least some resonances with the rites of other churches crafting prayers in an ecumenical spirit:

> Wesley's study of patristics had led him beyond the negativisms of the sixteenth-century Reformation on eucharistic sacrifice. Indeed, a major portion of the eucharistic hymns is entitled 'the Holy Eucharist as it Implies Sacrifice' and the imagery of the hymns is replete with Old Testament images of sacrifice. I think it was important that, by using Hebrews 9 and 13, Romans 12, and Augustine, I was allowed to make a strong positive statement of the Eucharist as sacrifice, perhaps for the first time in a Protestant liturgy. This I consider an important ecumenical step that Wesley encouraged.[17]

The liturgy that White produced reflected some especially novel concerns too, including quite directly White's own sustained concern with liturgy and justice, as he himself admits. The concern with justice comes out in certain stresses in the prayer-texts themselves, such as the memory of Jesus' citation of Isaiah 61 in the record of his speech in the synagogue in Luke 4: good news for the poor, release for captives, and liberating activities recalled by Christ from Isaiah are set alongside remembrance also of his healing of the sick, feeding of the hungry and eating with sinners.[18]

The connections between liturgy and justice in White's work

complement Saliers's interest in worship and ethics. White has used several forums to state his belief that liturgy demands and generates justice, in one place, for instance, writing characteristically of his conviction that 'the Church's contribution to social justice derives largely from its power of making God's love visible in the world through the sacraments'.[19] The post-Communion dialogue of the liturgy is especially significant for another insight into White's particular contribution to the rite: he introduced at this point a prayer from his own pen which echoes much of his more academic prose about the sacraments as 'God's self-giving': 'Eternal God, we give you thanks for this holy mystery in which you have given yourself to us. Grant that we may go into the world, in the strength of your Spirit, to give ourselves for others . . .'

Sperry-White draws attention to a number of other distinctive features of the rite, after first reiterating a point we have just seen illustrated in the recollection of Jesus' reading in the synagogue in the prayer's anamnesis:

> [T]he 1972 and subsequent texts included the recitation of salvation history, epiclesis, and eschatological dimension so often found in early Christian eucharistic prayers but also almost totally lacking in Protestant traditions. Thus the text moved the celebration of the Eucharist away from an exclusively theological focus on the death of Christ by crafting a wider euchological framework for proclaiming the content and meaning of Christ's saving work. The invocation of the Spirit signalled a return to a Wesleyan emphasis on the work of the Spirit in the Lord's Supper, and the euchological note in the prayer also drew on a dominant theme in Wesleyan eucharistic spirituality. Finally, the 1972 text highlighted the character of the Lord's Supper as a joyful feast celebrating the resurrection, not the mournful remembrance of the death of Jesus which the Lord's Supper had become for many American Methodists.[20]

Apart from this most obvious influence on the popular celebration of liturgy, White's significance can be gauged in other ways. It may well be the case that White has enjoyed 'arguably a larger readership than any other Protestant author in those fields at that time', and that 'the *Introduction* . . . may someday be celebrated as the foremost liturgical primer of its era'.[21]

These achievements indicate the felt-tension which White at times articulates, between scholarship and activism, 'love for both Church and academy'[22] and their resolution in his enjoyment of the nearness of theory and practice in liturgical studies: 'That is one thing that makes it a joy to teach. One touches both the *Apostolic Tradition* and next Sunday.'[23] As White suggests in the introduction to his most accessible book, the *Introduction to Christian Worship*, in his thinking and writing 'the whole thrust is always in a pastoral direction for strengthening the worship leadership of Christian communities'.[24] Yet scholar 'in the trenches' is a quite appropriate designation for one who can also assert that he 'would like to think I have helped shape the teaching of the subject through my textbook . . . source book . . . and my doctoral students'.[25]

Relishing diversity[26]

White has been deeply immersed in the liturgical renewal of his particular ecclesial tradition, the United Methodist Church. Indeed the circle of UMC liturgists, of which White was at the centre, working in the 1980s towards ecumenically-minded liturgical reform of their tradition were apparently known as the 'liturgical mafia'.[27] He writes,

> I attend a United Methodist Church in South Bend, Indiana, where every Sunday service for the last twenty years or more has been a Eucharist. I am fond of saying that the only difference between our worship according to the official United Methodist 'service of Word and Table' and the Roman Catholic Mass is that they use real wine and we use real bread. So similar have the revised rites become in recent decades that

an analysis of the texts would not yield any real significant theological differences and not many in structure.[28]

He observes that 'four centuries of antagonism' have collapsed into 'five decades of rapprochement'.[29] As might be imagined from his approach to Eucharistic sacrifice, White was keen to

> encourage Protestants to see and listen to what goes on in the rites and ceremonial of their sacraments ... We must be willing to go beyond the Reformation of the sixteenth century. No longer can we rest content with the resolution of practices and understandings in that time, any more than Roman Catholics now can be satisfied with that of the Council of Trent. A true Catholicism cannot be limited to any century or culture. Our concern here is with reformation of the present, not reformation as past.[30]

This key-note statement from *Sacraments as God's Self-Giving* gives theoretical weight to his praxis in the compilation of the rite. As Sperry-White notes, '*Sacraments* moves Protestant theological discourse about sacraments into a more complex understanding of the relationship between the lex orandi and the lex credendi'.[31]

This is a move dependent upon his involvement in discussions of liturgy as primary theology, most probably appropriated from the Roman Catholic context in which he taught, and promoted in that context by Aidan Kavanagh in particular, who went on to publish *On Liturgical Theology*.[32] What may be distinctive about White's understanding of primary theology will emerge shortly. At this point, it may be noted that White's writings on the history and theology of Christian worship have consistently insisted that 'a strong conviction of mine is that practice often shapes reflection',[33] and that this conviction comes to a particular focus in his most systematic work, as he develops and employs what he terms the liturgical cycle:

> We begin the circle by observing what the church says and does in its gatherings for worship. These experiences are considered very significant expressions of the faith of the church.

On the basis of such observation, we then move to theological reflection, as to the meaning of the faith expressed. We complete the circle by using such reflection as the basis for suggesting worship reforms by which faith can be expressed in more effective ways. Practice leads to theology, which then returns to practice.[34]

This, he admits, is a 'functional' approach. However, there have been some considerable shifts in his thinking as his thought has matured. For instance, he has always given due attention to the traditions of mainstream Protestantism – what he terms the MELP traditions: Methodist, Episcopalian, Lutheran and Presbyterian – but increasingly he has come to admit that it is important to recognize also 'the gifts of the younger churches' – Quaker, Pentecostal and Frontier, among others, as well as manifestations of mainstream and marginal traditions beyond the dominant continents. He writes, 'we can no longer think of Protestantism in purely European or North American terms'.[35] Moreover, it is often the case that the churches of other parts of the world have not marginalized the sacraments and aspects of liturgical history and celebration now being recovered and emphasized, because unlike those in the West the churches of the developing world have not been as dominated by the Enlightenment legacy.[36] So they may therefore have much to teach Christians in the West diminished by cultural confines imposed by the Enlightenment.

Reflecting upon his own role in developing 'the law of prayer' in his own tradition, White notes that 'in the whole process of liturgical revision one question keeps coming back to haunt me: "What right do we have to change the way people pray?" It is the only liturgical question that ever keeps me awake at night.'[37] However, in answering his own question, White gives a four-fold response as to why he regards making such changes necessary:

The first is to make liturgical or personal prayer reflect more accurately the true nature of God and God's relation to humans. For example, prayer addressed to God as the purveyor of success needs change. Second, prayer must be made to reflect and teach justice, though it ought not to preach. Prayers in former wedding services, which prayed that the woman alone 'fortify herself against weakness', certainly need replacing. In the third place, the language must be made accessible to all, not just to those who understand what it is to be 'sore let and hindered'. 'Plight thee my troth' always made me think of how we feed hogs, hardly what Cranmer intended! And fourth, the way we pray has to be shaped to relate to the prayer of all Christians. Christian prayer demands the company of many voices, present or unseen. We proclaim the same story and implore God's continuance of the same work.[38]

Yet while White's 'uncompromising ecumenical stance' may have been expected from his ecclesial and academic contexts – that is, the 'importance of listening to as many of the voices of the churches as possible'[39] – he has over time come to criticize aspects of the ecumenical 'convergence movement' in which he had participated so fully. Notwithstanding his appreciation of many positive aspects of the convergence movement, such as the fact that 'the blending of charismatic and holiness liturgical practices with a rich sacramental and liturgical life drawing on the resources of the so-called classical traditions certainly signals a trend unforeseen twenty years ago',[40] White has in the past twenty years become increasingly aware and articulate of some of its downsides. In particular, a critique of liturgical theology has emerged from this point. This critique comes into sharpest focus in some of his most recent writing, particularly his contribution to the Don Saliers festschrift *Liturgy and the Moral Self*, in which White challenges the 'natural assumption of ecumenism that homogeneity is better than heterogeneity'.[41] Questioning the appropriateness of this assumption in turn sets question marks against the achievements of the World Council of Churches, particularly as represented by a document such as *Baptism, Eucharist and Ministry*, and the work of individual theologians to focus a core *ordo* of shared practice and understanding. Gordon Lathrop's *Holy Things*, though 'brilliant', 'beautifully written' and 'the finest available description of classical Christian worship' is used as an example.[42] For while these writings and those of others – he cites his former colleague Kavanagh, other Roman Catholics such as David Fagerberg, Kevin Irwin and David Power, and fellow Methodists Saliers and Wainwright – may 'represent magnificent theological achievements', 'unfortunately, most liturgical theology tends to be historically naïve',[43] based upon 'a single period of a single tradition', often 'idealized' at that, and usually in its present-day manifestations, reflecting a construct of 'post-Vatican II Roman Catholic worship or its near counterparts'.[44] This point is enormously important, and derives from his studies of particularities in different Christian traditions as represented especially by his collection of books on Protestant and Roman Catholic worship.

White himself 'consider[s] the most important of my books to be *Protestant Worship: Traditions in Transition* and *Roman Catholic Worship: Trent to Today*'.[45] In quite distinct contrast to efforts at convergence, these books suggest the breadth not only between these two major worshipping traditions but also within them, especially as is revealed by Catholicism conceived historically and Protestantism surveyed for its manifold contemporary forms. As he sums up his point in *Liturgy and the Moral Self*:

> The fact that there are at least twelve major traditions of Eastern and Western Christian worship in North America alone makes generic statements almost impossible. And when one considers the multitude of ethnic and cultural styles within those traditions, generalities become still more difficult. One can do liturgical theology for a carefully defined tradition at a given time and place . . . But one cannot make normative statements on that basis for any other Church. At best, one can be descriptive: this is prayed and believed by these people in this time and place. But one cannot leap to a normative declaration: this is what all Christians believe.[46]

It is the descriptive task to which his later books on Protestant and Roman Catholic worship each attend, and these later books quite clearly stand in some contrast to his own earlier work as well as to those of other liturgical scholars. For instance, *Sacraments as God's Self-Giving* includes a great deal of prescription, whereas the phase of his work beginning with *Protestant Worship* is marked by the desire to attend in much greater detail to worship 'as it happens for ordinary worshipers'.[47] He describes the shift as follows:

> The greatest conversion experience in my own teaching has come about in moving from a normative approach to a descriptive approach. After years of trying to reform United Methodist worship I came to feel maybe I should have spent those two decades listening to United Methodists.[48]

What his studies of Protestant worship seemed to have impressed upon him is the great diversity of contemporary Protestant worshipping styles, and also their very significant distinctive features as opposed to the post-Vatican Two Roman Catholic paradigm. This suggests to him at least that 'if we come to liturgical theology with normative judgements already made in advance, the result will be highly predictable',[49] but also demands the constructive proposal that a broader and more comprehensive approach is necessary to do liturgical theology, and one which includes Protestant worship as a major and necessary source of data.

White takes the point that Paul Bradshaw's work *The Search for the Origins of Christian Worship* impressed upon studies of liturgy in the early period, that 'history turns up no facile homogeneity',[50] also needs a contemporary application. And so he draws attention to the fact that 'the study of Protestant worship has been conducted by methods derived from the study of Roman Catholic worship',[51] with greatest emphasis on liturgical texts and the centrality of the Eucharist. These two central themes together pressed focus on the texts of Eucharistic prayers as a (if not the) key source of primary theology. But, as White points out, this gives a distorted image of a great deal of Protestant worship, which may value extempore prayer forms above inherited, written texts; involve a good deal more spontaneity in liturgical structure than its Roman Catholic 'equivalents'; and celebrate Eucharist, by whatever name, with much less frequency than Roman Catholics celebrate mass. Indeed, the history of Protestant practice may suggest that worship may be 'strong and vital but not primarily sacramental',[52] at least in the 'narrow' sense of referring only to either two or seven sacraments. White suggests that in Protestant traditions, preaching and singing of hymnody may be the appropriate key sources for liturgical theology, and that his characteristic stress on architecture should also play a part: for 'to confine attention to printed texts as the sole documentation is to miss much, if not most of the reality of worship',[53] apart from being 'totally irrelevant to the worship of most Protestants in America and other lands as well'.[54]

Notwithstanding that 'it is not always easy to mark the edges of a tradition',[55] White believes it is possible conceptually to organize the variety of Protestant worship into a number of families or traditions. He sees Protestant history as being marked by an explosion of new traditions close to its origins – with five new traditions emerging in the 50 years from 1520 to 1570, and followed by the emergence of one enduring tradition in each successive century. 'It is significant that each century has found new possibilities of worship necessary, resulting in the origination of a new tradition.' In so far as he is able or attempts to explain this, he suggests that 'perhaps this reflects a slow process of liberation as more peoples successively achieve power to worship in ways they find natural'.[56] In addition to this hypothesis, White notes that within existing and established Protestant traditions 'change . . . does not seem to lessen a tradition's sense of identity as long as it is change that comes from within that tradition'.[57] Together these comments amount to a conviction that Protestant worship has recognized that historical realities shape people in different ways,[58] and that the worship within Protestant traditions should be conceived in its pioneering capacity: 'It is the peculiar vocation of Protestant worship to adapt Christian worship in terms of people as their social contexts and very beings change.'[59] Ultimately, what Protestant worship may insist upon is that people are the primary liturgical document.[60]

These features of White's thinking begin to show how his conception of liturgical theology is dependent upon liturgical scholarship which is committed to help identify the distinct characteristics of particular traditions, which he asserts are vulnerable to abuse and misunderstanding when they are undocumented. And against the stream of thinking and activity aimed at convergence between traditions, White has come to hold that, 'if convergence becomes too prominent, we must ask whether some of the richness of the variety of Protestant worship will suffer. The richness of Protestant worship consists in its diversity and its consequent ability to serve a wide variety of peoples.'[61] So *Protestant Worship*, after first of all noting some features of 'medieval worship and Roman Catholic worship' considers in turn Lutheran, Reformed, Anabaptist, Anglican, Separatist and Puritan, Quaker, Methodist, Frontier and Pentecostal practices.[62] While White insists, in continuity with his earlier work, and the focus of others, that 'Protestants can learn much from contemporary Roman Catholic reformers, and the enormous changes they have brought about in sacramental practice and faith', he continues, 'there are enormous riches in the various Protestant traditions that more Protestants would cherish greatly if they were aware of their value'.[63] This is a corrective to much liturgical theology, yet 'if we profess that the way people worship establishes the way they believe, we have to accept the consequences'. Moreover, his revised account of 'the purpose of worship reform' is in his later work defined as being 'not the elimination of multiplicity or the achievement of administrative efficiency. It is simply to enable people to worship with deeper commitment and participation – which may require more denominations and traditions rather than less.'[64]

It is exactly this that attempts at convergence may not concede, as they may indeed 'have the effect of ignoring the worship of most North American Christians'.[65] White states his point forcibly in the form of this question, 'Do we want to say that what happens in most churches in the United States on a Sunday morning is "baby worship," since it does not match up to some ecumenical or historical standard?'[66] White also turns the features of this critique on the Roman Catholic tradition, in order to shatter the myth that the worship forms of the Catholic tradition have been a static reality. White's studies suggest that a historical approach to its development reveals the deep ambiguity of seeing the tradition too much in the light of contemporary concerns alone, which may be one of the failures of much liturgical theology; and in parallel with his stress on diversity within Protestantism, he is also well aware that 'Catholic' itself refers to a diverse range of traditions, including those Catholic churches following eastern rites rather than Roman ones,[67] though he chooses to attend to the latter.

For White, then, descriptive accounts of liturgy can challenge both the notion of the 'benign abnormality' of infant baptism and also take fully into account the kind of reality acknowledged in the recognition that through much of the southern US, believers' baptism is normative, apart from the fact that under the increasing influence of the church growth movement, the sacraments themselves may be being marginalized from the experience of Christian worshippers, whatever a contemporary appropriation of a classical *ordo* may imply. As Sperry-White rightly asserts, 'White's more recent insistence in the variety of Protestant worship traditions . . . points to a significant ideological shift in North American liturgical studies'.[68]

Understanding the 'Americanization' of liturgy

White's observance of worship in the North American context has already been noted. Quite clearly, he has helped greatly to create 'what might be called "a North American school of liturgical history"',[69] through his teaching and doctoral supervision. In so far as this is the case, White has done much to redress the point that North American liturgical history had been neglected by European scholars. For instance, attention to Quaker and Pentecostal worship was unusual enough at the time of *Protestant Worship*'s publication, but his survey and reflections upon the Frontier tradition were virtually unique.

Adding to his critique of the convergence movement, White admits that much of American Christianity is 'doing well' without ecumenism, in which it shows 'no interest':[70] 'Many Protestant groups, especially within the Quaker, Frontier, and Pentecostal traditions, seem to be continuing in their own distinctive ways, little affected by recent tendencies among other Protestants and Roman Catholics.'[71] If liturgical scholars ignore them, White asserts, they violate the *lex orandi* they profess to be primary, when proper attention to its implementation should in fact demand much greater respect for the younger traditions and change liturgical theology in turn. Yet White himself is not enchanted by the prospect of what this may in fact mean in relation to recent developments in the Megachurch movement:

> In our own times the Frontier tradition has continued to grow in variety and skill. I interpret the latest manifestation of it to be the emergence of the Church Growth Movement and the disciples of Donald McGavran (1897–1990). It passes under names such as the Mega-church movement or the seekers' service model and I would like to call it high-tech worship.[72]

'Entertainment evangelism' is another commonly used term for this form of assembly. The Willow Creek Community Church outside Chicago is a 'flagship' representative of the phenomenon, marked as it is by highly 'culture specific' form and purpose: to 'reach out to men between twenty-five and fifty'.[73] Quite deliberately, minimal cultural and linguistic barriers are imposed in the effort to 'reach the unchurched' and whatever sense of 'community' as may be possible is formed around the notion of the '"homogeneous unit principle" – i.e., individuals are attracted by those like themselves'.[74]

> In this movement inculturation has become a fine science. Perhaps Anscar Chupungco and other Roman Catholic champions of inculturation would have second thoughts if they could visit Willow Creek. The premises are not all that

different from those in use at Mobil Oil headquarters down the road and worshippers must feel quite at home on Sunday just as they do at corporate headquarters on Monday. There is not a single Christian symbol visible in the auditorium. Maybe it is time to stop theorizing about inculturation. It is here and its results are dramatic.[75]

To White's mind, this 'extreme example of inculturation . . . makes one wonder whether successful inculturation is all that desirable. We may now have to show its limits!',[76] though these comments should be set alongside his critique of 'centralization' in the Roman Catholic tradition, of which he is equally critical. In *Protestant Worship* he laments the fact that the Vatican document *Declaration on Eucharistic Prayers and Liturgical Experimentation* of 1988 curtails local innovation in liturgical celebration, noting sardonically that a full quarter century after the *Constitution on the Sacred Liturgy* mandated inculturation (in paragraphs 37–40), the 1988 document's still unfulfilled promise of 'guidelines on the adaptations to the cultures and traditions of peoples' hardly suggests that the production of such guidelines or the granting of freedom to embrace the implications of inculturation is a high priority.[77] In *Roman Catholic Worship* he makes a similar critique of 'the grip which the Congregation for Worship has increasingly tightened' around liturgical inculturation.[78]

In a climate in which liturgical studies is evolving as a discipline, and in which theological approaches to the liturgy are making more impact on a scene dominated by a historical approach,[79] James White has done much to define the realities of the practice of worship in different historical eras, as well as revealing the diversity at given times and places. He has also offered important correctives and direction to the future of the discipline of liturgical theology, defined in the stricter sense of 'theology derived from the liturgy'.

Engaging the debate about *Patterns for Worship*

The implications of White's views for debate around *Patterns for Worship* are important, not least in implying that attention to the actual practice of churches that have departed from the authorized provisions of liturgical commissions and such like is significant. Yet an appreciation of heterogeneity in liturgy that is knowledgeable of the mainstream traditions and its merits as well as its potential weaknesses, and which grounds convictions about heterogeneity in liturgy in recovery of aspects from the edges of the tradition's history is a different thing to an embrace of heterogeneity without such historical insight. White's convictions about variety in worship are not licence for laissez-faire, thoughtless presentations of liturgy. His critique of the trends of the Megachurches in his own North American context are witness to that, as is the attention he gave to the sacraments throughout his career – notably in reflecting ecumenical agendas in his construction of the UMC Eucharistic rite, and in his concern with the sacraments in his most recent major work, *The Sacraments in Protestant Practice and Faith*, at a time when the Megachurches and the drift from the sacraments which they represent are still increasing in their influence on the North American Christian scene. Clearly, then, White's revision of earlier perspectives on ecumenical convergence was not whole scale, but rather selective. And, very significantly, White's intention in seeking to broaden liturgists' appreciation of worshipping traditions and styles continued to focus on the notion of participation. As he wrote in relation to the later Protestant traditions, his view of the 'purpose of worship reform . . . is simply to enable people to worship with deeper commitment and participation . . .'. So his was indeed a shift, but it was not an abandonment of convictions long held both by himself and others associated with the ecumenical vision of liturgical renewal. White's liturgical constructs were not detached from his sense of the freedoms and demands of liturgical history. He represented a series of important reminders, then, that encourage resistance to footloose liturgical construction for and with urban persons, young persons and others.

What White, with Lathrop and Saliers each in their own way, might do to focus thought about worship with and for young or urban persons, however, is to call attention to the potential of non-textual aspects of liturgical celebration. For White, with Saliers and Lathrop, pioneered an approach to liturgy that moves beyond the earlier emphasis on texts and in particular the Eucharistic prayer. Contrasting White's concerns with architecture for instance as constitutive of liturgy with the concerns of a prime example of the previous generation of liturgical scholars, such as Josef Jungmann, with his massive stress on the Roman canon, reveals an attempt to concentrate on a more diffuse centre latterly, of which White was representative. This contrast can be paralleled with the shift in the English Anglican prayer books of the late twentieth century, even between the approach of the *Alternative Service Book 1980*, with its texts and rubrics, and *Patterns for Worship* under a decade later, in which liturgy was presented in a quite different way – with the Service of the Word simply a set of guidelines with notes, and the novel commentary section introducing reflection on architectural influences and other non-textual considerations. White's interest in the architectural setting of liturgy finds its own parallels in Lathrop's fascination with vessels, objects and 'things', and in Saliers's stress on affective involvement as just one partial way of approaching that most diffuse constituent of liturgy – people. White, with Saliers and Lathrop, offers considerable material for reflection towards an approach to liturgy and liturgical theology that simply was not imagined before their time, and the ways in which they have expanded the orbit of their discipline has much to yield to congregations constructing worship simply on the basis of guidelines and notes, and plotting their way through a wide range of options for possible inclusion in rites, so freed from narrow attention to texts alone. For instance, White's thinking about architecture as and in liturgy might fruitfully be brought into conversation with the kinds of perspectives on the influence of architecture on urban subjectivity as Robert Orsi understands it:

> City folk do not live in their environments; they live through them. Who am I? What is possible in life? What is good? These are questions that are always asked, and their answers are discerned and enacted, in particular places. Specific places structure the questions, and as men and women cobble together responses, they act upon the spaces around them in transformative ways.[80]

How the architectural environment of liturgy interacts with the 'stoops, fire escapes, rooftops, and hallways' to which Orsi calls attention is a question congregations might not have considered in their hope to be free of liturgy understood narrowly as text alone.

White's emphasis on relishing diversity may also provide the most valuable tools for justifying age-streamed congregations, if and when attempts at inclusivity fail, as is so often the case, despite aspirations to the contrary.[81]

Above all, White can help contemporary liturgical thinking revitalize the point for contemporary appropriation made by James Baldovin in the unfolding of his study of the ancient liturgy's encounters with the cultures in which it was set: 'worship never takes place outside of a specific context, a context which reflects the social, political and economic condition of its participants.'[82]

Lathrop, Saliers and White in dialogue

In our survey of the three theologians' work, we have seen especially with reference to James White that over time they have changed their minds, and Saliers and Lathrop may of course do so again. Yet I have explored their work because I perceive James White, Don Saliers and Gordon Lathrop, both in relation and distinction to one another, to open up a wide range of topics in contemporary liturgical theology. To my mind, they convincingly suggest the richness and fruitfulness of their discipline.

One of my reasons for the exploration of Saliers, Lathrop and White's work has been to reveal the comparative paucity of argument in the Church of England's Liturgical Commission, not least with respect to *Patterns for Worship* – yet in such a way as to hint how the Church of England's thinking can find new and steady direction. For instance, Lathrop's exploration of the way in which he believes abiding liturgical patterns to be 'bound up with who Christ is', revealing the self of Jesus, as it were, might potentially strengthen the view that the bishops and Liturgical Commission promote in both *Patterns* and the *Renewal of Common Prayer*. Similarly, Saliers's attention to the affective dimensions of worship might improve argument for the retention or loss of particular patterns of worship. It can, I believe, aid discernment about which aspects of liturgy might yield under contemporary cultural pressures, and which might be especially valuable in order to engage with the maladies of our given time in different places. While the subtleties of Lathrop and Saliers' perceptions cannot of course be reduced to the possible contributions I have just cited, I believe these to be the heart of how they might clarify and assist conversations about liturgy in the Church of England that are comparatively underdeveloped. However, as Chapter 7 has shown, the thrust of James White's considered position is to offer a fierce challenge to any attempt to overcentralize liturgical provision. The abrasion of his own earlier and later views and of White's views against the views of Lathrop and Saliers where they differ with one another also foster sensitivity to the question of how a properly contextualized understanding of liturgy and liturgical theology can mature. So at least the following questions emerge from the conversation I have attempted to facilitate in this work to this point: How might White, Lathrop and Saliers's contributions to the wider discipline of liturgical theology be appropriated in a particular situation concerned with liturgy engaging deprived urban Christians in modern Britain, or involving children? How do actual celebrations of liturgy in particular urban assemblies, or congregations constituted by significant numbers of children, reflect the classical *ordo*? How might the culture of urban or age-inclusive congregations manage the subtle juxtapositions of which Lathrop speaks? What kind of judgement on the 'durability' of the classical *ordo* might contextually alert urban or age-inclusive liturgy represent? What kind of 'characterizing activity' (in Saliers's phraseology) do these particular urban or age-inclusive celebrations promise? What might urban or age-inclusive worship learn from the 'newer' or 'non-liturgical' traditions? What affectional or ethical 'fruit' may be jeopardized by omission of traditional components of the *ordo*? I think that *Patterns for Worship* – and then other Church of England liturgies – might well be approached and employed with these questions in mind.

Notes

1. James F. White, *The Cambridge Movement: The Ecclesiologists and the Gothic Revival*, Cambridge: Cambridge University Press, 2nd edn, 1979.
2. Grant S. Sperry-White, 'Tribute: James F. White: Historian, Liturgist, and Teacher', Karen B. Westerfield-Tucker, *The Sunday Service of the Methodists: Twentieth-Century Worship in Worldwide Methodism: Studies in Honor of James F. White*, Nashville: Kingswood, 1998, pp. 333–46, p. 334; also, James F. White, 'Some Lessons in Liturgical Pedagogy', *Christian Worship in North America, a Retrospective 1955–1995*, Collegeville: Liturgical Press, 1997, pp. 307–18, p. 314.
3. James F. White, 'Liturgical Space Forms Faith', *Christian Worship in North America*, pp. 211–15, p. 212. White's statement may be modelled on a similar one in Bishops' Committee on the Liturgy, *Music in Catholic Worship*, Chicago: Liturgy Training Publications, 1977, p. 6: 'Good celebrations foster and nourish faith. Poor celebrations may weaken and destroy it.' James F. White, *Protestant Worship and Church Architecture: Theological and Historical Considerations*, New York: Oxford University Press, 1964.
4. Sperry-White, 'Tribute', p. 335.
5. James F. White, *Introduction to Christian Worship*, Nashville: Abingdon Press, 3rd edn 2000.

6. James F. White, *Documents of Christian Worship: Descriptive and Interpretive Sources*, Louisville: Westminster John Knox, 1992.

7. James F. White, *A Brief History of Christian Worship*, Nashville: Abingdon Press, 1993.

8. James F. White, *Protestant Worship: Traditions in Transition*, Louisville: Westminster John Knox, 1989.

9. James F. White, *Roman Catholic Worship: Trent to Today*, New York: Paulist, 1995.

10. James F. White, *The Sacraments in Protestant Practice and Faith*, Nashville: Abingdon Press, 1999.

11. James F. White, *Sacraments as God's Self-Giving*, Nashville: Abingdon Press, 1982.

12. James F. White and Susan J. White, *Church Architecture: Building and Renovating for Christian Worship*, Akron: Order of St Luke, 2nd edn, 1998.

13. Hoyt L. Hickman, Don E. Saliers, Laurence Hull Stookey and James F. White, *The (New) Handbook of the Christian Year*, Nashville: Abingdon Press, 1986, 2nd edn 1992.

14. Sperry-White, 'Tribute', p. 333.

15. White, 'Shaping the 1972 United Methodist Eucharistic Rite', *Christian Worship in North America*, pp. 143–53, p. 143.

16. See Frederick R. McManus, 'Reform, Liturgical, of Vatican II', Peter Fink, ed., *New Dictionary of Sacramental Worship*, Collegeville: Liturgical Press, 1991, pp. 1081–97.

17. James F. White, *Christian Worship in North America, A Retrospective: 1955–95*, Collegeville: Liturgical Press, 1997, p. 151.

18. The standard Great Thanksgiving for the Service of Word and Table Order 1; *United Methodist Book of Worship*, Nashville: United Methodist Publishing House, 1989, p. 37.

19. White, *Sacraments as God's Self-Giving*, p. 109.

20. Sperry-White, 'Tribute', p. 338.

21. Sperry-White, 'Tribute', p. 335.

22. James F. White, Preface, *Christian Worship in North America*, pp. vii, ix.

23. White, 'Some Lessons', p. 309.

24. White, *Introduction to Christian Worship*, p. 11.

25. James F. White, 'Thirty Years of the Doctoral Program in Liturgical Studies at the University of Notre Dame, 1965–1995', Nathan Mitchell and John F. Baldovin, eds, *Rule of Prayer, Rule of Faith: Essays in Honor of Aidan Kavanagh OSB*, Collegeville: Liturgical Press, 1996, pp. 324–42, p. 333.

26. White, *A Brief History of Christian Worship*, p. 180, cf. p. 11.

27. James F. White, 'A Short History of American Methodist Service Books', *Christian Worship in North America*, pp. 93–102, p. 101;

also, White, 'Shaping the 1972 United Methodist Eucharistic Rite', p. 150.

28. James F. White, 'Roman Catholic and Protestant Worship in Relationship', *Christian Worship in North America*, pp. 3–15, p. 3.

29. White, 'Roman Catholic and Protestant Worship in Relationship', pp. 4 and 10.

30. White, *Sacraments as God's Self-Giving*, p. 9.

31. Sperry-White, 'Tribute', p. 340.

32. Aidan Kavanagh, *On Liturgical Theology: The Hale Memorial Lectures of Seabury-Western Theological Seminary, 1981*, New York: Pueblo Pub. Co., 1984.

33. White, *Sacraments in Protestant Practice and Faith*, p. 10.

34. White, *Sacraments as God's Self-Giving*, p. 10.

35. White, *Sacraments in Protestant Practice and Faith*, p. 142.

36. White, *Sacraments in Protestant Practice and Faith*, p. 142.

37. White, 'Response', p. 143.

38. White, 'Response', pp. 144–5.

39. Sperry-White, 'Tribute', p. 345.

40. Sperry-White, 'Tribute', p. 345.

41. James F. White, 'How Do We Know It Is Us?', E. Byron Anderson and Bruce T. Morrill, eds, *Liturgy and the Moral Self: Humanity at Full Stretch before God: Essays in Honor of Don E. Saliers*, Collegeville: Liturgical Press, 1998, pp. 55–65, p. 56.

42. White, 'How Do We Know . . . ?', pp. 56–7.

43. White, 'How Do We Know . . . ?', p. 56.

44. White, 'How Do We Know . . . ?', p. 56.

45. James F. White, 'Thirty Years of the Doctoral Programme in Liturgical Studies at the University of Notre Dame, 1965–95', eds Nathan Litchell and John F. Baldovin, *Rule of Prayer, Rule of Faith: Essays in Honour of Aidan Kavanagh OSB*, Collegeville: Liturgical Press, 1996, pp. 324–42.

46. White, 'How Do We Know . . . ?', p. 57.

47. White, *Protestant Worship*, p. 15.

48. White, 'Some Lessons', p. 315.

49. White, *Protestant Worship*, p. 15.

50. White, 'Some Lessons', p. 314; also White, 'Thirty Years', p. 334.

51. White, *Protestant Worship*, p. 13.

52. White, *Protestant Worship*, p. 212.

53. White, *Protestant Worship*, pp. 13–14.

54. White, *Protestant Worship*, p. 13. For a related discussion, see James F. Kay, 'The *Lex Orandi* in Recent Protestant Theology', David S. Cunningham, Ralph Del Colle and Lucas Lamdrid, eds, *Ecumenical Theology in Worship, Doctrine and Life: Essays*

Presented to Geoffrey Wainwright on His Sixtieth Birthday, New York: Oxford University Press, 1999, pp. 11–23.

55. White, *Protestant Worship*, p. 18.
56. White, *Protestant Worship*, p. 210.
57. White, *Protestant Worship*, p. 211.
58. White, *Protestant Worship*, p. 17.
59. White, *Protestant Worship*, p. 215.
60. This perspective has clear resonances with the contribution made to pastoral studies by Anton Boison in his insistence on attention to human beings as 'living human documents' to be studied alongside authoritative inherited sacred texts.
61. White, *Protestant Worship*, p. 212.
62. The procedure of study is much the same as that attempted by Evelyn Underhill a generation earlier in her *Worship*, London: Collins, 1936, of which chapters 12–15 discuss, respectively: 'Catholic Worship: Western and Eastern', 'Worship in the Reformed Churches', 'Free Church Worship' and 'The Anglican Tradition'. See also Ann Loades, *Evelyn Underhill*, London: Fount, 1997.
63. White, *Sacraments as God's Self-Giving*, p. 10.
64. White, *Protestant Worship*, p. 213.
65. White, 'How Do We Know . . . ?', p. 57.
66. White, 'How Do We Know . . . ?, pp. 57–8.
67. White, *Roman Catholic Worship*, pp. 1–3.
68. Sperry-White, 'Tribute', p. 334.
69. Sperry-White, 'Tribute', p. 335; also White's own comments about justifying a study of liturgical history from a North American perspective, for the twofold reason of rectifying the oversights of Eurocentric liturgical study, and allowing the importance of American liturgical experience as it has been 'exported' in missionary endeavour to be traced, in *Brief History*, p. 11.
70. White, 'How Do We Know . . . ?', p. 58.
71. White, *Protestant Worship*, p. 35.
72. James F. White, 'Evangelism and Worship from New Lebanon to Nashville', reprinted in *Christian Worship in North America*, pp. 155–72, p. 161.
73. White, 'Evangelism and Worship', p. 162.
74. James F. White, 'Protestant Public Worship in America: 1935-1995', *Christian Worship in North America*, Collegeville: Liturgical Press, 1997), 115–33, p. 132.
75. White, 'Evangelism and Worship', p. 162.
76. White, 'Some Lessons', p. 313.
77. White, *Protestant Worship*, p. 215.
78. White, *Roman Catholic Worship*, pp. 143–4.

79. White, 'Thirty Years', p. 340.
80. Robert A. Orsi, ed., *Gods of the City: Religion and the American Urban Landscape*, Bloomington, Indiana: Indiana University Press, 2000, pp. 43–4.
81. White's historical perspectives are helpfully allied to Mark R. Francis's account of the growing trend towards ethnic parishes in the contemporary North American context, in Mark R. Francis, *Shape a Circle Ever Wider: Liturgical Inculturation in the United States*, Chicago: LTP, 2000.
82. James F. Baldovin, *The Urban Character of Christian Worship: The Origins, Development and Meaning of Stational Liturgy*, Rome: Pontifical Institutum Studorum Orientium, 1987, p. 253.

Part Four

Constructing Liturgical Theology:

Concluding Case Study

Part Four consists of a case study that applies some of what I think there is to be learned from the preceding discussions to the planning and presentation of worship events, and particularly with respect to the shaping of worship in the urban British context and among children. It shows how the conversation begun in this book translated into the worshipping life of a Christian community. It does this by exploring the issues raised in the questions with which I closed Part Three in relation to my own practice of ministry in the particular place and context in which this work was conceived, Gateshead.

This Part of the work, then, suggests some practical applications based on contextualized experience. It is in no sense intended as a manual, but rather as simply one model of relating liturgical theology and contextual sensitivity that may act as an invitation to the reader to reflect on the practice of liturgy in the particularity of their own context.

CASE STUDY:
LITURGICAL CONSTRUCTION
IN GATESHEAD

Recollecting the conversation

Part One of this work began by identifying the notion of participation as central to liturgical theology (Chapter 1, above).
It then studied *Patterns for Worship* as one example of concern
with participation in the Church of England, especially among
the urban poor and among children (Chapter 2). The first section of the book suggested how *Patterns for Worship*, *Faith in
the City* and *Children in the Way*, and their successive and sup-
portive legacies in related documents of the Church of England,
raised important and provocative questions for the Church. In
the course of exploration of these documents I asserted that, at
the present time, not all of the questions they bring into focus
are receiving the attention they merit. In part, *Worship in Context* is an attempt to redress the lack of connection between the
various reports that have emerged from the Church of England
in the period that I have considered. An obvious instance of the
lack of connection is that neither *Youth a Part* nor *God in the
City* paid attention to *Patterns for Worship*, despite the fact
that the authors of the former could have been greatly encouraged by what was to be found in and elaborated from *Patterns
for Worship* if they had done so.

Part Two of this work introduced a number of complexities
to my task, and I traced the trajectories through to the present
day of *Faith in the City* and *Children in the Way*'s respective
concerns with urban life (Chapter 3) and with the young (Chapter 4). While recognizing much of continuing relevance in the
documents, these chapters stated some ways in which the focus

of the original documents now requires a shift – for instance, by acknowledging globalization as being of major importance to contemporary urban theology, and by embracing opportunities now presented by widespread shifts to allow the 'sacramental belonging' of children. The force of the chapters is that such shifts are necessary if the documents and their legacies are to continue to possess interpretative power.

Worship in Context then turned to resources that I think might assist in understanding and encouraging the participation in liturgy with which *Patterns for Worship* was concerned, especially with the young and the urban poor. So Part Three, 'Exploring Liturgical Theology', looked in detail at the writings of Gordon Lathrop (Chapter 5), Don Saliers (Chapter 6) and James White (Chapter 7). These chapters showed that read alongside each other, White, Saliers and Lathrop are in some instances mutually affirming, and in other instances mutually critical. They went on to suggest that in the coherence of the three theologians' work, and in their questions of one another's perspectives, the contours of a liturgical theology can be discerned that helpfully expands the horizons of the Church of England's public thinking about its worship. In my own appropriation of the work of the three theologians, I developed a series of questions that I think might fruitfully be brought into dialogue with developments in Anglican liturgy represented by *Patterns for Worship*: for example, how might White, Lathrop and Saliers's contributions to the wider discipline of liturgical theology be appropriated in a particular situation concerned with liturgy engaging deprived urban Christians in modern Britain, or involving children? How do actual celebrations of liturgy in particular urban assemblies, or congregations constituted by significant numbers of children, reflect the classical *ordo*? How might the culture of urban or age-inclusive congregations manage the subtle juxtapositions of which Lathrop speaks? What kind of judgement on the 'durability' of the classical *ordo* might contextually alert urban or age-inclusive liturgy represent? What kind of 'characterizing activity' (in Saliers's phraseology) do these particular urban or age-inclusive celebrations promise? What might urban or age-inclusive worship learn from the 'newer' or 'non-liturgical' traditions? What affectional or ethical 'fruit' may be jeopardized by omission of traditional components of the *ordo*? These are the kinds of questions that liturgies with children, and liturgies in the city, need to engage.

A Gateshead case study

In drawing towards a conclusion, a case study attempts to show some of the merit of asking these kinds of questions in a particular place. It narrows the focus on Gateshead in a very specific way,[1] as I relate parts of the preceding conversation explicitly to a liturgical text used in our parish's worship. In what follows, I intersperse that text (congregational text for prayer, and related rubrics) with a commentary that shows how liturgical resources and reflection were developed in a very specific situation that has formed my convictions and practice.

The text presented is that used in Eucharistic worship through the Easter season. It belonged to a series of related orders of service presented in a very similar style: each was typeset in the font used in *Common Worship* (Gill Sans) and each was presented in the 'house-style' of contemporary Church of England publications, using the Church of England logo, and so on. All of these related orders were organized around a clear, stable *ordo*, separated into four sections corresponding to the major sections of the Eucharistic service – gathering, word, table, sending – and so although the elements within that fourfold structure were variable, a very clear and fixed structure linked the different orders used throughout the year. Although images interspersed the texts, only the texts are presented here.

The variable content of the different orders was decided upon by a group of lay and clergy people working together with the range of available authorized resources, and was then 'trial run' over a year through which the coherence of text and ceremony was tested, and the feedback – appreciative and critical – of the congregation led to a number of amendments. The liturgies were themselves, then, very much the product of conversation. The process began in 1998, shortly after the first publication of *Common Worship* resources, and was settled a little over 12 months later, in 2000. It is the texts in their final form that are presented here.

In the development of our local liturgy, it was decided that only officially authorized texts would be used where these were required according to the Church of England's canons, but that at 'soft-spots' – where rubrics indicated alternatives could be used – wider resources would be drawn in. The *New Zealand Prayer Book* was the main source used at these opportunities. Use of only authorized texts when required, and use of wide resources when permitted, were both seen as ways of expressing the relationship of a particular congregation to others, as gestures of catholicity. The decision related to a sense, among some members of the congregation, of feeling 'inferior' if special exemptions were seen to be necessary in their case, without being evidently necessary for other Church of England congregations.

The liturgies were always closely related to catechesis, and that in different contexts. The exercise of preparing liturgies in conversation was itself a key means of catechesis but opportunity for learning and practising liturgy took place not in the kind of meetings that made decisions about the inclusion or exclusion of variable texts, but in training for those involved in public ceremonial or vocal roles in liturgy, and with the congregation as a whole. A particular impetus for all-age catechesis in liturgy was generated by opportunity in the diocese for children to begin to receive Communion. As part of the parish's own move to introduce children to Communion, provision of sacramental catechesis for church members of all ages was built in to all of the parish's policies about the Eucharist, and part of this involved a commitment to partake in regular 'instructed Eucharists' at which the sermon of the day would be located at a particular point in the service (for example, the intercessions) where reflection would be centred. These instructed Eucharists happened several times a year.

The following text and commentary focus points made throughout this book thus far, and show the ways in which one local liturgy was structured around the patterns of the *ordo*, while taking into account a range of factors particular to our context. However, perhaps inevitably, the text and commentary do not convey very well how environmental, architectural and musical aspects of liturgy were employed. The text, however, is developed as commended in *Patterns for Worship*, as a 'people's' or congregational text that includes only what the congregation require, rather than a fuller text that might be used by the minister. This is of obvious benefit in a context of low literacy. So long presidential prayers are omitted from the – congregational – text presented here. The use of any larger blocks of texts is confined to cherished prayers that many members of the congregation had found possible, and rewarding, to commit to memory, and hence wanted to encourage others to do the same.

WE GATHER IN GOD'S PRESENCE

Peaceful greeting

The risen Lord came and stood among his disciples and said:
Peace be with you.
And he showed them his hands and his side.
They were glad when they saw the Lord. (John 20)
The peace of the Lord be always with you.
And also with you.

Please move around greeting others.
A song of praise may be sung.

The minister welcomes everyone to the celebration
and this or another opening prayer may be said:

Loving Lord, fill us with your life-giving,
joy-giving, peace-giving presence,

that we may praise you now with our lips
and all the day long with our lives,
through Jesus Christ our Lord. Amen.

In the Easter season, services began with the greeting of peace. In catechesis, this position for the peace was related to the biblical narratives of the risen Christ appearing unexpectedly to disciples gathered together behind locked doors. The abrupt beginning of the service without any kind of formal or informal introduction therefore attempted to relate something of the surprise of resurrection appearances. In the liturgical context of Gateshead, beginning abruptly with the peace was meant to be a faint 'aftershock' of such appearances, now into the mêleé of our gathering.

At different times of the year, the position of the peace shifted, and this functioned, along with changes in environmental colours, as one of the main indicators of a change in liturgical season. Throughout the year, the position of the peace varied through all of the options suggested by the notes of *Common Worship*. In ordinary time, it was positioned in the 'classical' position suggested by Justin Martyr's early witness, between intercession and preparation of the table for Communion. During Advent and Lent, the peace replaced the closing dismissal, underlining the theme of reconciliation as a mark of these seasons. During Christmas and Epiphany, it was positioned in the commonplace Roman Catholic position between the Lord's Prayer and the breaking of bread. This was, in the context of Gateshead, a small attempt to relate different senses of the body of Christ, people being closely juxtaposed to sacramental matter. In this position the peace was meant to function as an invitation to relate to neighbours who necessarily interrupted the privacy of individual preparation for Communion immediately before reception.

During the Easter season, the peace was introduced from the west end of the church, behind people sat in preparation for worship. In all seasons, a procession led from the west to the east end during the opening hymn, with adults and children forming the procession to carry a lectern Bible and lights before presider and assistant. Services always had a clear presider (distinguished by vesture), and the presider was always accompanied by an assistant. At a Eucharist, the presider was always a priest, although at other times (such as services of the word), ordained persons assisted lay presiders as a gesture of shared ministry.

In the Easter season, an alternative opening prayer from *Patterns for Worship* replaced the more familiar Collect for Purity (which was used in ordinary time).

Invitation to repentance

Christ Jesus says: Do you love me? (John 21)
Spirit of God, search our hearts.

In silence, we remember our need to be forgiven . . .

**God our Father, long-suffering, full of grace and truth,
you create us from nothing and give us life.
You give your faithful people new life
in the water of baptism.
You do not turn your face from us,
nor cast us aside.
We confess that we have sinned against you
and our neighbour.
We have wounded your love
and marred your image in us.
Restore us for the sake of your Son,
and bring us to heavenly joy,
in Jesus Christ our Lord. Amen.**

The minister declares God's forgiveness.

The Collect

The presider calls everyone to prayer and after a silence, collects all our offerings in a special prayer for the day.

Through most of the liturgical year, confession and absolution formed part of the gathering rites.[2] The response 'Spirit of God, search our hearts', from the *New Zealand Prayer Book*, consistently provided the congregational response to the range of scriptural sentences used throughout the year as an invitation to repentance. In the Easter season, the sentence echoed the risen Christ's question to Peter, as above. During ordinary time, the 'great' and 'new' commandments from Matthew 22 were used as our 'standard fare' with the New Zealand response repeated after each. In Advent and Lent, a version of the ten commandments was used, again using the New Zealand response. In the 'kingdom season' from All Saints through to the Reign of Christ (the Sunday before Advent), the Johannine sentence 'If you love me, keep my commandments' was used. The response, 'Spirit of God . . .' amplified the collect for purity and allowed a connection to the sense of that cherished prayer even when it was not actually used.

A range of forms of confession was used throughout the year, drawing mainly on *Patterns for Worship* resources, and using responsive *kyries*, variable from week to week, through the long season of ordinary time. In the Easter season, an authorized confession amplifying baptismal imagery was used, anticipating a special focus on baptism later in the service. (It is notable that with only one exception – the Nicene Creed, used for the short Kingdom season – this was the longest single block of congregational text used at any point in the year.) Absolutions were never prescribed in the local order, allowing reference to a range of authorized forms.

In every season, the collect marked the close of the gathering rites.[3]

WE HEAR GOD'S WORD

Bible reading

At the end of the reading:

The word of the Lord.
Thanks be to God.

A song of praise may be sung.

Gospel reading
When the reading is introduced:

Alleluia, alleluia!
I am the first and the last, says the Lord, the living One;
I was dead, and behold I am alive for evermore.
Alleluia! (Revelation 1)
Hear the good news of our Lord Jesus Christ according to . . .
Glory to you, O Lord.

At the end of the reading:

The gospel of the Lord.
Praise to you, O Christ!

Sermon

*The sermon may be followed by questions and comments
or silence or instrumental music for reflection.*

Statement of Christian faith

Brothers and sisters, I ask you to profess with me
the faith of the Church in the saving death
and resurrection of our Lord Jesus:
Christ died for our sins
in accordance with the Scriptures;
He was buried;
he was raised to life on the third day
in accordance with the Scriptures;
Afterwards he appeared to his followers,
and to all the apostles:
this we have received and this we believe. Amen.
(1 Corinthians 15)

Scripture readings were always read by lay people – often children – and this often required patience while readers took time over the readings, given that many – especially adults – could but didn't read. Scripture readings would sometimes involve members of the congregation encouraging readers with pronunciation and 'long words'. If only to find volunteers to read, it was essential to encourage a culture in which participation was valued whatever the 'standard' of the contribution. This proved an ongoing task that was in fact crucial to raising the standard as people participated and received encouragement, improving in quality over time.

The gradual hymn was, with the exception of ordinary time, fixed for each season and used each week through the season. For instance, in Eastertide, 'Come, Sing and Dance to Jesus' Lead' from *Music for Liturgy*, the imaginative hymnal from Saint Gregory of Nyssa, San Francisco, might be used.[4] This, with changing colour, and the shifting position of the peace, lent a sense of marking time. Sometimes a Gospel procession to the church door at the west end of the building was incorporated, as a gesture of proclamation to those 'outside' as well as present, and a sign of attempting to link liturgy and the rest of life.

Sermons were often accompanied by projected artwork and were always followed by a brief time of communal reflection, 'chaired' by either presider or assistant, though highly informal in tone. Children participated in these discussions alongside adults, and this reflective time was a chief means of shared catechesis in the congregation, often involving testimony and encouragement by one to others.

Creedal statements varied through the year. The normative Eucharistic creed, that based on the Nicaean statement, was in fact used only through the short Kingdom season. A responsive form of the shorter Apostles' Creed, drawn from *Patterns for Worship*, was used through ordinary time. In Advent and Lent, the *Patterns for Worship* version of the 'Christ-psalm' of Philippians 2 was used, emphasizing as it does both kenosis and sacrifice with their connections to the incarnation and the triduum for which these seasons respectively prepare. In Christmas and Epiphany, the *Patterns* version of the 'prayer' from Ephesians 3 ('I bow my knees before the Father . . .') was used, linking the season marking the childhood of Christ to an affirmation of all as children of God. Through these seasons, this connection was strengthened by having children from the congregation introduce this particular affirmation of faith, so addressing others of very different ages as 'brothers and sisters'. In the Easter season, another scriptural creedal statement was used, 1 Corinthians 15 as presented in *Patterns for Worship*, and this provided a set of biblical imagery that juxtaposed that of the 'Christ-psalm' used through the previous season.

Prayers of God's people

We pray for the needs of the world, the renewal of the church, and grace for one another.

Your kingdom come,
Your will be done.

At the end of the prayers:

Hasten, Lord, the day
**when people will come from east and west,
from north and south, and sit at table
in your kingdom and we shall see your Son
in his glory. Amen.**

A song of praise may be sung.

Intercessions were on most occasions led by lay members of the congregation, including children who prepared prayers with family members or other adults. Often the intercessions were accompanied by visual imagery presented on screens. The habit grew of inviting specific responses from the congregation – naming the sick, the recently bereaved, local concerns, world events and so on – as a means by which people could participate in a way which was often felt to be personally significant.

The collect gathering the various intercessions changed with the seasons of the year. Through Easter this prayer, with others through the service, especially emphasized some inclusive 'global' imagery. This became especially significant in shaping response to the many asylum seekers who became the neighbours of many of the congregation – almost 1000 asylum seekers became resident in the town in under 12 months from July 1999 – and several of them joined the congregation. Some of the church's most focused work in the community came to be in response to asylum seekers' needs, and various 'drop ins' and visiting schemes were established – some shared with the local interfaith forum, and some developed independently. The catechetical point to which this and other prayers were related was linked to the baptismal associations of Eastertide, stressing common identity as 'children of God' when much of the wider culture was emphasizing difference and division between longstanding inhabitants of Gateshead and the influx of asylum seekers.

The offertory hymn was often one drawn from a pool of hymns which members of the congregation identified as their favourites. Such hymns were often acknowledged as a particular person's most cherished hymn, and that person would often at this point in the service, as the hymn was sung, be involved in the offertory procession, alongside both other adults and/or other children. Identifying hymns as favourites of members of the congregation at least partly enabled use of a wider repertoire of music in worship than might otherwise have been the case had hymns not been so closely associated with particular people. At least, tolerance of others' cherished music could be encouraged because critics of particular styles of music would themselves become vulnerable to criticism when their favourite hymnody was used and they were identified with it in the community's ritual. Over time, this strategy for encouraging inclusive approaches to music did begin to change the way diverse kinds of music were evaluated, because music was always identified with names and faces, and had to be judged with that in mind.

WE CELEBRATE AT GOD'S TABLE

Prayer of great thanksgiving

The Lord is here.
His Spirit is with us.
Lift up your hearts.
We lift them to the Lord.
Let us give thanks to the Lord our God.
It is right to give thanks and praise.

In a special prayer led by the presider,
we give thanks to God for all his goodness,
especially in the life of Jesus the Saviour.
We join the praise of the saints and angels of heaven, saying:

Holy, holy, holy Lord, God of power and might,
heaven and earth are full of your glory,
hosanna in the highest.

We recall Jesus' command to remember him with bread and
wine.
These responses are used:

This is his story:
This is our song. Hosanna in the highest.

This is our story:
This is our song. Hosanna in the highest.

We pray for the outpouring of the Holy Spirit, ending
Blessing and honour and glory and power
be yours for ever and ever. Amen.

Sharing the Lord's prayer

We pray with Jesus, present with us now:
Our Father, who art in heaven,
hallowed be thy name;
thy kingdom come, thy will be done,
on earth as it is in heaven.
Give us this day our daily bread.
And forgive us our trespasses
as we forgive those who trespass against us.
And lead us not into temptation
but deliver us from evil.
For thine is the kingdom, the power,
and the glory for ever and ever. Amen.

Breaking of bread

As the grain once scattered in the fields
and the grapes once dispersed on the hillside
are now reunited on this table in bread and wine,
So, Lord, may your whole Church
soon be gathered together
from the corners of the earth
into your kingdom.

Invitation to the table

The presider invites the people to share the bread and wine
as the signs of Christ's love. Everyone is welcome to share the
sacramental gifts.

During communion, songs of praise may be sung.

Patterns for Worship's presentation of sample services, which
eliminate all text needed only by the presider were used as
models followed in the local Gateshead orders, as this Eucharis-

tic prayer shows. Through the year, the full range of authorized Eucharistic prayers from *Common Worship* were used.

Adults and children together prepared the altar-table, setting out bread (baked by a member of the congregation) and pouring out wine. They also gathered together around the altar with the presider for Eucharistic prayer and the Lord's prayer. As a means of gesturing shared ministry, no spaces of the building were reserved for ordained persons, and children shared all the spaces accessed by adults. The ritual at this point intended to suggest the equality of adults and children in the community, and children and adults both acted as 'prompter' during Eucharistic prayer, in the case of prayer D used through Eastertide, announcing the trigger-phrase 'this is our story' to invite congregational response.

The version of the Lord's Prayer used was one of the two options permitted by *Common Worship*, the 'traditional language' version. Our choice of the traditional form of the prayer reflected the sense among some in the congregation that a measure of change was tolerable if some aspects of the liturgy remained untouched – and the Lord's Prayer was the most deeply cherished prayer in the latter category. While other things about our liturgy changed, the fact that this (if little else) remained unchanged was itself a gesture of inclusivity. Furthermore, the fact that the prayer in its traditional form was more widely known among the young – where it was known at all – also fed into our decision to retain the traditional form of the prayer.

The words at the fraction in the Easter season, drawn from the *Didache*, consolidated the 'global' emphasis that other prayers through the order also sought to express.

Different arrangements of liturgical space, within a range of limited options, allowed for different patterns of sharing Communion. An important principle to try to embody was that children might administer the sacramental gifts, given that latterly they were deemed to be as eligible as adults to receive them. However, diocesan policies on this matter had not yet been reformed in the light of new openness to children receiving

Communion and, regrettably, the administration of Communion was reserved to those over 16 years old.

The shift to sharing Communion with children also raised a wider range of issues about sharing Communion with others who also had not been confirmed. The issue came into focus particularly at occasions like baptisms, when many non-churched persons were present, although, in fact, the issues were felt almost every time a visitor or guest attended a Eucharistic service. Worship in Gateshead, as in so many other places, had been influenced by the Parish Communion Movement, and a pattern of weekly Eucharist had been long established. What had not been a focus of attention in Gateshead, as in so many other places, was that despite the benefits of regular Eucharist, other foci from the Church's 'repertoire' of worship had been lost, not least baptism. Furthermore, such Eucharistically based worship presents the demanding problem of how hospitality can be offered in such a context, particularly in a wider culture in which patterns of significant decline in church attendance may well predate the influence of the Parish Communion Movement, when services of the word of various kinds, perceived to be more hospitable than the Eucharist as a rite of commitment, were the main acts of weekly worship. Sacramental catechesis focused on biblical memories of Jesus' table fellowship with outcasts and sinners led to an unwritten policy that all would be invited to share Communion with 'no questions asked'. Although this practice in fact stepped beyond the legalities of Anglican Eucharistic hospitality, a number of precedents shaped the convictions that began to emerge. For instance, Eucharistic services at St Gregory of Nyssa, San Francisco, always include the invitation to 'all, without exception', to share the sacramental gifts, with a rationale for such practice clearly linked to the Gospel traditions of Jesus' meals in contradistinction from the 'worthy reception' traditions elaborated from Pauline material that are often the focus of more traditional Anglican approaches to the issues.

The practice of an 'open table' developed in Gateshead in response to the widespread perception among visitors that the

Eucharist divided members of the church from those who were more casual attenders. Our emerging practice of inviting all to Communion was meant to contest the perceived lack of hospitality at Eucharistic events, and also spurred a quest to widen out the sacramental focus of most of our gatherings, particularly in terms of recovering a greater role for baptism.

Before turning more specifically to the matter of recovering baptism, it is worth noting that hospitable practice at the Eucharist had particular implications among the asylum seekers attending worship. Not all were Christian: some Muslims attended sporadically, before being put in contact with other Muslims worshipping locally. They attended Christian worship on the basis of their sense that Christians and Muslims 'both believe in one God'. Some shared the Eucharist. Also, some Buddhists attended, some of whom eventually of their own accord converted, and were baptized, although they had been sharing Communion for some time before that formal mode of sacramental initiation. Again, St Gregory of Nyssa's provided some points with which we linked this practice: their icon project, 'the Dancing Saints', which surrounds their altar-table, includes figures from non-Christian religions and people of no faith as well as Christians. Clearly, our practice of admitting members of other religions, at their request, to the Eucharistic table introduced a measure of confusion to our sacramental practice. We did so, however, while recognizing that of course the practice of baptism and Eucharist in Gateshead was already very 'messy' long before numbers of believers of other faiths began to worship with us.

WE ARE SENT TO SERVE IN GOD'S NAME

Prayer after communion

A time of silence is kept for personal thanksgiving,
and this or another prayer may be said:

We thank you, Lord,
that you have fed us in this sacrament,

united us with Christ,
and given us a foretaste of the heavenly banquet
prepared for all peoples. Amen.

Sending out

Water is poured into the font as the people of God recall
God's gift of baptism and the new life to which Christ calls
his people.

Those who are baptised
are called to worship and serve God:

Will you continue in the apostles' teaching
and fellowship, in the breaking of bread,
and in the prayers?
With the help of God, I will.

Will you persevere in resisting evil,
and, whenever you fall into sin,
repent and return to the Lord?
With the help of God, I will.

Will you proclaim by word and example
the good news of God in Christ?
With the help of God, I will.

Will you seek and serve Christ in all people,
loving your neighbour as yourself?
With the help of God, I will.

Will you acknowledge Christ's authority
over human society, by prayer for the world
and its leaders, by defending the weak,
and by seeking peace and justice?
With the help of God, I will.

May Christ dwell in your hearts through faith,
that you may be rooted and grounded in love
and bring forth the fruit of the Spirit. **Amen.**

*The service ends as people come to the font as a song of praise
is sung.*
*Each person uses the water to sign themselves with the cross,
saying,*
'I belong to Christ. Amen.'

As with prayers used earlier in this service, the post-Communion
prayer emphasized the 'global' scope of divine love, and was
related in catechesis especially in response to the many asylum
seekers who were becoming resident in Gateshead and members of the church during the period in which the services were
constructed.

In the Easter season, services closed with an explicit connection to the longstanding practice of baptism at Eastertide. Baptisms in the parish were themselves clustered around four nodal
points in the year – the festival of the baptism of Christ, Easter,
Pentecost and All Saints, as *Common Worship* suggests they
might be. *Common Worship*'s resources for remembering baptism, particularly the affirmations used at confirmation, were
used throughout the Easter season, however. The responses
from confirmation were used in part to try to secure a role for
confirmation when its place was being renegotiated in relation
to questions about access to the Eucharistic table. By employing these responses for a whole season of the liturgical year, the
concrete implications of the personal commitment represented
by confirmation were underlined.

Emphasis on baptism through the Easter season was also
an attempt to widen out the congregation's sacramental
spirituality from an almost exclusive focus on the Eucharist.
The decline in the number of actual celebrations of baptisms,
and their celebration outside the main (Eucharistic) event of
worship each week meant that baptism certainly did not have a
central place in the communal life of the Church. Yet recovering

baptism came to be considered central both to underlining the place of children in the Church, and to encouraging evangelism, one key means of which was the pastoral offices in which both lay and clergy members were involved with many in the wider community.

The ritual of pouring water and inviting worshippers to mark themselves with the sign of the cross of course has wide ecumenical resonances. It recalls the aspersion that may form a central part of the gathering in the Roman rites (and latterly the gathering of the *Common Worship* funeral service in which the coffin of the deceased may be sprinkled), and it also draws on various Protestant traditions' recently recovered means of remembering baptism. In our practice, the recollection of baptism in the Easter season was often accompanied by the aspersion common to both Roman and Uniting Church rites, as well as signing with the cross that is also shared by both Protestant and Roman traditions. These ecumenical resonances were themselves a matter for catechesis and a variant trajectory of the 'global' theme developed throughout the services of the Easter season. The baptismal focus of the conclusion also helped to serve as a reminder to the Church that children baptized among us belong among us, and, more particularly, powerfully gestured this to those children who actually were present.

By concluding this study with commentary on an actual order of service used in Gateshead, I have shown one attempt to foster 'full, conscious and active participation' in worship, such as has been the vision of ecumenical liturgical renewal, and a special concern of *Faith in the City* in its influence on *Patterns for Worship* (Chapter 1, *passim*). Moreover, the case-study has touched a number of specific issues that relate to how liturgical celebration may communicate the hospitality of God. Resonance with divine hospitality is, I believe, the possibility and challenge at the centre of liturgical theology.

The Gateshead liturgies, of which the above case study forms a part, were an attempt to enact that hospitality to both adults and children in the context of our particular urban setting, with all its attendant demands. The Gateshead liturgies were constructed in the context of my conversation with the writings of Lathrop, Saliers and White and with a congregation conscious of some of its needs and open to catechesis. So the liturgies represent the meshing of some of the key insights of these three theologians with the challenging context of a living community. Importantly, the Gateshead liturgies were themselves the product of a conversation in which a number of members of a congregation participated, and they represent a communal response to our wider circumstances. In this, the liturgical resources of *Patterns for Worship* were certainly helpful, as, I believe, were Saliers, White and Lathrop's insights insofar as they offered the possibility of enriching understanding of the issues *Patterns* sought to address in the English Anglican context.

Recalling the questions introduced at the end of Part Three, the liturgies were intended to engage with and reflect the classical resources of Christian worship known as the *ordo*. They were intended to allow different juxtapositions in the *ordo* to animate the faith of participants in liturgy in our setting. At times, the liturgies embodied Saliers and White's encouragement to learn from the newer 'non-liturgical' traditions. The liturgies were an attempt to wrestle with a range of issues that are often overlooked in writing about worship, and moreover with issues that represent some deep challenges to the *ordo* which may not be apparent when the *ordo* is discussed abstractly, detached from particular challenges facing actual communities. The liturgies were an attempt to identify clearly some of the characteristics of the *ordo* and to make these available to a particular congregation, and to facilitate affective response to divine hospitality in such a way as to enable participants to engage with others generously in the midst of ethical challenges that confronted us as we came to share our space in new ways with those with particular needs and in very specific kinds of difference.

Even so, good practice in Gateshead was sometimes discerned but not properly or effectively enacted, sometimes begun but not finished, and certainly never perfect. And, because my examples are contextual, the reflection developed in this chapter is necessarily partial. Nevertheless, the present case study may, I hope, be a helpful conversation partner for those in other settings, although it makes no claim that its reflection is 'transferable' in any simple sense – and, if at all, perhaps in terms of resonance which readers in other situations may recognize or find intriguing. Still, I hope that it might help to generate sensitivity to the demands of other situations and the quest for transformation in the particularity of their otherness, for the challenge of enacting, in some partial measure, the divine hospitality that is the heart of liturgy's saving work must be undertaken in each and every place.

Despite the necessary limits of the case study, it has intended to advance the development in the Church of England's liturgical life represented by *Patterns for Worship*, enriched by the kinds of consideration that arise from exploration of contemporary liturgical theology such as we have encountered in the thought of Don Saliers, Gordon Lathrop and James White. In its modest and piecemeal way, may it suggest how engagement with liturgical theology can engender both an inclusive vision and hospitable practices in the life of the local church, and at the very least, hint that the *ordo* is worth attention, rather than jettisoning it as in so much worship with children and among the urban deprived, apart from others.

Notes

1. For further reflections on this particular context, see Stephen Burns, *Welcoming Asylum Seekers*, Cambridge: Grove Books, 2004. Ellen Clark-King's excellent study of the outlook of a range of Christian women in a geographically adjacent and culturally similar area, *Theology by Heart: Women, the Church and God*, Peterborough: Epworth Press, 2004, merits and repays close attention.
2. My reflections on Jacques Pohier's *God in Fragments*, London: SCM Press, 1985, esp. pp. 212–22, generated some reserve about this in my mind. In one season, the brief Kingdom season, the confession was moved to an alternative position after intercession, so that it

formed part of the response to the ministry of the word. A place much nearer the beginning, as in the Easter order, was, however, felt by most of the congregation to be the preferable place for confession. Perhaps this relates to the observation made earlier (in relation to art and music, for instance) about joyfulness being more difficult to express in some urban contexts than bleaker emotions.

3. The collects were the element from the texts of *Common Worship* that were experienced as particularly difficult in Gateshead. The problems with them are widely recognized and documented, and they are now being radically recrafted for later editions of the prayer book. The collects were in fact the one point where we in Gateshead departed from our decision to use only authorized texts. Generally, the Joint Liturgical Group's edition of the collects for the Roman sacramentary, published as *Opening Prayers*, Norwich: Canterbury Press, 1998, were used.

4. *Music for Liturgy: A Book for All God's Friends*, San Francisco: St. Gregory of Nyssa Episcopal Church, [2] 1999.

ACC. NO. 973786 05	FUND THEOLS
LOC. ET	CATEGORY STAN	PRICE £8·16
2 6 FEB 2014		
CLASS No. 264·0083 BUR		
OXFORD BROOKES UNIVERSITY LIBRARY		